Teach Yourself VISUALLY™

Macromedia®
Flash™ MX 2004

by Sherry Willard Kinkoph

Visual™

From

maranGraphics®

&

Wiley Publishing, Inc.

Teach Yourself VISUALLY™ Macromedia® Flash™ MX 2004

Published by
Wiley Publishing, Inc.
111 River Street
Hoboken, NJ 07030-5774

Published simultaneously in Canada

Copyright © 2004 by Wiley Publishing, Inc., Indianapolis, Indiana

Certain designs and illustrations Copyright © 1992-2003 maranGraphics, Inc., used with maranGraphics' permission.

maranGraphics, Inc.
5755 Coopers Avenue
Mississauga, Ontario, Canada
L4Z 1R9

Library of Congress Control Number: 2003116120

ISBN: 0-7645-4334-2

Manufactured in the United States of America

10 9 8 7 6 5 4 3 2 1

1K/RS/QR/QU/IN

Trademark Acknowledgments

Important Numbers

For U.S. corporate orders, please call maranGraphics at 800-469-6616 or fax 905-890-9434.

For general information on our other products and services or to obtain technical support please contact our Customer Care Department within the U.S. at 800-762-2974, outside the U.S. at 317-572-3993 or fax 317-572-4002.

Permissions

maranGraphics:
Certain text and illustrations by maranGraphics, Inc., used with maranGraphics' permission.

Wiley Publishing, Inc.

U.S. Corporate Sales	U.S. Trade Sales
Contact maranGraphics at (800) 469-6616 or fax (905) 890-9434.	Contact Wiley at (800) 762-2974 or fax (317) 572-4002.

Some comments from our readers...

"I have to praise you and your company on the fine products you turn out. I have twelve of the *Teach Yourself VISUALLY* and *Simplified* books in my house. They were instrumental in helping me pass a difficult computer course. Thank you for creating books that are easy to follow."

– *Gordon Justin (Brielle, NJ)*

"I commend your efforts and your success. I teach in an outreach program for the Dr. Eugene Clark Library in Lockhart, TX. Your *Teach Yourself VISUALLY* books are incredible, and I use them in my computer classes. All my students love them!"

– *Michele Schalin (Lockhart, TX)*

"Like a lot of other people, I understand things best when I see them visually. Your books really make learning easy and life more fun."

– *John T. Frey (Cadillac, MI)*

"I have quite a few of your Visual books and have been very pleased with all of them. I love the way the lessons are presented!"

– *Mary Jane Newman (Yorba Linda, CA)*

"I write to extend my thanks and appreciation for your books. They are clear, easy to follow, and straight to the point. Keep up the good work!"

– *Seward Kollie (Dakar, Senegal)*

"I am an avid fan of your Visual books. If I need to learn anything, I just buy one of your books and learn the topic in no time. Wonders! I have even trained my friends to give me Visual books as gifts."

– *Illona Bergstrom (Aventura, FL)*

"Thank you for making it so clear. I appreciate it. I will buy many more Visual books."

– *J.P. Sangdong (North York, Ontario, Canada)*

"I was introduced to maranGraphics about four years ago and YOU ARE THE GREATEST THING THAT EVER HAPPENED TO INTRODUCTORY COMPUTER BOOKS!"

– *Glenn Nettleton (Huntsville, AL)*

"Compliments to the chef!! Your books are extraordinary! Or, simply put, extra-ordinary, meaning way above the rest! THANK YOU THANK YOU THANK YOU! for creating these."

– *Christine J. Manfrin (Castle Rock, CO)*

"I just purchased my third Visual book (my first two are dog-eared now!) and, once again, your product has surpassed my expectations. The expertise, thought, and effort that go into each book are obvious, and I sincerely appreciate your efforts. Keep up the wonderful work!"

– *Tracey Moore (Memphis, TN)*

"Thank you, thank you, thank you...for making it so easy for me to break into this high-tech world. I now own four of your books. I recommend them to anyone who is a beginner like myself. Now...if you could just do one for programming VCR's, it would make my day!"

– *Gay O'Donnell (Calgary, Alberta, Canada)*

"You're marvelous! I am greatly in your debt."

– *Patrick Baird (Lacey, WA)*

Dec '02

maranGraphics is a family-run business located near Toronto, Canada.

At **maranGraphics**, we believe in producing great computer books — one book at a time.

maranGraphics has been producing high-technology products for over 25 years, which enables us to offer the computer book community a unique communication process.

Our computer books use an integrated communication process, which is very different from the approach used in other computer books. Each spread is, in essence, a flow chart — the text and screen shots are totally incorporated into the layout of the spread.

Introductory text and helpful tips complete the learning experience.

maranGraphics' approach encourages the left and right sides of the brain to work together — resulting in faster orientation and greater memory retention.

Above all, we are very proud of the handcrafted nature of our books. Our carefully-chosen writers are experts in their fields, and spend countless hours researching and organizing the content for each topic. Our artists rebuild every screen shot to provide the best

clarity possible, making our screen shots the most precise and easiest to read in the industry. We strive for perfection, and believe that the time spent handcrafting each element results in the best computer books money can buy.

Thank you for purchasing this book. We hope you enjoy it!

Sincerely,

Robert Maran
President
maranGraphics
Rob@maran.com
www.maran.com

CREDITS

Project Editor
Maureen Spears

Acquisitions Editor
Jody Lefevere

Product Development Manager
Lindsay Sandman

Copy Editor
Kim Heusel

Technical Editor
Kyle Bowen

Editorial Manager
Robyn Siesky

Permissions Editor
Laura Moss

Manufacturing
Allan Conley
Linda Cook
Paul Gilchrist
Jennifer Guynn

Indexer
Joan Griffitts

Special Help
Adrienne Porter

Book Design
maranGraphics®

Production Coordinator
Nancee Reeves

Layout
Beth Brooks
Carrie Foster
LeAndra Hosier
Kristin McMullan

Screen Artist
Jill A. Proll

Illustrators
Karl Brandt
Ronda David-Burroughs
Kelly Emkow
David E. Gregory
Rashell Smith

Proofreaders
John Greenough
Susan Moritz

**Vice President and
Executive Group Publisher**
Richard Swadley

Vice President and Publisher
Barry Pruett

Composition Services Director
Debbie Stailey

ABOUT THE AUTHOR

Sherry Willard Kinkoph has written over 50 books over the past 8 years covering a variety of computer topics ranging from hardware to software, from Microsoft Office programs to the Internet. Her recent titles include *Teach Yourself VISUALLY Premiere 6, Master VISUALLY Dreamweaver MX and Flash MX*, and *Teach Yourself VISUALLY Restoration and Retouching with Photoshop Elements 2*. Sherry's on-going quest is to help users of all levels master the ever-changing computer technologies. No matter how many times they — the software manufacturers and harward conglomerates — throw out a new version or upgrade, Sherry vows to be there to make sense of it all and help computer users get the most out of their machine.

AUTHOR'S ACKNOWLEDGMENTS

Special thanks go out to publisher, Barry Pruett, for always keeping me busy pursuing exciting software like Flash; to acquisitions editor, Jody LeFevere, for allowing me the opportunity to tackle this project; to project editor, Maureen Spears, for her dedication and patience in guiding this project from start to finish, and for keeping her sense of humor intact the entire time; to technical editor, Kyle Bowen, for skillfully checking each step and offering his valuable input; and finally to the production team at Wiley for their able efforts in creating such a visual masterpiece.

To my father-in-law, James Kinkoph, who set such an example of love, kindness, and perseverance while battling Parkinson's disease. You will be dearly missed.

TABLE OF CONTENTS

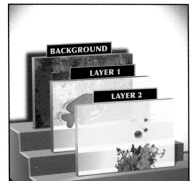

Chapter 4

WORKING WITH IMPORTED GRAPHICS AND VIDEOS

Chapter 5

WORKING WITH TEXT

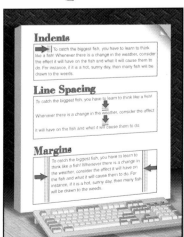

TABLE OF CONTENTS

Chapter 6

WORKING WITH LAYERS

Chapter 7

WORKING WITH FLASH SYMBOLS AND INSTANCES

Chapter 8

CREATING ANIMATION IN FLASH

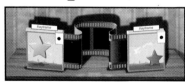

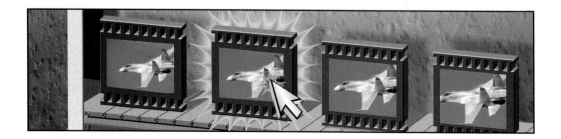

Chapter 9

CREATING ANIMATION BY TWEENING

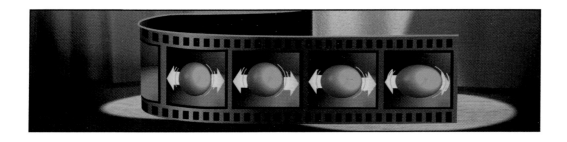

TABLE OF CONTENTS

Chapter 10

ADDING FLASH ACTIONS

Chapter 11

CREATING INTERACTIVE BUTTONS

Chapter 12

ADDING SOUND

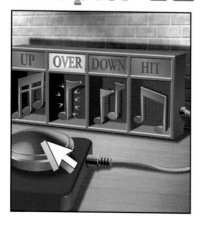

Chapter 13

EXPORT A MOVIE

Animated GIF   EPS   Adobe Illustrator

HOW TO USE THIS BOOK

Teach Yourself VISUALLY Flash MX 2004 contains straightforward sections, which you can use to learn the basics of creating, editing, and publishing your animated movies. This book is designed to help a reader receive quick access to any area of question. You can simply look up a subject within the Table of Contents or Index and go immediately to the section of concern. A *section* is a set of self-contained units that walk you through a computer operation step-by-step. That is, with rare exception, all the information you need regarding an area of interest is contained within a section.

The General Organization of This Book

Each section contains an introduction, a set of screen shots, and, if the task goes beyond 1 page, a set of tips. The introduction tells why you want to perform the task, the advantages and disadvantages of performing the task, and references to other related tasks in the book. The screens, located on the bottom half of each page, show a series of steps that you must complete to perform a given section. The tip portion of the section gives you an opportunity to further understand the task at hand, to learn about other related tasks in other areas of the book, or to apply alternative methods.

The Organization of Each Chapter

Teach Yourself VISUALLY Flash MX 2004 has 13 chapters. Chapter 1 tells you what you need to know to operate Flash, including how to use the Properties Inspector, the Flash Window, and the Flash Timeline. Chapter 2 and 3 show you how to create, enhance, and edit the objects and shapes you will eventually use in your animation projects. Chapter 4 discusses how to import graphics and video into Flash. In Chapter 5, you learn all about how to place text into your animation, or how to use text as an animation. Chapter 6 shows you how to organize your work into layers, and Chapter 7

shows you how to work with Flash symbols and instances. In Chapter 8 and 9, learn to take your illustrations and convert them into animation. Chapter 10, 11, and 12 discuss how to make your amimations interactive and interesting by adding Flash Actions, buttons, and sounds. Finally, in Chapter 13, you learn how to take your Flash movie and distribute it to the masses!

Who This Book Is For

This book is highly recommended for the visual learner who wants to learn the basics of Flash, and who may or may not have prior experience with a computer.

What You Need To Use This Book

To perform the tasks in this book, you need a computer installed with Flash MX 2004.

Mac Requirements

- 500 MHz PowerPC(r) G3 processor or better
- Mac OS X system software version 10.2.6
- 128 MB RAM (256 MB recommended)
- 215 MB available disk space

Windows Requirements

- 600 MHz Intel Pentium III processor or equivalent
- Windows 98 SE, Windows 2000, or Windows XP
- 128 MB of RAM (256 MB recommended)
- 215 MB of available disk space

Conventions When Using the Mouse

This book uses the following conventions to describe the actions you perform when using the mouse:

Click

Press and release the left mouse button. You use a click to select an item on the screen.

Double-click

Quickly press and release the left mouse button twice. You double-click to open a document or start a program.

Right-click

Press and release the right mouse button. You use a right-click to display a shortcut menu, a list of commands specifically related to the selected item.

Click and Drag, and Release the Mouse

Position the mouse pointer over an item on the screen and then press and hold down the left mouse button. Still holding down the button, move the mouse to where you want to place the item and then release the button. Click and dragging makes it easy to move an item to a new location.

The Conventions In This Book

A number of typographic and layout styles have been used throughout Microsoft Office XP to distinguish different types of information.

Bold

Indicates text, or text buttons, that you must click in a menu or dialog box to complete a task.

Italics

Indicates a new term being introduced.

Numbered Steps

Indicate that you must perform these steps in order to successful perform the task.

Bulleted Steps

Give you alternative methods, explain various options, or present what a program will do in response to the numbered steps.

Notes

Give you additional information to help you complete a task. The purpose of a note, which appears in italics, is three-fold: It can explain special conditions that may occur during the course of the task, warn you of potentially dangerous situations, or refer you to tasks in the same, or a different chapter. References to tasks within the chapter are indicated by the phrase "*See the section...*" followed by the name of the section. References to other chapters are indicated by "*See Chapter...*" followed by the chapter number.

Icons

Icons in the steps indicate a button that you must click to perform a section.

Operating System Difference

If you are using a Mac, this book assumes that you have OS X installed on your computer. If you have a PC, this book assumes that you have Windows XP installed on your computer. Other OS and Windows versions may give different results than those presented in this book.

Also, although Macromedia Flash MX 2004 is available for use on both the Mac and PC, this book only illustrates its use on a PC. If you are using Flash on a Mac, and there are differences between the PC and Mac operations, the steps indicate this. PC operations are listed first and are immediately followed by the Mac operation in parentheses. For example:

4 Press **Enter** (**Return**).

CHAPTER 1

Flash Fundamentals

Are you ready to start using Flash MX 2004? In this chapter, you learn all the basics for starting Flash files and finding your way around the program window.

INTRODUCING FLASH

Macromedia Flash has quickly become the standard for creating lively vector art and animation on the Web, and the latest version—Flash MX 2004—offers more versatility and workflow enhancements than ever before.

Flash is the perfect tool for both new and experienced Web page designers who want to create expressive, dynamic Web page elements. With the program's many tools, you can add interactivity to page elements, create movies, and coordinate accompanying sounds.

Create Animation Content

Flash includes a variety of tools you can use to draw your own objects to use in your animations. Flash-created vector graphics are much smaller in file size than raster graphics, such as JPEGs and GIFs. Vector graphics display much faster on a downloading Web page and are a more efficient method of delivering images over the Internet. For more on creating objects, see Chapters 2 and 3. To include text in your content, see Chapter 5. For more on importing graphics and video, see Chapter 4.

Work with Symbols

After creating new objects, or importing objects from other sources, you can turn objects into symbols to reuse in your Flash movie. Every time you use a symbol, you use an instance of the original object. If you make changes to the original, the instance changes as well. Flash keeps track of your symbols in the file's Library. For more on creating symbols and instances, see Chapter 7.

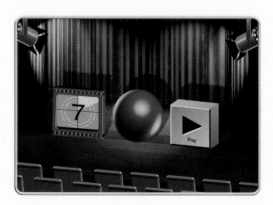

Build Animation Sequences

You can use the Flash animation tools to create all kinds of animation effects, from making an object move across the screen to complex animations that follow paths and action commands. You can create animations using frames. A frame stores content and the total number of frames determine the length of your movie. For more on creating animation, see Chapters 8 and 9. For more on adding sound to your animation, see Chapter 12.

Organize with Layers

You can use layers in your Flash movies to organize content and add depth to your animations. Each layer acts like a transparent sheet, allowing you to view underlying layers. You can manage layers in the Flash Timeline window. For more on working with layers in Flash, see Chapter 6.

Add Interactive Elements

You can also use the Flash tools to create interactive elements in your movie and assign actions. For example, you can add a button that, when clicked, activates another movie. A programming language, called ActionScript, controls interactivity in Flash. For more on working with actions, see Chapter 10. For more on creating interactive buttons, see Chapter 11.

Publish Your Movies

There are a variety of ways you can share your animations with others. Flash includes options for publishing movies to Web pages, as Flash movie files, or as self-extracting animations. The program also includes features to help you preview a movie before publishing, test download performance, and more. For more on publishing your movie, see Chapter 13.

NAVIGATE THE FLASH WINDOW

The Flash program window has several components for working with graphics and movies. Take time to familiarize yourself with the on-screen elements. If you use Flash on a Macintosh computer, the program elements may look a bit differently than those displayed in the Windows example below.

Tools Panel

Contains the basic tools needed to create and work with vector graphics.

Title Bar

Displays the name of the open file.

Menu Bar

Displays Flash menus which, when clicked, reveal commands.

File Tab

The tab at the top of the work area represents the current file. If two or more files are open, you can switch from file to file by clicking a file name.

Timeline

Contains all the frames, layers, and scenes that make up a movie.

Work Area

The area surrounding the Stage. Anything placed on the work area does not appear in the movie.

Stage

The area where a movie or graphic displays, where you can view a frame's contents and draw graphic objects.

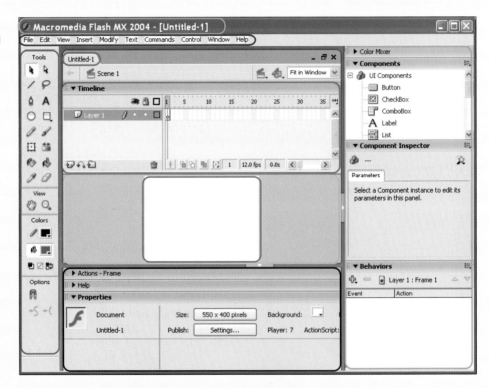

Properties Inspector

Use this panel to view and edit properties of the current object.

Panels

Allow quick access to options for controlling and editing Flash movies.

UNDERSTANDING THE FLASH TIMELINE

The Flash Timeline contains the frames, layers, and scenes that make up a movie. You can use the Timeline to organize and control your movies. By default, the Timeline appears docked near the top of the program window. If you are new to Flash, take a moment and familiarize yourself with the Timeline elements.

Frame Numbers

Frames appear in chronological order in the Timeline, and each frame has a number.

Playhead

Marks the current frame displayed on the Stage.

Timeline Control

Displays a menu of customizing options for controlling how frames are displayed in the Timeline.

Current Scene

Displays the name of the scene on which you are currently working.

Layer Controls

Display the status of a layer, such as hidden, locked, or outlined.

Frames

Lengths of time in a Flash movie are divided into frames. They enable you to control what appears in animation sequences and which sounds play.

Layers

Use layers to organize artwork, animation, sound, and interactive elements. Layers enable you to keep pieces of artwork separate and combine them to form a cohesive image, such as a company logo that includes a layer of text and another layer with a graphic shape.

Timeline Buttons

Scattered around the Timeline are buttons for controlling frames, layers, and movies.

Layer Buttons

Click to add and delete layers.

START AND EXIT FLASH

When you first open the Flash program window, a welcome window, also called a start page, appears in the Stage area. You can click the links in this window to open new files, existing files, templates, or access the Flash help system.

The start page appears by default unless you turn the feature off.

START AND EXIT FLASH

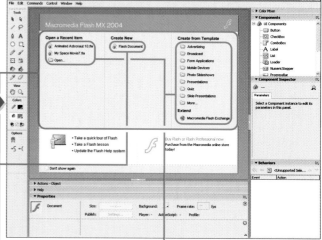

START FLASH

1 Click **start**.

2 Click **All Programs**.

3 Click **Macromedia**.

4 Click **Macromedia Flash MX 2004**.

■ The Flash program window opens along with the start page.

5 Click an option.

■ To start a new file, click the **Flash Document** link.

■ To open an existing file, click the file name.

■ To open a template, select a template folder and choose a template.

How do I open Flash MX 2004 on a Mac?

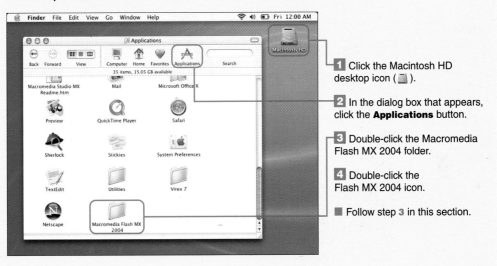

1 Click the Macintosh HD desktop icon ( ).

2 In the dialog box that appears, click the **Applications** button.

3 Double-click the Macromedia Flash MX 2004 folder.

4 Double-click the Flash MX 2004 icon.

■ Follow step **3** in this section.

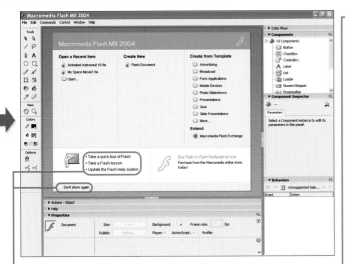

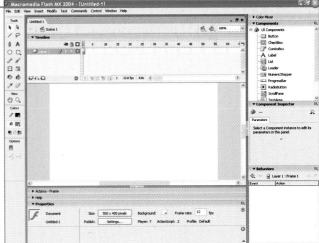

■ To access the help system, select a help link.

■ To keep the start page from opening again, click the **Don't show again** check box (changes to).

■ Flash opens the option you selected.

EXIT FLASH

1 Click the program window's ✕ button.

■ On a Mac, click **Flash**, and then **Quit Flash**, or press ⌘+Q.

■ The Flash program window closes.

Note: If you have not saved your work, Flash prompts you to do so before closing. See the task "Save and Close a Flash File" to learn more about saving your work.

OPEN A FLASH FILE

Flash files are called *documents* or *movies*. When you save a file, you can open it and work on it again. You can make Flash files as simple as a drawing you created using the Flash drawing tools, or as complex as an animation sequence consisting of scenes and interactive elements.

You can also start a new Flash file at any time, even if you are currently working on another file. Every new file you start uses a default Stage size.

OPEN A FLASH FILE

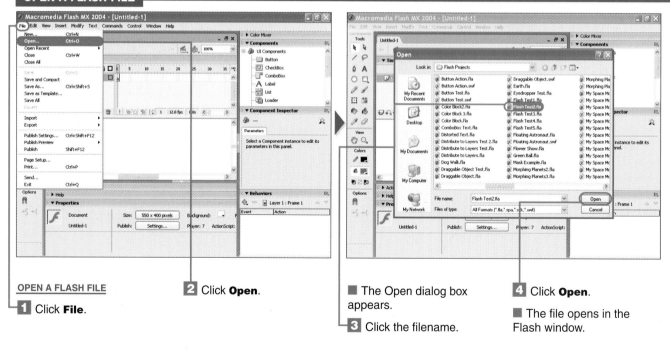

OPEN A FLASH FILE

1 Click **File**.

2 Click **Open**.

■ The Open dialog box appears.

3 Click the filename.

4 Click **Open**.

■ The file opens in the Flash window.

Why does Flash not show a Main toolbar?

The Main toolbar includes access to common commands, such as Open and Save. For example, to open a file, click the Open button (📁). By default, Flash does not display the Main toolbar, but you can turn it on if you like. Click **Windows**, **Toolbar**, and then **Main**.

Is there a limit to how many Flash files I can have open?

No. However, the more files you open, the slower your computer becomes. Graphics files, such as those you author in Flash, can take up more processing power than other programs. Unless you are sharing data between the files, it is a good idea to close Flash files you are no longer using.

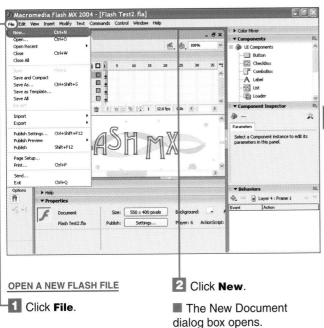

OPEN A NEW FLASH FILE

1 Click **File**.

2 Click **New**.

■ The New Document dialog box opens.

3 Click **Flash Document**.

4 Click **OK**.

■ A blank document appears in the Flash window.

■ You can have several Flash files open and switch between them via the **Window** menu.

SAVE AND CLOSE A FLASH FILE

As you create movies in Flash, you need to save them to work on them again. By default, Flash saves all files in the FLA file format. Because Flash does not offer an automatic save feature, it is a good practice to save your work frequently.

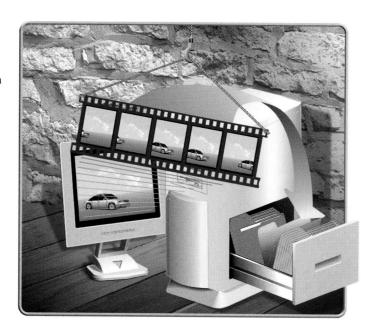

You can close Flash files no longer in use to free up computer memory. Be sure to save your changes before closing a file.

Saving graphics to the Flash Library works a bit differently than saving a file. See Chapter 7 for more information about saving symbols.

SAVE AND CLOSE A FLASH FILE

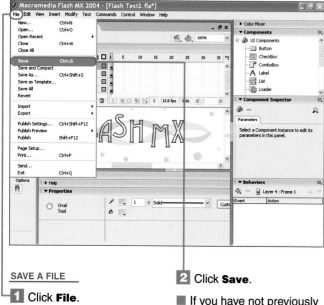

SAVE A FILE

1 Click **File**.

2 Click **Save**.

■ If you have not previously saved your file, the Save As dialog box appears.

3 Type a unique name for the file.

■ By default, Flash saves your files to the My Documents folder.

■ To save to another folder, click ▾ and select another location.

4 Click **Save**.

■ Flash saves your file.

How do I save a previously saved file under a new name?

You can copy a previously saved file and save it under a new filename. You can then make changes to the file copy without worrying about changing the original file. To do so, click **File**, then click **Save As**. This opens the Save As dialog box. Type a new name for the file and click **Save**.

Can I save a Flash file in another format?

Yes. However, you cannot use the Save command unless you want to save the file in an older Flash program version. Instead, you must export the movie to another file format. See Chapter 13 to learn how.

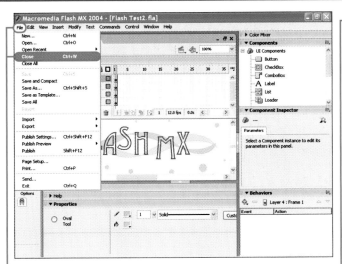

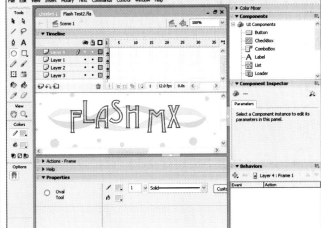

CLOSE A FLASH FILE

1 Save your file.

2 Click **File**.

3 Click **Close**.

■ Flash closes the file you were working on, but the program window remains open.

Note: If you have not saved your changes, Flash prompts you to do so before closing a file.

USING THE CLOSE BUTTON

1 Save your file.

2 Click the Close button (⊠).

Note: Clicking the program window's ⊠ button closes the Flash application entirely and might result in lost files.

Note: If you have not saved your changes, Flash prompts you to do so before closing a file.

CHANGE THE STAGE SIZE

The *Stage* is the on-screen area where you can view the contents of a frame and draw graphic objects. You can control the size and appearance of the Stage. The size of the Stage determines the size of your Flash movie screen.

It is a good idea to set your movie Stage size before adding any content to your frames. If you set a size after creating your movie, you may end up needing to reposition objects to fit the new Stage size.

CHANGE THE STAGE SIZE

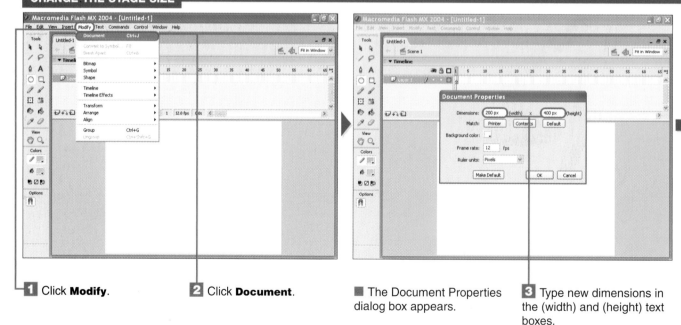

1 Click **Modify**.

2 Click **Document**.

■ The Document Properties dialog box appears.

3 Type new dimensions in the (width) and (height) text boxes.

14

How do I specify different units of measurement for the Stage?

From the Document Properties dialog box, click the Ruler units ⌄ and then click the unit of measurement you want to apply. The unit of measurement immediately changes in the width and height text boxes and you can now set the appropriate measurements.

How do I set a new background color?

By default, Flash sets the Stage background color to white. To set another background color, click the Background Color button (⬜) in the Document Properties dialog box. A palette of color choices appears. Click the color you want to apply and the color becomes the new background color throughout your movie.

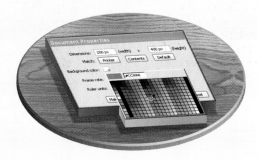

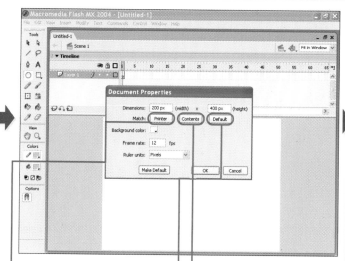

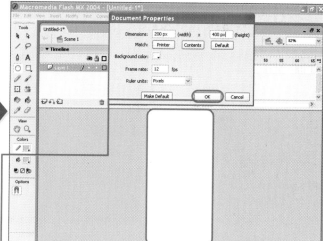

■ You can click **Printer** if you want to match the Stage dimensions to the maximum available print area size for your printer.

■ You can click **Contents** to change the Stage dimensions to match the contents of your movie, with equal spacing all around.

■ You can click **Default** to return the Stage size to the default size.

4 Click **OK**.

■ Flash resizes the Stage area according to your new settings.

USING THE PROPERTIES INSPECTOR

You can use the Properties inspector to see and edit the properties of the object with which you are currently working. The Properties inspector changes to reflect the properties associated with the object you select on the Stage.

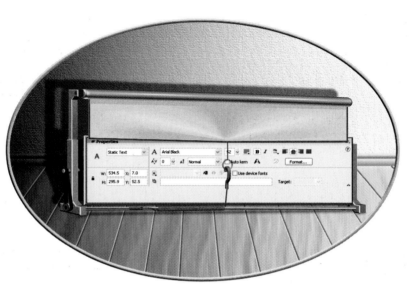

The Properties inspector acts as a panel, which you can collapse, hide from view, or move. By default, Flash docks the Properties inspector at the bottom of the program window. You can collapse the Properties inspector when you do not need it to free up workspace.

USING THE PROPERTIES INSPECTOR

COLLAPSE THE PROPERTIES INSPECTOR

■1 Click the Collapse button (▼ becomes ▶).

■ You can also click on the panel name or anywhere on the inspector's title bar.

Note: This example shows the text properties listed in the Properties inspector.

■ The Properties inspector collapses.

EXPAND THE PROPERTIES INSPECTOR

■2 Click the Expand button (▶ becomes ▼).

■ You can also click on the panel name or anywhere on the inspector's title bar.

■ The Properties inspector expands.

Can I close the Properties inspector entirely?

Yes. To close any panel, click the panel's Options Menu control (▦) to display a pop-up menu, and then click **Close Panel**. The Properties inspector panel closes completely. You can also right-click the panel's title bar and click **Close Panel**. To reopen the panel again, click the **Window** menu and click **Properties**.

Can I move the Properties inspector panel?

Yes. Like all panels in Flash, you can move the Properties inspector to create a floating panel, or you can dock the panel on another side of the screen.

■ To move the panel, click and drag the upper-left corner of the panel.

■ To collapse a floating panel, simply click the panel's title bar. To expand it again, click the bar again.

SHOW AND HIDE PROPERTIES

1 Click the Expand/Collapse button (△). (△ becomes ▽.)

■ A portion of the Properties inspector collapses.

2 To view all properties again, click ▽ again (▽ becomes △).

WORK WITH PANELS

You can use the Flash panels to access additional controls. Flash offers over a dozen different panels, each displaying options related to a specific task. Panels can appear docked or they can appear as floating panels. When you no longer need them, you can close panels to free up on-screen workspace.

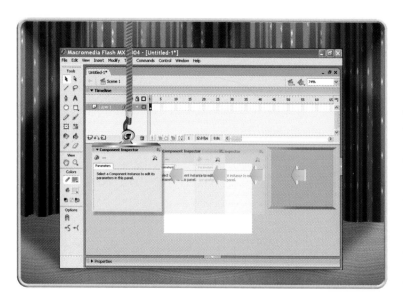

When you open Flash for the first time, the Default Layout panel set appears. This panel set includes the Components, Component Inspector, Behaviors, and Help panels as well as the Properties inspector. You can replace the Default Layout panel set with another panel set.

WORK WITH PANELS

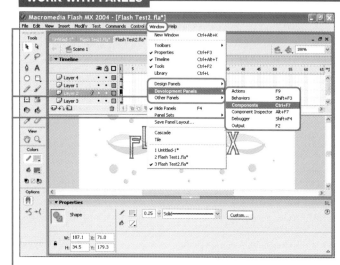

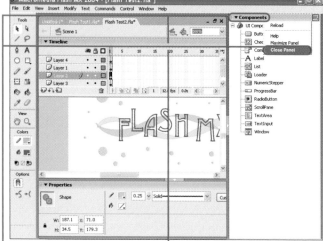

OPEN PANELS

1 Click **Window**.

2 Click a panel set group.

3 Click the panel you want to open.

■ A check mark (✔) indicates the panel is open; no check mark indicates the panel is closed.

■ The panel appears on-screen.

CLOSE PANELS

1 Right-click over the panel's title bar.

2 Click **Close Panel**.

■ The panel closes.

■ To hide a panel instead of closing it, you can click the panel's title bar.

Can I hide all the panels at once?

Yes. Click the **Window** menu and click **Hide Panels**. Flash closes all the panels, including the Drawing toolbar.

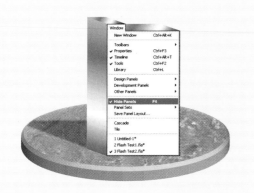

Can I undock or resize a panel?

Yes. Click and drag the panel's drag area, the upper left corner of the panel. To collapse a floating panel, simply click the panel's title bar. To expand it again, click the bar again. To resize a panel, move the mouse pointer over the edge of the panel (➤ changes to ⬍), then drag the panel border to a new size.

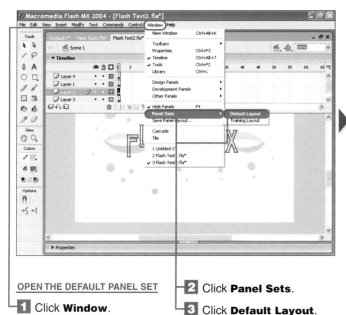

OPEN THE DEFAULT PANEL SET

1 Click **Window**.

2 Click **Panel Sets**.

3 Click **Default Layout**.

■ Flash displays the default panel set.

Note: Your screen resolution determines how the panel set affects the layout of your Flash work area and Stage.

■ You can also click the Show/Hide buttons to hide the default panels without closing them completely.

ZOOM OUT OR IN

When working with various elements on the Stage, you can zoom out or in for a better view. For example, you may need to zoom in to see the details of an object you are editing, or you might need to zoom out to see the entire Stage area.

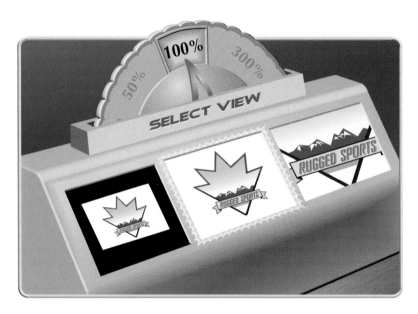

Zooming your view merely changes the magnification of the Stage area and does not change the size of the objects you are viewing.

ZOOM OUT OR IN

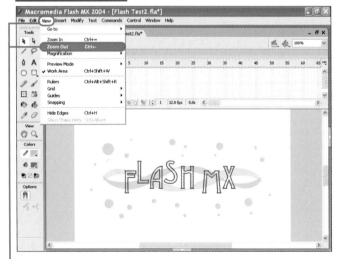

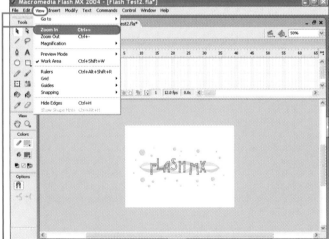

ZOOM OUT

1 Click **View**.

2 Click **Zoom Out**.

■ Flash zooms your view of the Stage.

■ You can select the command again to zoom out another magnification level.

ZOOM IN

1 Click **View**.

2 Click **Zoom In**.

■ Flash zooms your view of the Stage.

■ You can select the command again to zoom in another magnification level.

How do I use the Zoom tool button?

You can also use the Zoom button on the
Drawing toolbar to change the magnification.

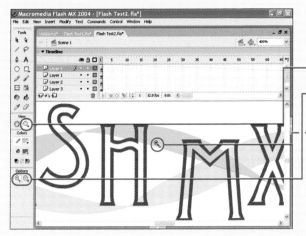

1 Click the Zoom button (🔍).

2 Click the Enlarge (🔍)
or Reduce (🔍) buttons.

3 Click the area of the Stage
you want to view.

■ The area enlarges or reduces.

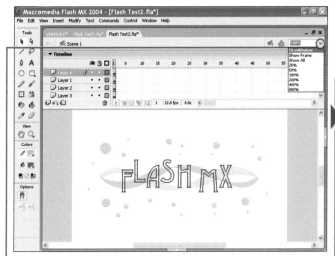

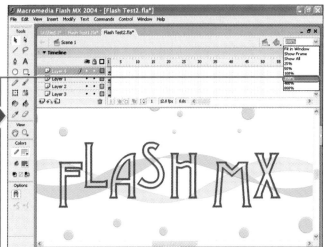

<u>SELECT A ZOOM PERCENTAGE</u>

1 Click the ⌄ of the
Zoom box.

2 Click a magnification
percentage.

■ Flash immediately
adjusts the view.

■ In this example, the
window zooms to 200
percent.

USING RULERS AND GRIDS

To help you draw with more precision, turn on the Flash rulers and grid lines. Both tools can help you position objects on the Stage. The rulers and grids do not appear in the final movie.

You can use rulers to measure the various elements on the Stage. You can use gridlines to help you quickly position elements on the Stage.

USING RULERS AND GRIDS

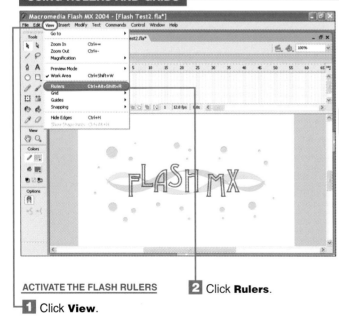

ACTIVATE THE FLASH RULERS

1 Click **View**.

2 Click **Rulers**.

■ Flash opens a horizontal and vertical ruler in the Stage area.

■ You can repeat steps **1** and **2** to turn off the ruler.

How can I precisely align objects with the grid?

Use the Snap tool to help you quickly align objects to the grid lines. To activate the tool, click **View**, and then click **Snap**. You can also click **View**, click **Grid**, and then click **Snap To Grid**.

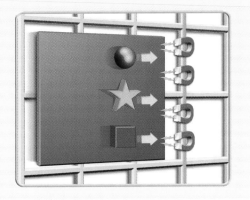

What are guides?

Guides are lines that appear as you move items on the stage to help with positioning. You can turn on the Flash guides as another tool to help you position objects on the Stage. To display the guides, click **View**, click **Guides**, and then click **Show Guides**. You must also turn on the Flash rulers in order to use guides. To add a guide to the Stage, drag a guide line off of the ruler and onto the Stage. To remove a guide, drag it back to the ruler.

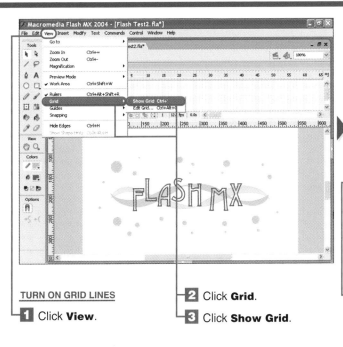

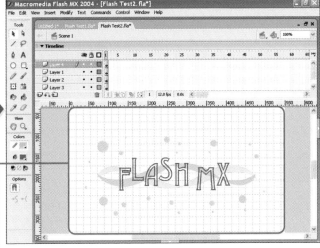

TURN ON GRID LINES

1 Click **View**.

2 Click **Grid**.

3 Click **Show Grid**.

■ Grid lines appear on the Stage.

■ You can repeat steps **1** to **3** to turn off the grid lines.

FIND HELP WITH FLASH

When you run across a program feature or technique that you do not understand, consult the Flash Help system. The Flash help files offer a wide variety of topics ranging from basic Flash features, such as how to use on-screen buttons and drawing tools, to advance features, such as how to write scripts using ActionScript.

You display the Flash Help information in the Help panel. Like the other panels available in Flash, you can move, resize, collapse, and expand the Help panel. See the section "Work with Panels" to learn more.

FIND HELP WITH FLASH

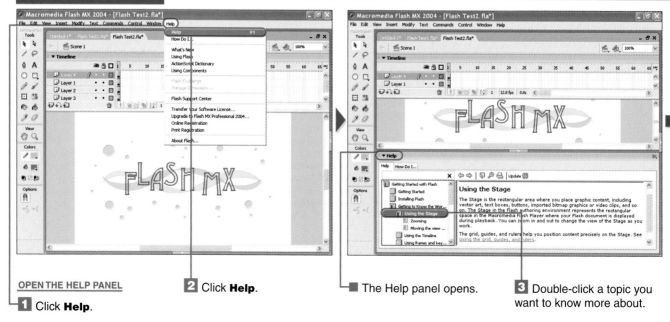

OPEN THE HELP PANEL

1 Click **Help**.

2 Click **Help**.

■ The Help panel opens.

3 Double-click a topic you want to know more about.

Where else can I find Flash help?

Macromedia's Web site (www.macromedia.com/support/flash/) is a good place to start if you are looking for additional information about the Flash program. To access the site from Flash, click Help, and then click **Flash Support Center**. This opens your default Web browser. You may need to log onto your Internet connection first. You can also find numerous sites on the Internet dedicated to Flash users by performing a simple search for the keyword *Flash* using your favorite search engine.

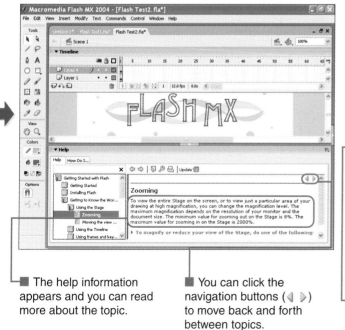

■ The help information appears and you can read more about the topic.

■ You can click the navigation buttons (◁ ▷) to move back and forth between topics.

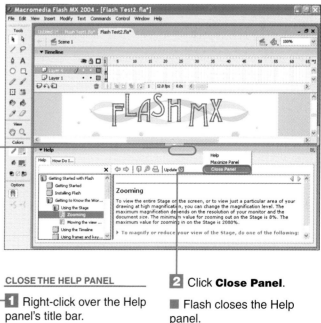

CLOSE THE HELP PANEL

1 Right-click over the Help panel's title bar.

2 Click **Close Panel**.

■ Flash closes the Help panel.

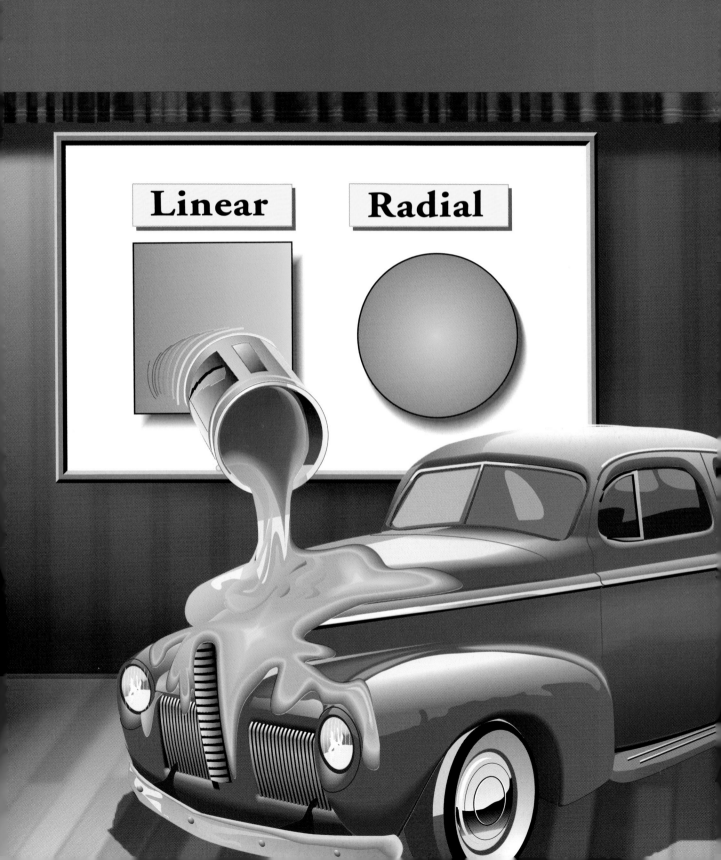

CHAPTER 2

Creating Shapes and Objects

Do you want to draw your own illustrations to animate? Flash offers many tools you can use to make all sorts of illustrations.

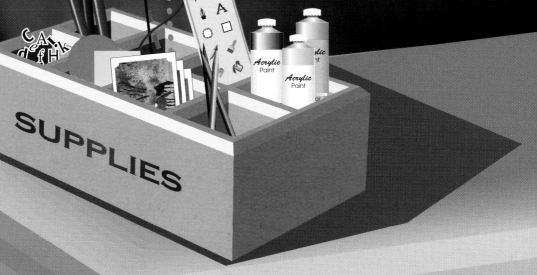

INTRODUCING FLASH OBJECTS

You can create all kinds of drawings in Flash. The program includes a variety of tools for creating simple shapes or complex images to use in your Flash movies. Flash drawings are composed of lines, also called *strokes*, and solid colors that fill the interior of connected lines. An item you draw is called an *object*.

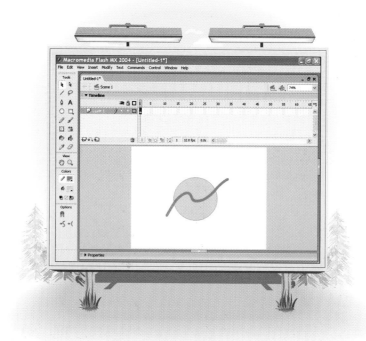

Shape Recognition

It is not always easy to draw with a computer mouse, but Flash makes it simpler with shape recognition. Draw a rough idea of a shape, and Flash automatically cleans it up for you. The shape recognition feature is turned on by default.

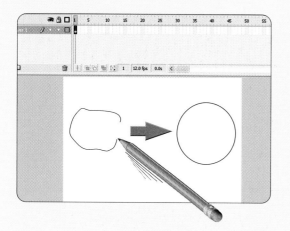

Segments

When you draw overlapping lines or shapes, the areas that overlap divide the object into segments. You can then manipulate the segments separately, if needed. For example, if you draw a line though an oval, the line becomes segmented everywhere it overlaps the oval.

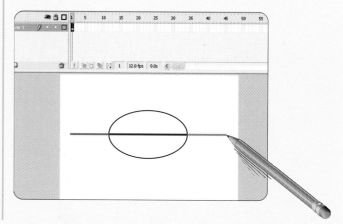

Manipulating Objects

You can combine simple objects to create drawings, or remove parts to create new shapes. You can change an object's color, scale, and positioning. You can also stack objects on top of other objects to give your drawings depth.

Overlay Level

The *overlay level* is like a transparent sheet of paper on top of the stage level. Any object you place on the overlay level floats on top and does not interact with stage-level objects. Overlay-level objects include items you group together to act as a single unit, symbols you create for reuse throughout your movie, text blocks, and imported graphics.

Stage Level

When working with objects on the Stage, there are two levels: the stage level and the overlay level. The *Stage level* is the bottom level on the Stage and any objects you place there can interact. For example, a line and a shape can connect. Stage-level objects include anything you draw with the drawing tools.

Breaking Apart Objects

Flash makes it easy to break apart overlay-level objects and turn them into stage-level objects you can manipulate and edit. For example, you can turn text into graphic shapes you can resize and rotate.

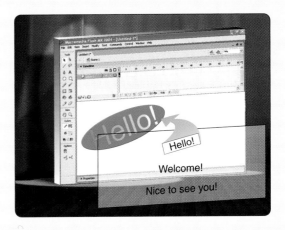

USING THE TOOLS PANEL

Packed with tools, the Tools panel helps you create and work with graphic and text objects. By default, it appears docked on the far left side of the program window. To hide the Tools panel at any time, click Windows, then Tools.

Selection
You can use this tool to grab, select, and move items on the Stage.

Subselection
Displays edit points you can adjust to change a line's shape.

Line
Draws straight lines.

Lasso
Use to select irregularly shaped objects on the Stage.

Pen
Use to draw precise curves.

Oval
Draws circle and oval shapes.

Pencil
Use to draw freeform lines.

Free Transform
Use to rotate, scale, skew, or distort objects.

Text
Draws text boxes.

Rectangle
Draws square and rectangle shapes, or, when you click the button's ▾, you can draw polygon shapes.

Brush
Draws with a fill color, much like a paintbrush.

Fill Transform
Use to edit a fill color or pattern.

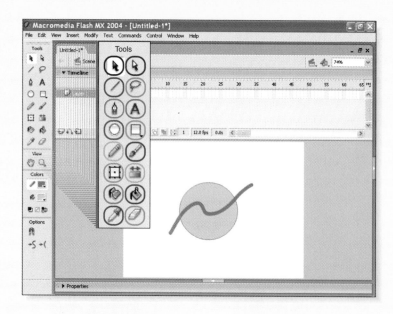

Ink Bottle
Use to change the style, thickness, and color of lines.

Paint Bucket
Fills shapes or lines with color.

Eyedropper
Use to copy the attributes of one object to another.

Eraser
Erases parts of a graphic object.

View Tools

Hand

Use to move your view of the objects on the Stage or in the work area.

Zoom

Magnifies your view or zooms out for a better look at the Stage.

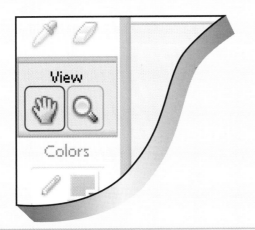

Option Tools

Some of the drawing tools you select might offer modifiers that enable you to set additional controls for the tool.

See Chapter 1 to learn how to display or hide the Tools panel.

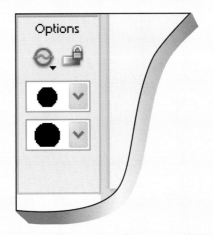

Color Tools and Controls

Line Color controls

Click to display a palette of colors for lines.

Fill Color controls

Click to display a palette of colors for fills.

Black and White

Changes the line color to black and the fill color to white.

No Color button

Use to draw shapes without fill colors.

SWAP Colors

Switches the line color to the fill color and vice versa.

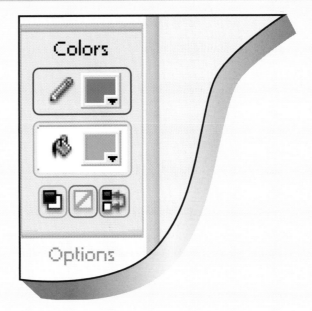

DRAW LINE SEGMENTS

You can draw all sorts of objects with lines. The easiest way to draw straight lines in Flash is to use the Line tool. To draw a freeform line, use the Pencil tool. Lines, also called *strokes* in Flash, can connect with other lines and shapes to create a drawing.

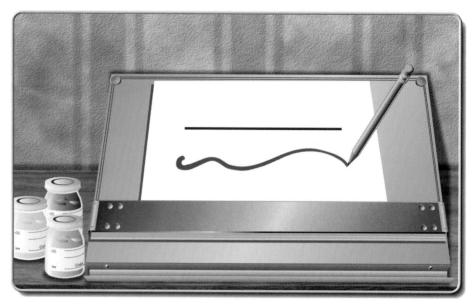

DRAW LINE SEGMENTS

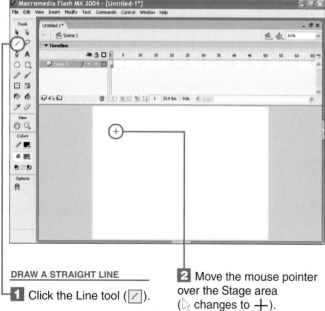

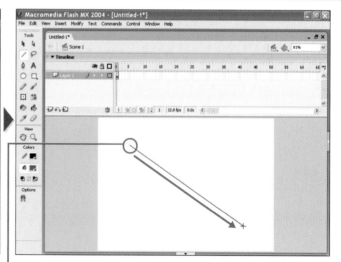

DRAW A STRAIGHT LINE

1 Click the Line tool ().

2 Move the mouse pointer over the Stage area (⟍ changes to +).

3 Click and drag to draw a line to your desired length.

4 Release the mouse button.

■ The line appears to your specifications.

How do I control the line thickness?

You can set a line thickness before you start drawing the actual line segment. Open the Properties inspector, if it is not already open. See Chapter 1 to learn more about this panel. The Properties inspector displays options for controlling line thickness, style, and color. To change the thickness, drag the thickness slider up or down. You can apply a new line thickness to an existing line by first clicking the line to select it and then dragging the slider.

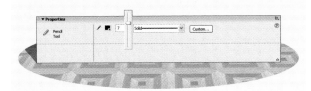

How do I keep a straight line vertical or horizontal?

Using the Line tool, hold down `Shift` and draw a line that is pretty much vertical or horizontal. Flash makes the line perfectly vertical or horizontal. This trick also works when drawing a 45-degree line.

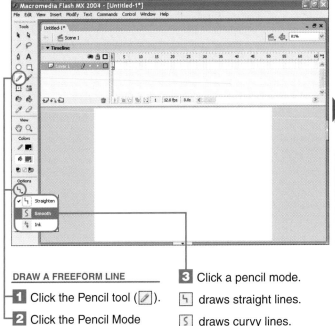

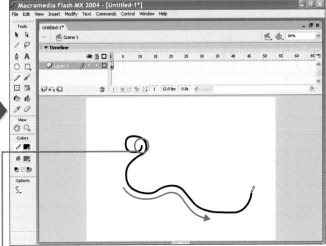

DRAW A FREEFORM LINE

1 Click the Pencil tool (✏️).

2 Click the Pencil Mode button (🔽).

3 Click a pencil mode.

🔽 draws straight lines.

⑤ draws curvy lines.

🖌 draws freeform lines.

4 Click and drag your cursor on the Stage to draw the line (cursor changes to ✏️).

5 Release the mouse button.

■ The line appears to your specifications.

DRAW LINES WITH THE PEN TOOL

You can draw precise lines and curves with the Pen tool. Using this tool takes some getting used to, but with a little practice, you can draw lines easily. Lines that you create with the Pen tool are composed of points, which appear as dots on the line segment and represent changes in the line's curvature.

The quickest way to draw curves is to drag the Pen tool along with its control handle on the Flash Stage. The *control handle* is a straight line with two solid points at either end. You can rotate the bar to create different degrees of curvature.

DRAW LINES WITH THE PEN TOOL

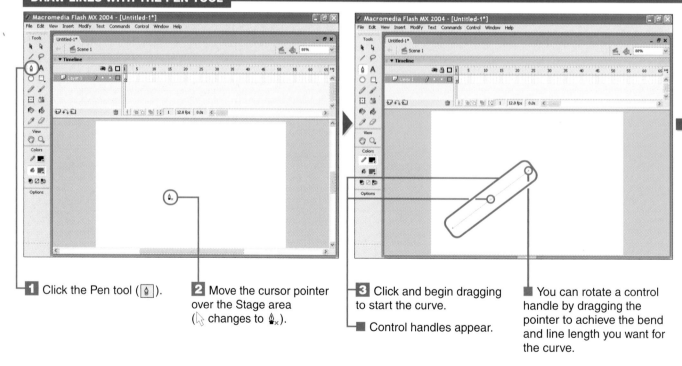

1 Click the Pen tool (👆).

2 Move the cursor pointer over the Stage area (👆 changes to 👆ₓ).

3 Click and begin dragging to start the curve.

■ Control handles appear.

■ You can rotate a control handle by dragging the pointer to achieve the bend and line length you want for the curve.

How can I edit points on a curved line?

Use the Subselection tool to make changes to a curved line you created using the Pen tool. Click [↖] and move the cursor over an edit point on the line or at the end of the line. Drag to reposition and reshape the line or curve.

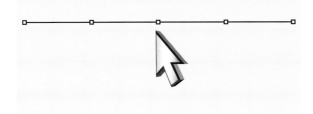

Is there a way to constrain the degree of curvature?

Yes. You can press and hold down [Shift] while dragging the Pen tool to keep the curves at 45-degree angles.

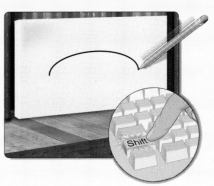

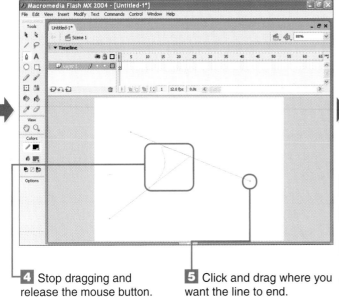

4 Stop dragging and release the mouse button.

5 Click and drag where you want the line to end.

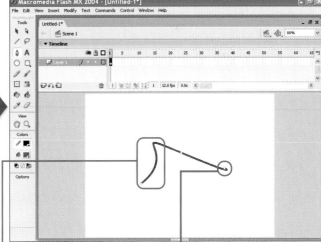

6 Release the mouse button.

■ The curved line appears on the Stage.

■ You can add more curves to an existing curved line as long as the Pen tool is still active by simply dragging another line segment.

■ Flash automatically attaches the second line segment to the first curved line.

DRAW OVAL AND RECTANGLE SHAPES

You can create simple shapes in Flash and then fill them with a color or pattern or use them as part of a drawing. You can create shapes using many of the tools on the Tools panel, but for more uniform shapes, such as circles, ovals, squares, and rectangles, you can use the Oval or Rectangle tools.

DRAW OVAL AND RECTANGLE SHAPES

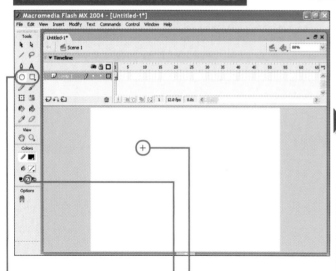

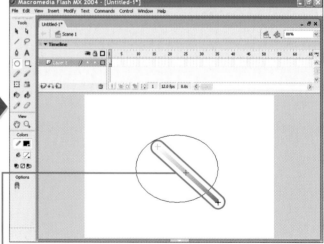

DRAW AN EMPTY SHAPE

1 Click the Oval (⬭) or Rectangle (⬜) tool.

■ To draw a polygon, click the Rectangle tool's ·, click **PolyStar Tool**, and then draw the shape.

2 Move the cursor over the Stage area (⬚ changes to ✛).

■ You can draw a shape without a fill by clicking the No Color button (⬚).

3 Click and drag to draw the shape you want.

4 Release the mouse button.

■ Flash completes the shape.

How do I draw a rectangle with rounded corners?

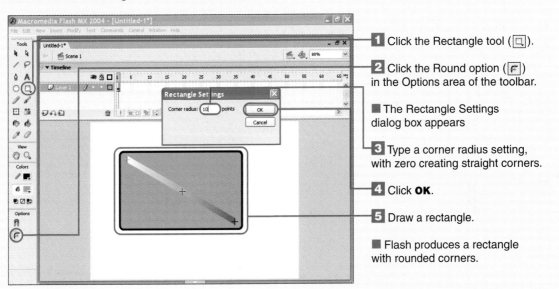

1 Click the Rectangle tool (▭).

2 Click the Round option (⌐) in the Options area of the toolbar.

■ The Rectangle Settings dialog box appears

3 Type a corner radius setting, with zero creating straight corners.

4 Click **OK**.

5 Draw a rectangle.

■ Flash produces a rectangle with rounded corners.

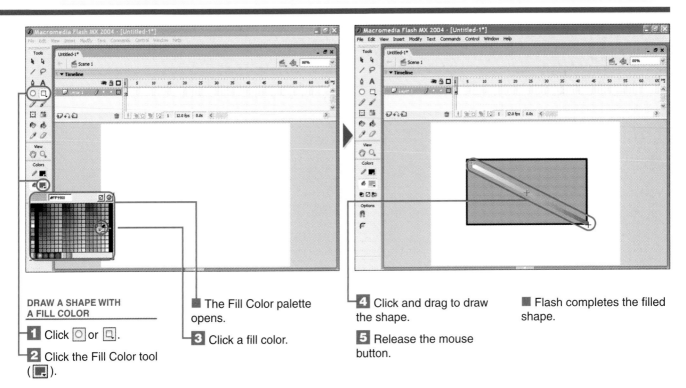

DRAW A SHAPE WITH A FILL COLOR

1 Click ○ or ▭.

2 Click the Fill Color tool (▣).

■ The Fill Color palette opens.

3 Click a fill color.

4 Click and drag to draw the shape.

5 Release the mouse button.

■ Flash completes the filled shape.

DRAW OBJECTS WITH THE BRUSH TOOL

You can use the Brush tool to draw with brush strokes, much like a paintbrush. You can control the size and shape of the brush as well as how the brush strokes appear on the Stage.

DRAW OBJECTS WITH THE BRUSH TOOL

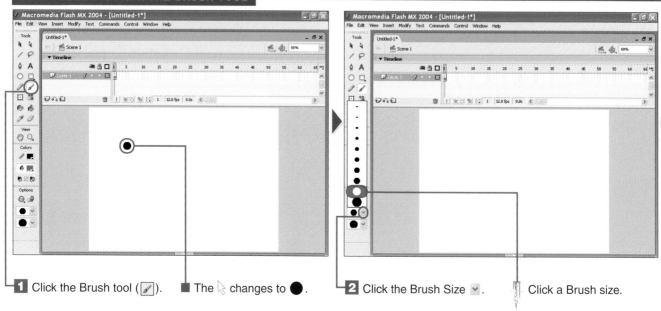

1 Click the Brush tool (🖌).

■ The ⏳ changes to ●.

2 Click the Brush Size ☑.

Click a Brush size.

What do the brush modes do?

You can find five brush modes by clicking the Brush Mode button
(⬛) at the bottom of the Tools panel toolbar.

⬤ **Paint Normal**	⬤ **Paint Fills**	⬤ **Paint Behind**	⬤ **Paint Selection**	⬤ **Paint Inside**
Lets you paint over anything on the Stage.	Paints inside fill areas but not on lines.	Paints beneath any existing objects on the Stage.	Paints only inside the selected area.	Begins a brush stroke inside a fill area without affecting any lines.

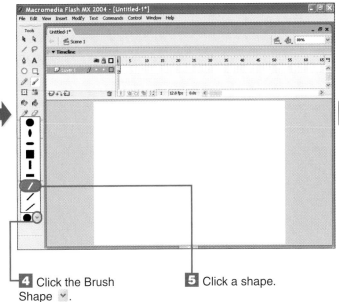

4 Click the Brush
Shape ☑.

5 Click a shape.

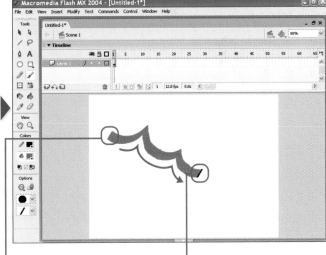

6 Move your cursor over
the Stage.

■ The mouse pointer
displays the brush size and
shape you selected.

7 Click and drag to begin
drawing.

■ A brush pattern appears
to your specifications.

FILL OBJECTS WITH THE PAINT BUCKET TOOL

You can use the Paint Bucket tool to quickly fill in objects, such as shapes. You can fill objects with a color, a gradient effect, or even a picture. The Flash Color palette comes with numerous colors and shades, as well as several premade gradient effects from which to choose.

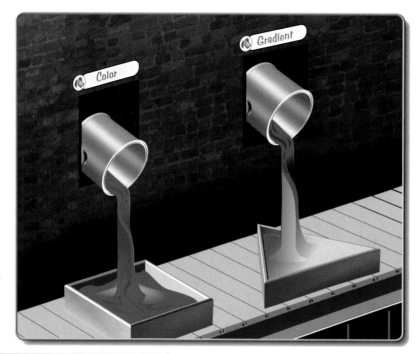

A gradient is two or more colors that blend together. See Chapter 3 to learn more about creating new gradient effects.

FILL OBJECTS WITH THE PAINT BUCKET TOOL

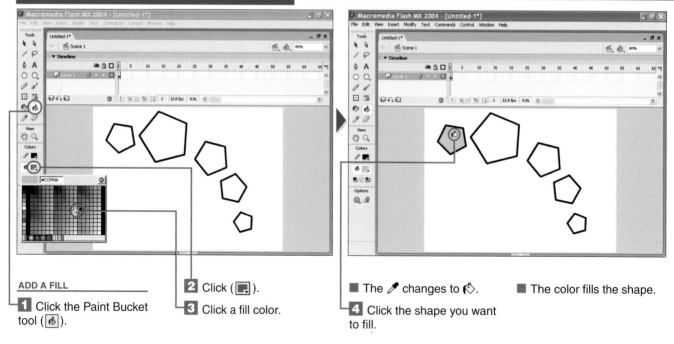

ADD A FILL

1 Click the Paint Bucket tool (🪣).

2 Click (▦).

3 Click a fill color.

■ The ✏ changes to 🪣.

4 Click the shape you want to fill.

■ The color fills the shape.

What is a gradient effect?

A *gradient effect* shows one or several colors of different intensities, creating a three-dimensional effect. With Flash, you can create a linear gradient effect that intensifies color shading from left to right or top to bottom, or create a radial gradient effect that intensifies color shading from the middle to the outer edges or vice versa.

What does the Gap Size modifier do?

When you select the Paint Bucket tool, the Gap Size modifier (🔘) appears in the Options tray at the bottom of the Tools panel. Click 🔘 to display a menu list of four settings. These settings determine how the Paint Bucket tool treats any gaps that appear in the shape you are trying to fill. For very large gaps, you may need to close the gaps yourself before applying the fill color.

- ○ Don't Close Gaps
- ✓ ○ Close Small Gaps
- ○ Close Medium Gaps
- ○ Close Large Gaps

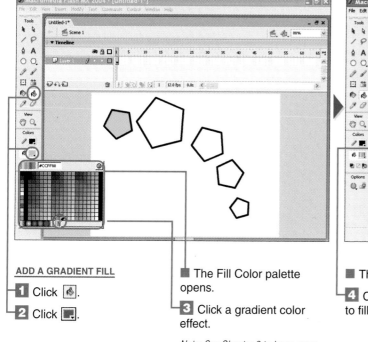

ADD A GRADIENT FILL

1 Click 🖊.

2 Click 🔲.

■ The Fill Color palette opens.

3 Click a gradient color effect.

Note: See Chapter 3 to learn more about creating new gradient effects.

■ The 🖊 changes to 🖐.

4 Click the shape you want to fill.

■ The gradient colors fill the shape.

Enhancing and Editing Objects

Need to enhance your drawn object or give it some depth? This chapter shows you how to use a variety of editing tools to enhance shapes and lines, as well as adjust stacking order, change fill colors, and format strokes. You can also use these same tools to edit graphics you import.

SELECT OBJECTS

To work with objects you draw or place on the Flash Stage, you must first select them. The more lines and shapes you place on the Stage, the trickier it is to select only the ones you want. There are several techniques you can use for selecting objects.

You can use the Selection tool to quickly select any single object, such as a line segment or fill. To select several objects, you can drag a marquee around the items.

SELECT OBJECTS

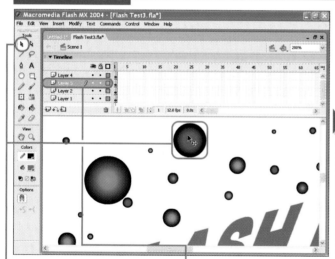

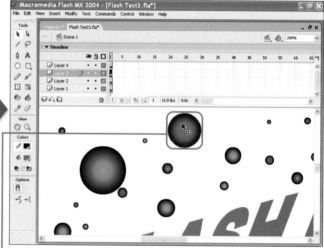

CLICK TO SELECT OBJECTS

■1 Click the Selection tool (🖈).

■2 Click the object you want to select.

■ You can select a fill and its surrounding line border by double-clicking the fill.

■ When working with multiple layers, click the layer containing the object you want to select, and then click the object.

Note: See Chapter 6 to learn about layers.

■ Selected objects appear highlighted with a pattern.

■ You can now edit the object.

How do I select multiple objects?

Hold down Shift while clicking objects when you want to select more than one at a time. For example, if you have a line with several segments, you can select all of them for editing. Click ▶; then hold Shift and click each line segment you want to select.

How do I select everything on the Stage?

Click **Edit** and then click **Select All**. You can also press Ctrl + A (⌘ + A) on the keyboard.

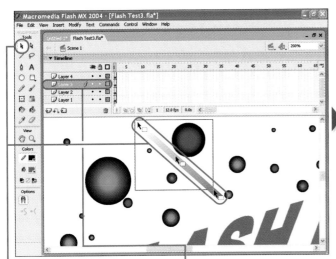

SELECT BY DRAGGING

1 Click ▶.

2 Click and drag a square selection box around the object you want to select.

■ When working with multiple layers, click the layer containing the object you want to select, and then click the object.

Note: See Chapter 6 to learn more about layers.

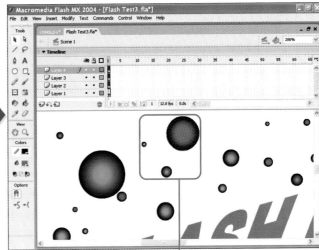

3 Release the mouse button.

■ Flash selects everything inside the selection box.

CONTINUED ▶

SELECT OBJECTS

You can use the Lasso tool to select irregular objects. The Lasso tool draws a freehand "rope" around the item you want to select. This allows you to select an oddly shaped object or just a small portion of an object.

You must drag the Lasso tool completely around the item you want to select. If you make a mistake and lasso a part of the drawing you do not want to select, click anywhere on-screen and try again.

SELECT OBJECTS (CONTINUED)

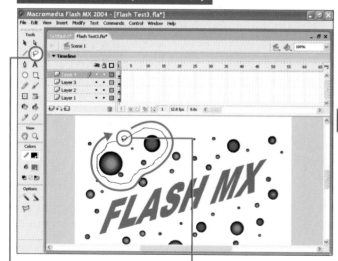

LASSO AN IRREGULARLY SHAPED OBJECT

1 Click the Lasso tool (🔲) (🖐 changes to 🅿).

2 Click and drag 🅿 completely around the object until you reach the point where you started.

■ When working with multiple layers, click the layer containing the object you want to select, and then click the object.

Note: See Chapter 6 to learn more about layers.

3 Release the mouse button.

■ Flash highlights anything inside the lasso shape.

How can I select complex shapes?

Drawing around irregular items with the Lasso tool can be difficult. For additional help, use the Lasso tool's Polygon Mode modifier (⬡). Click the Lasso tool (⬡) and then click ⬡ in the Modifier Tray. Now click your way around the object you want to select. Every click creates a connected line to the last click. To turn off the Polygon Mode, double-click the icon.

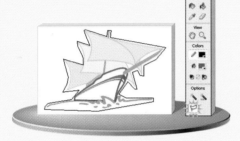

How do I select just a fill and not its border?

Simply click the fill to select it. To select both the fill and the fill's border, double-click the fill.

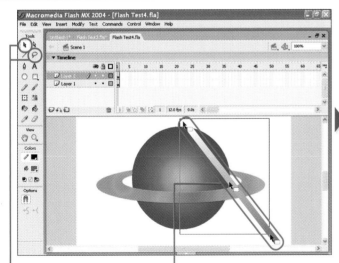

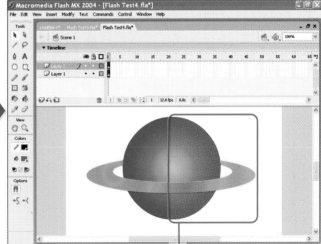

__SELECT PART OF AN OBJECT__

1 Click ⬡ or ⬡.

■ You can click ⬡ for simple shapes or lines.

■ You can click ⬡ for irregularly shaped objects.

2 Click and drag ⬡ to surround the object part you want to select.

3 Release the mouse button.

■ Flash selects everything inside the area over which you dragged.

EDIT LINE SEGMENTS

You can change a line by adjusting its length or reshaping its curve. For example, you may want to change the angle of a line, extend a curved line to make it appear longer, or just simply make the curve more curvy. You can edit any line segment by altering its end points.

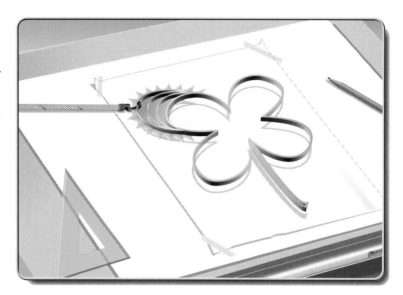

Unlike other editing techniques, you do not need to first select the line in order to modify its end points.

EDIT LINE SEGMENTS

CHANGE A LINE'S LENGTH

1 Click [↖].

2 Move ↖ over an end of the line.

Note: Do not click the line to select it.

■ A ⌐ appears next to the ↖.

3 Click and drag the end of the line to shorten or lengthen the segment.

■ As you drag ↖⌐ in any direction, you can change the line's angle.

4 Release the mouse button.

■ Flash resizes the line.

48

How do I draw perfect vertical and horizontal lines?

You may find it difficult to keep a steady hand while drawing a line on the Stage. You can draw perfectly straight horizontal and vertical lines if you hold `Shift` down while dragging the Line tool across the Stage.

Can I see precise edit points on a line?

Yes. Click the Subselection tool (▸) and then click the line. Edit points appear at either end of the line, and if the line consists of more than one segment, edit points also appear at each change of the segment. You can drag any edit point to reshape the line.

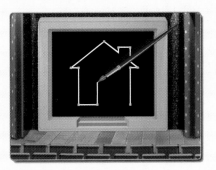

RESHAPE A LINE SEGMENT

1 Click ▸.

2 Move the ▸ over the area of the line you want to curve.

Note: Do not click the line to select it.

■ A ∪ appears next to the ▸.

3 Click and drag the line to add or reshape the curve.

4 Release the mouse button

■ Flash reshapes the line.

49

SMOOTH OR STRAIGHTEN LINE SEGMENTS

You can create subtle or dramatic changes in your drawing by smoothing or straightening line segments. For example, perhaps you have painstakingly drawn a tree with several curving branches. You now decide a few of your branches need some modifications. You can use the Selection tool's Smooth or Straighten option buttons on the Tools panel to adjust your lines.

SMOOTH OR STRAIGHTEN LINE SEGMENTS

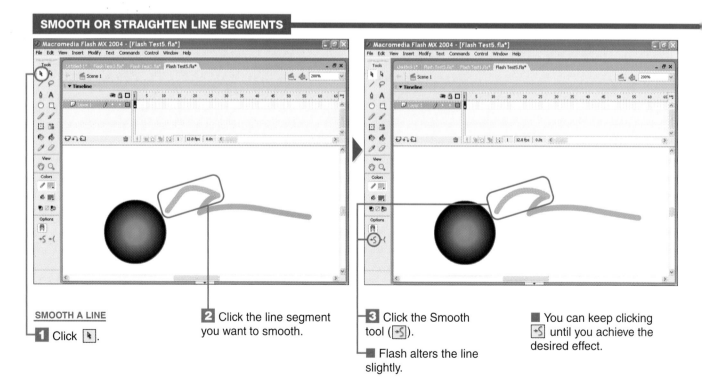

SMOOTH A LINE

1 Click ![cursor].

2 Click the line segment you want to smooth.

3 Click the Smooth tool (![icon]).

■ Flash alters the line slightly.

■ You can keep clicking ![icon] until you achieve the desired effect.

Why do my curved lines appear so rough?

A previous user may have made some adjustments to the program's preferences, which you can adjust via the Preferences dialog box:

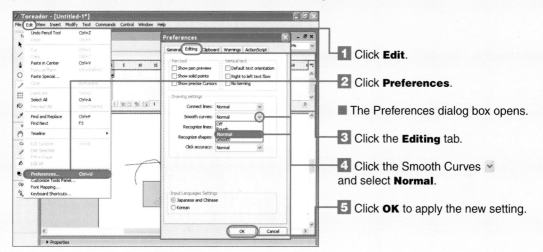

1 Click **Edit**.

2 Click **Preferences**.

■ The Preferences dialog box opens.

3 Click the **Editing** tab.

4 Click the Smooth Curves ⊻ and select **Normal**.

5 Click **OK** to apply the new setting.

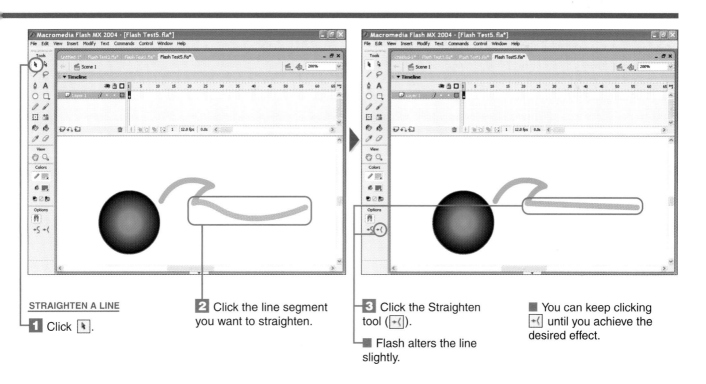

STRAIGHTEN A LINE

1 Click ▶.

2 Click the line segment you want to straighten.

3 Click the Straighten tool (⊣).

■ Flash alters the line slightly.

■ You can keep clicking ⊣ until you achieve the desired effect.

EDIT FILLS

With Flash, you can change a fill shape by adjusting the sides of the fill. A *fill* is a color or pattern that fills a closed outline or shape. You can also change the fill color at any time to create additional changes to the shape or object. For more on creating a fill object, see Chapter 2.

You must select the fill first in order to apply a new color. As long as you highlight the fill on the Stage, you can continue trying different colors from the Fill Color palette.

EDIT FILLS

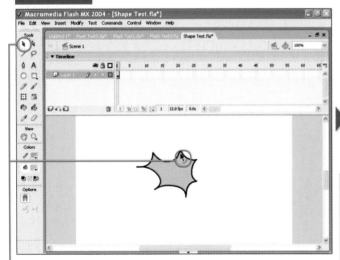

RESHAPE A FILL

1 Click [k].

2 Move the k over the edge of the fill.

Note: Do not select the fill.

■ A ⌒ or a ⌐ appears next to the k.

3 Click and drag the fill's edge in or out to reshape the fill.

How can I soften the edges of a fill shape?

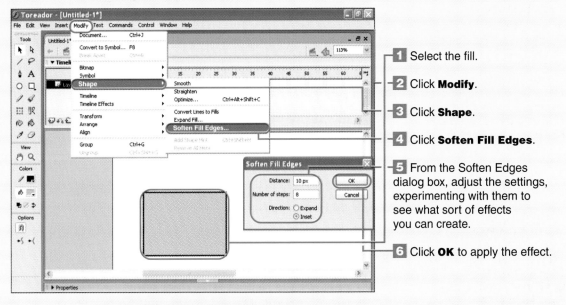

1 Select the fill.

2 Click **Modify**.

3 Click **Shape**.

4 Click **Soften Fill Edges**.

5 From the Soften Edges dialog box, adjust the settings, experimenting with them to see what sort of effects you can create.

6 Click **OK** to apply the effect.

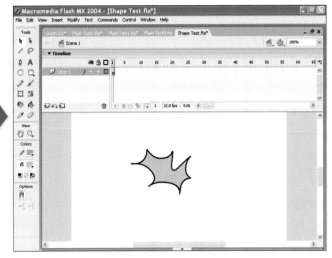

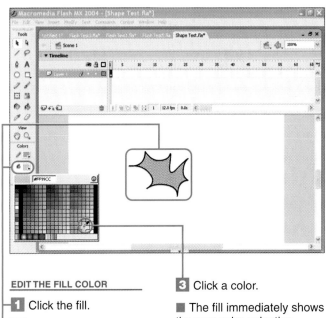

4 Release the mouse button.

■ Flash reshapes the fill.

EDIT THE FILL COLOR

1 Click the fill.

2 Click the Fill Color tool ( ) to open the color palette.

3 Click a color.

■ The fill immediately shows the new color selection.

Note: See the Section "Create Gradient Effects" to learn how to work with gradient fills.

MODIFY OBJECTS WITH THE FREE TRANSFORM TOOL

You can use the Free Transform tool in Flash to rotate, skew, scale, distort, and envelope objects, thus creating new shapes to use in your animations and Flash movies. The Free Transform tool, found on the Tools panel, includes four modifier tools: Rotate and Skew, Scale, Distort, and Envelope.

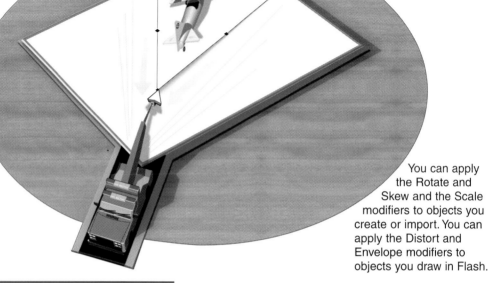

You can apply the Rotate and Skew and the Scale modifiers to objects you create or import. You can apply the Distort and Envelope modifiers to objects you draw in Flash.

MODIFY OBJECTS WITH THE FREE TRANSFORM TOOL

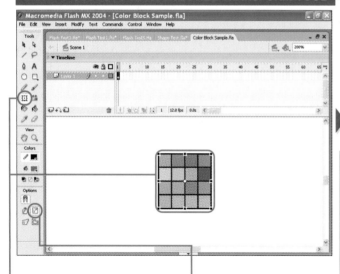

SCALE AN OBJECT

1 Select the object you want to resize.

2 Click the Free Transform tool (⊞).

3 Click the Scale tool (⊞).

■ Flash surrounds the object with edit points.

4 Click and drag an edit point to scale the object.

■ You can drag corner edit points to resize the object while keeping its proportions.

■ You can drag middle edit points to stretch or compress an object thus distorting its shape.

5 Release the mouse button.

■ The object resizes.

54

How do I set a precise size?

If you need to size an object to a precise measurement, use the Info panel. Click **Window**, **Design Panels**, and then **Info**. This opens the Info panel. Here you can set a precise size for the object using the width (W) and height (H) text boxes. Simply type in the measurement you want, then click outside the panel to see the changes take effect.

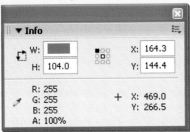

What happens if I resize an item beyond the Stage?

In some cases, the object you resize may reach beyond the Stage area. Not to worry, the object is still there. You may need to zoom out to see the object. You can move the item back onto the Stage or resize the Stage to fit the larger object. Any part of the object that hangs off the Stage is still considered in the work area; however, the part may not be visible when you play your Flash movie. See Chapter 1 to learn more about resizing the Stage area.

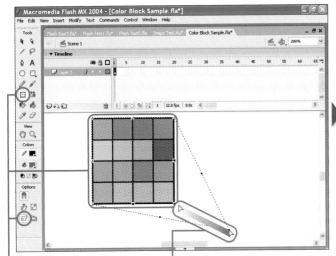

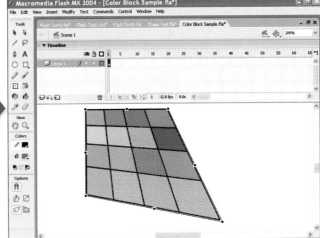

DISTORT AN OBJECT

■ **1** Select the object you want to distort.

■ **2** Click 🔲.

■ **3** Click the Distort button ✍.

■ Flash surrounds the object with edit points.

■ **4** Click and drag an edit point to distort the object (➤ changes to ▷).

■ **5** Release the mouse button.

■ The object distorts.

CONTINUED ▶

You can use the Free Transform tool's skew and envelope features to warp and distort an object or shape, which is useful for creating morphed elements for animations. The skew feature allows you to distort an object by slanting it on one or both axes. The Envelope modifier allows you to enclose the object with edit points, and then use the points to control the shape.

MODIFY OBJECTS WITH THE FREE TRANSFORM TOOL (CONTINUED)

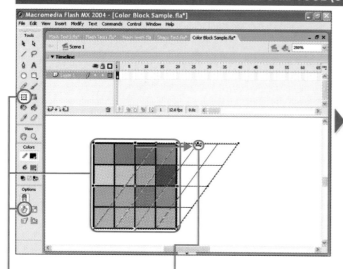

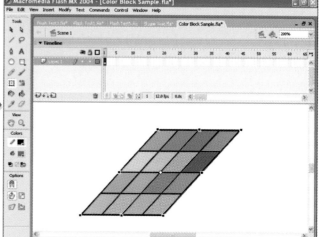

SKEW AN OBJECT

1 Select the object.

2 Click 田.

3 Click the Rotate and Skew tool (🔲).

■ Edit points appear around the selected object.

4 Click and drag an edge of the object to skew the object shape (🡤 changes to ⇌).

5 Release the mouse button.

■ The object skews.

How do I distort text in Flash?

Using the Break Apart command, you can break apart the strokes and fills that make up the letters in a word or words. You can then use the Envelope modifier to distort the shape of the text. To do so, click the text box, click **Modify**, and then **Break Apart**. When you repeat this step a second time, you can apply the Envelope modifier. See Chapter 5 to learn more about working with the Text tool.

What types of edit points does the Envelope modifier use?

The Envelope modifier uses two types of edit points: regular edit points and tangent handles. *Regular edit points* are square and when you manipulate them, they change the corners and sides of an object. *Tangent handles* are circles that adjust additional points along the edges of a selected object. You can only use the Envelope modifier to change shapes you create in Flash. You cannot use the feature to alter symbols, bitmaps, text boxes, or video objects. Learn how to use the rotate portion of the feature in the next section, "Rotate and Flip Objects."

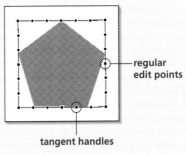

regular edit points

tangent handles

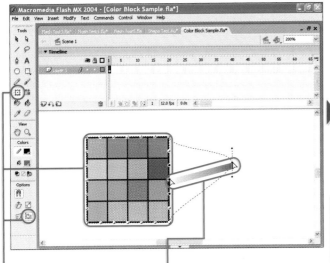

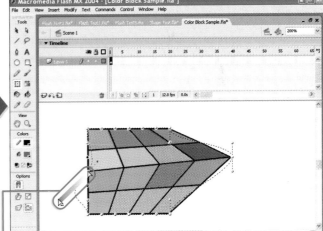

ENVELOPE A SHAPE

1 Select the shape.

2 Click ⊞.

3 Click the Envelope tool (▦).

■ Edit points surround the object.

4 Click and drag an edit point to change the object shape (↖ changes to ▷).

■ An outline of the object appears as you drag.

5 Release the mouse button.

■ The object reshapes.

6 Click and drag a tangent point to change the object shape (↖ changes to ▷).

■ An outline of the object appears as you drag.

7 Release the mouse button.

■ The object reshapes again.

ROTATE AND FLIP OBJECTS

Not every shape or line you draw has to remain as it is on the Stage. You can reorient objects to create different looks. You can spin an object based on its center point, or you can flip an object vertically or horizontally. Both actions enable you to quickly change an object's position in a drawing.

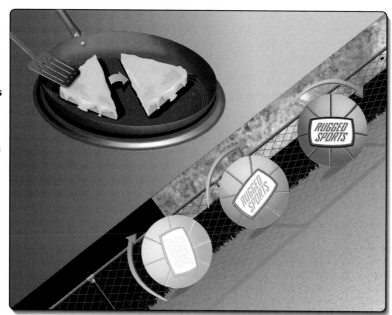

When you rotate an object on the Stage, you use the edit points, also called rotation handles, to reorient the object. When you flip an object, there are no edit points.

ROTATE OBJECTS

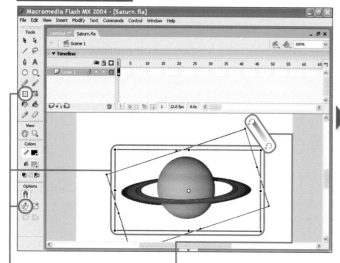

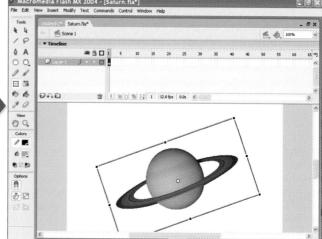

1 Select the object or shape you want to rotate.

2 Click 🔲.

3 Click 🔄.

■ Edit points appear around the selected object.

4 Click and drag an edit point to rotate the object (k changes to ⟳).

■ An outline of the object appears as you rotate.

5 Release the mouse button.

■ The object rotates.

Can I change an object's center point?

Although for most objects, the center point is truly the object's center, you may want the center point to reference another part of the object so that you can change the way in which Flash scales, aligns, or transforms an animation or object. To change the center point, select the object, and then click the Free Transform tool (). The center point appears as a tiny circle icon in the middle of the selected object. Drag the center point icon to a new location. Note: This only works on overlay-level, not stage-level, objects. See Chapter 2 to learn more about drawing levels.

Center Point

FLIP OBJECTS

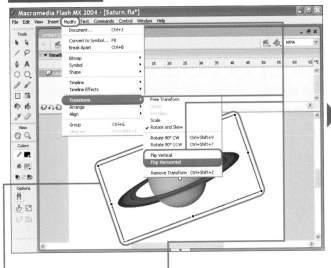

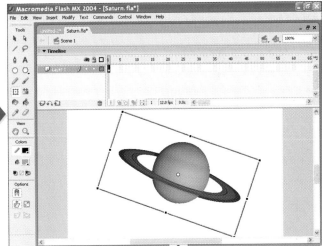

1 Select the object you want to flip.

Note: To learn more about selecting objects, see the section "Select Objects" in this chapter.

2 Click **Modify**.

3 Click **Transform**.

4 Click **Flip Vertical** or **Flip Horizontal**.

■ The object flips on the Stage.

USING THE ERASER TOOL

You can use the Eraser tool to erase stray parts of a drawing or object, or you can use it to create new shapes within an object. The Eraser tool has several modifiers you can use to control how the tool works.

Use the Eraser tool to erase strokes and fills on the stage level. You cannot erase grouped objects, symbols, or text blocks unless you apply the Break Apart command and make the items part of the stage level rather than the overlay level.

USING THE ERASER TOOL

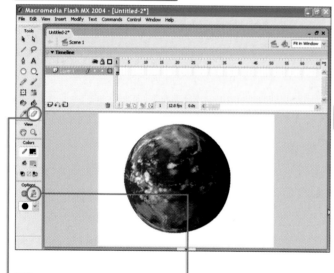

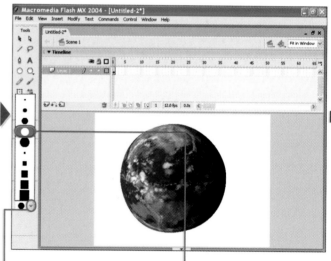

1 Click the Eraser tool ( ).

■ For a quick erase of entire lines or fills, you can click the Faucet tool ( ), and then click the item you want to erase.

2 Click ⌄ in the Erase size box.

3 Click a size or shape for the Eraser.

What do the Eraser modifiers do?

You can use one of five modifiers with the Eraser tool.

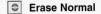

Erase Normal

Lets you erase over anything on the Stage

Erase Fills

Erases inside fill areas but not lines

Erase Lines

Erases only lines

Erase Selected Fills

Does just that — erases only the selected fill

Erase Inside

Erases only inside the selected area

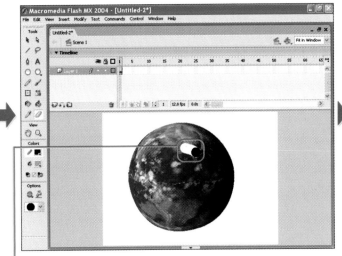

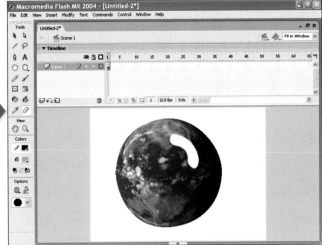

4 Click and drag to begin erasing.

■ The ⬍ displays the eraser size and shape you selected ●.

5 Release the mouse button.

■ An eraser path marks everywhere you dragged over the object.

CREATE A GRADIENT EFFECT

You can use gradient effects to add depth and dimension to your Flash drawings. A *gradient* effect is a band of blended color or shading. You can apply a gradient effect as a fill to any shape. By default, the Fill Color palette offers several preformatted gradient effects you can use. This task shows you how to create your own.

CREATE A GRADIENT EFFECT

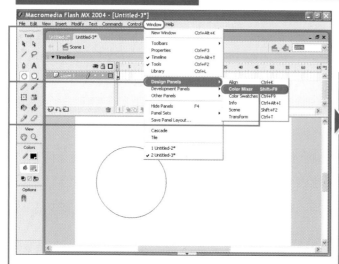

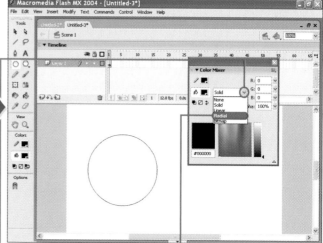

1 Click **Window**.

2 Click **Design Panels**.

3 Click **Color Mixer**.

■ The Color Mixer panel opens.

Note: See Chapter 1 to learn how to work with Flash panels.

4 Click the Fill Style ⊠.

5 Select **Linear** or **Radial**.

Can I make changes to an existing gradient in the palette?

Yes. You can select an existing gradient effect from the Fill Color palette and make modifications to the colors using the Color Mixer panel. You can make changes to the color markers or intensities and save the edits as a new gradient color swatch.

How can I delete a customized gradient effect I no longer need?

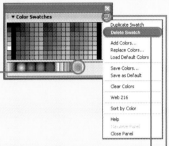

1 Follow steps **1** to **3**, selecting **Color Swatches** instead of **Color Mixer**.

■ The Color Swatches panel displays.

2 Click the gradient effect swatch you want to delete.

3 Click 🖼.

4 Click **Delete Swatch**.

■ Flash permanently deletes the gradient effect from all color palettes.

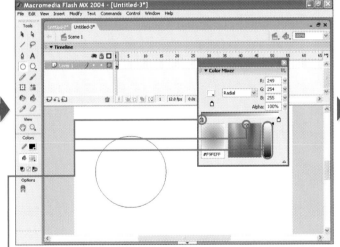

6 Click the color marker (🔒) you want to change.

7 Click a color.

8 Click a color shade.

■ The gradient bar changes color.

■ To add another 🔒 to the effect, click below the gradient bar.

■ To remove a 🔒, drag it off the panel.

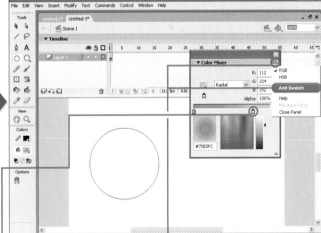

■ You can continue creating the gradient effect by adding color markers and assigning colors.

9 Drag the 🔒 left or right to adjust the color intensity bandwidth on the gradient.

10 To save the gradient, click the Panel Menu button (🖼).

11 Click **Add Swatch**.

■ The new gradient now appears as a swatch in the color palette.

TRANSFORM A GRADIENT FILL

You can use the Fill Transform tool to transform gradient fills. For example, a radiant fill radiates the fill color from the middle of the fill. With one gradient color appearing lighter than the other, it makes the object appear to be highlighted by an off-stage light source.

With the Fill Transform tool, you can change the position of the radiant center point to change the highlight.

TRANSFORM A GRADIENT FILL

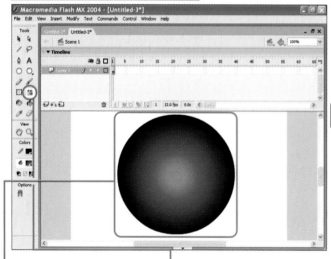

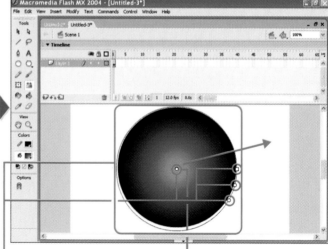

1 Assign a gradient fill to an object or shape.

Note: See Chapter 2 to learn how to fill an object.

2 Click 🖫.

3 Click the fill.

■ Four edit point controls appear on the fill.

4 Click and drag an edit point to transform the fill.

■ You can click and drag the center point to change the position of the highlight.

Can I change the size of a linear gradient effect?

No. When you apply the Fill Transfrom tool (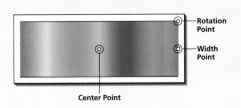) to a linear gradient, you only see three edit point controls. A linear gradient uses only the center, width, and rotation edit point controls, allowing you to change the gradient's center, direction or angle, and width of color bands in the linear gradient.

Rotation Point

Width Point

Center Point

My fill takes up the entire Stage and I cannot see the fill's edit points. How do I view the edit points to transform the fill?

Click the **View** menu, then click **Work Area**. You can also click the **View** menu, click **Magnification**, and click a zoom level to zoom out and see more of the work area.

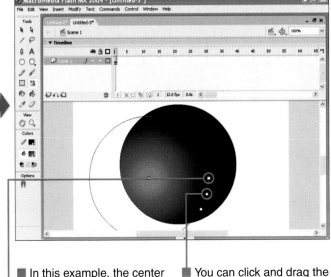

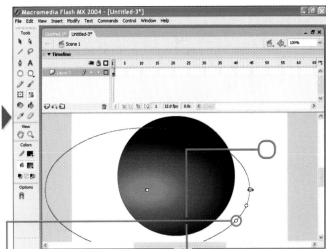

■ In this example, the center point moves down and left.

■ You can click and drag the width point (☐) to change the shape of the gradient effect.

■ You can click and drag the scale point (○) to change the size or radius of the gradient effect.

■ In this example, the scale point moves outward in the radial gradient.

■ You can click and drag the rotation point (○) to change the angle of the gradient.

5 Click anywhere outside the fill to turn off the Fill Transform feature.

■ Flash transforms your gradient.

EDIT A COLOR SET

You can customize the colors you use in Flash to create a unique color set to suit the projects you build. Flash comes with a default color set, but you can make new color sets based on the default set by removing colors you do not need for a particular project. You can then save the edited color set as a new color set for use in other Flash projects. You save color sets with the .clr file extension.

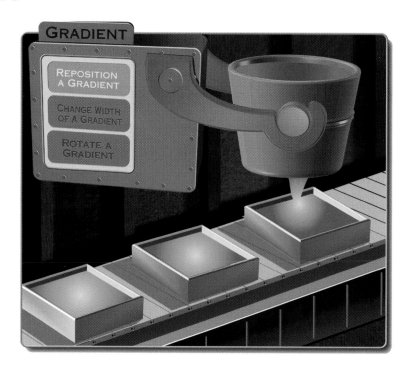

EDIT A COLOR SET

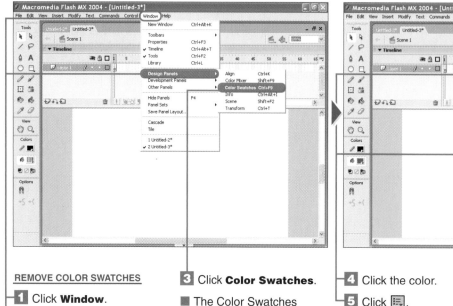

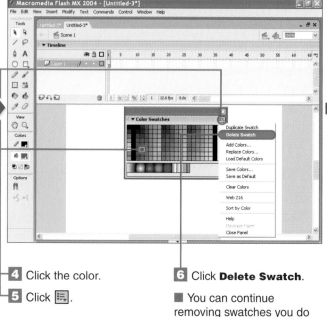

<u>REMOVE COLOR SWATCHES</u>

1 Click **Window**.

2 Click **Design Panels**.

3 Click **Color Swatches**.

■ The Color Swatches panel opens.

4 Click the color.

5 Click 📇.

6 Click **Delete Swatch**.

■ You can continue removing swatches you do not want as part of your color set.

TEACH YOURSELF

How do I load a color set?

After you create a color set, you can reuse it in any Flash file.

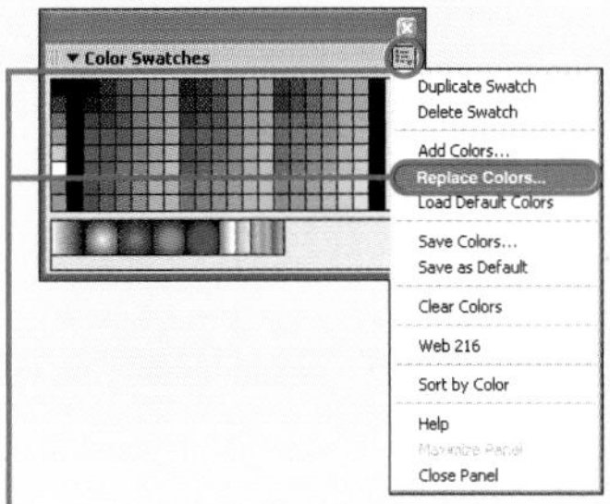

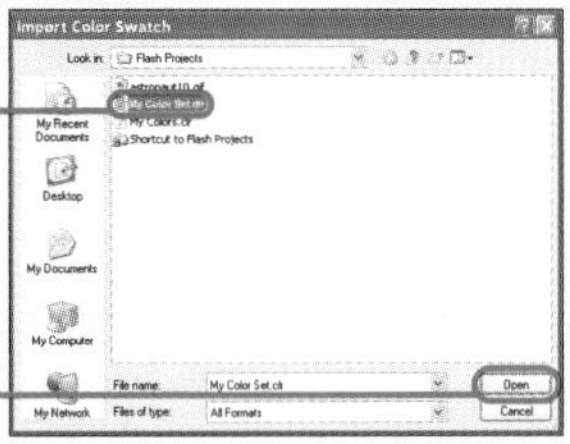

1 In the Color Swatches panel, click ☰.

2 Click **Replace Colors**.

■ This opens the Import Color Swatch dialog box.

3 Select the color set file you want to use.

4 Click **Open**.

■ The color set is now available.

TEACH YOURSELF

Which colors should I use for Web page designs?

To assure that your color selections are suitable for all browsers, designers developed a 216-color Web Safe color palette containing colors that are consistent in both Windows and Mac platforms for all the major Web browser programs. You access this palette by opening the Swatches panel, clicking ☰, and then clicking Web 216.

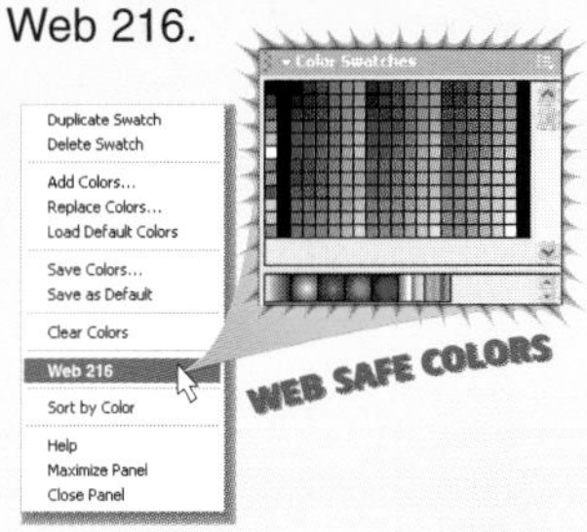

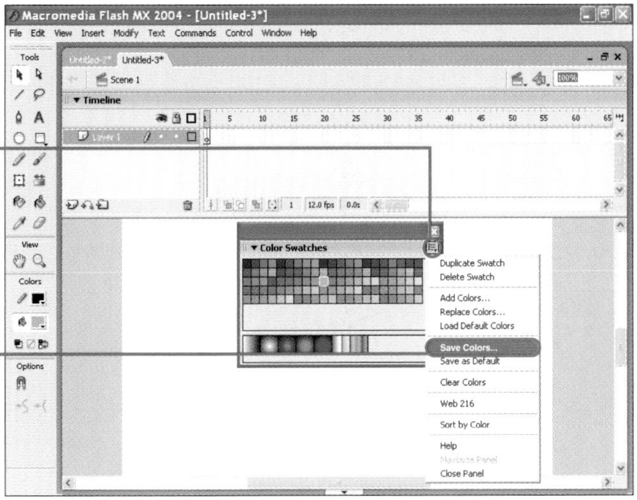

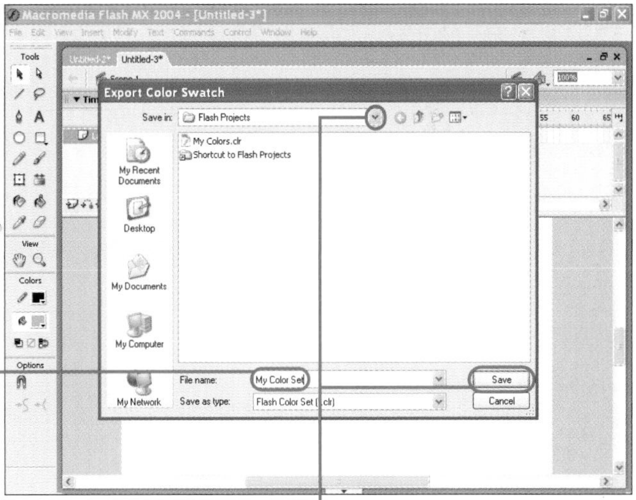

SAVE THE EDITED COLOR SET

7 Click ☰.

8 Click **Save Colors**.

■ The Export Color Swatch dialog box opens.

9 Type a name for the color set.

■ By default, Flash saves the color set in the My Documents folder.

■ You can save the file to another folder by navigating to the appropriate folder.

10 Click **Save**.

■ Flash saves the edited color set.

COPY ATTRIBUTES

You can use the Eyedropper tool to quickly copy attributes from one object to another. Copying attributes rather than reassigning them one at a time can save you time and effort. The Eyedropper tool copies fill and line attributes and enables you to copy the same formatting to other fills and lines.

COPY ATTRIBUTES

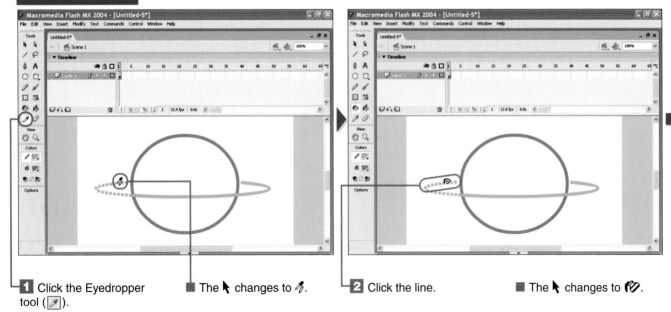

1 Click the Eyedropper tool ().

■ The ➤ changes to ✏.

2 Click the line.

■ The ➤ changes to 🖌.

Can I copy fill attributes, too?

You can copy fill attributes just like you copy line attributes. When you move the ⟋ over a fill, a tiny 🖌 appears next to it to show that you are over a fill. Click 🗒 to absorb the fill formatting. Move ⟋ over the fill you want to reformat, and click again. Flash immediately changes the second fill to match the first.

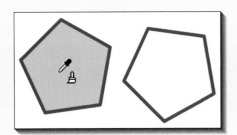

My Eyedropper tool does not work. Why not?

When copying line attributes, you cannot use the Eyedropper tool (🗒) on grouped lines. Be sure to ungroup the lines first and then try copying the line attributes to each line. See the section "Group Objects" for more information.

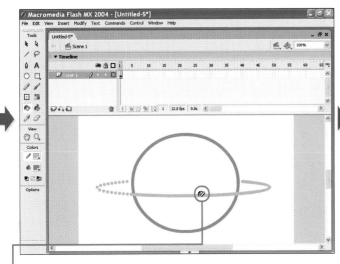

3 Move the 🗒 over the line to which you want to copy attributes.

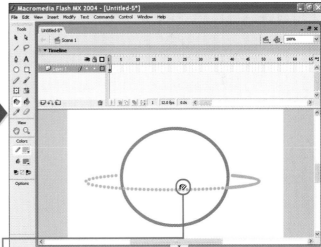

4 Click the line to which you want to copy.

■ Flash immediately applies the line formatting.

GROUP OBJECTS

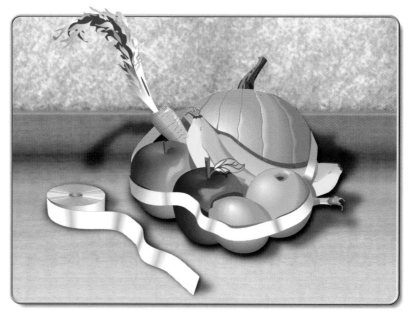

You can work on multiple items at the same time by placing the objects in a group. A group enables you to treat the items as a single unit. Any edits you make affect all items in the group. One of the prime benefits of grouping several objects is that you can move them all at once on the Stage instead of moving one object at a time.

You place grouped objects on the overlay drawing level in Flash. Grouped objects do not interact with objects on the stage level. See Chapter 2 to learn more about drawing levels.

GROUP OBJECTS

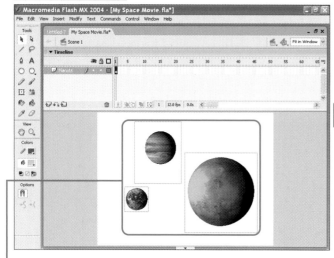

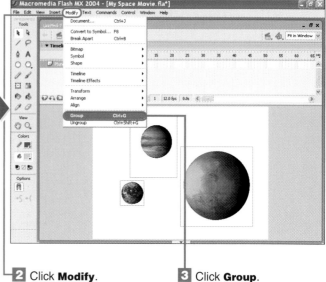

CREATE A GROUP

1 Select all the objects you want to include in a group.

Note: See the section "Select Objects" to learn more about selecting items on the Flash Stage.

■ You can select multiple items by pressing and holding **Shift** while clicking each item.

2 Click **Modify**.

3 Click **Group**.

How can I avoid accidentally changing a group?

If you worry about accidentally moving or changing a group, you can lock it. Click **Modify**, **Arrange**, and then **Lock**. To unlock the group again, click **Modify**, **Arrange**, and then **Unlock All**.

Can I have a group of one?

Yes. You can turn one object into a group to move it to the overlay level and keep it from interacting with other objects on the stage level.

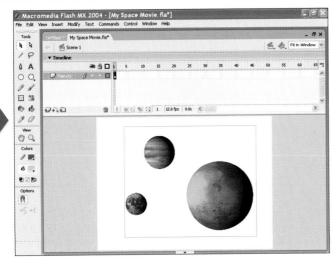

■ Flash groups the objects together and surrounds them with a blue box.

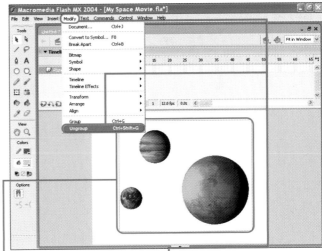

UNGROUP A GROUP

1 Select the group you want to ungroup.

Note: See the section "Select Objects" to learn more about selecting items on the Flash Stage.

2 Click **Modify**.

3 Click **Ungroup**.

■ Flash ungroups the objects.

STACK OBJECTS

You can stack objects you add to the Stage to change the appearance of drawings. When placing objects over other objects, you can control exactly where an object appears in the stack. You can place an object at the very back of a stack, at the very front, or somewhere in between.

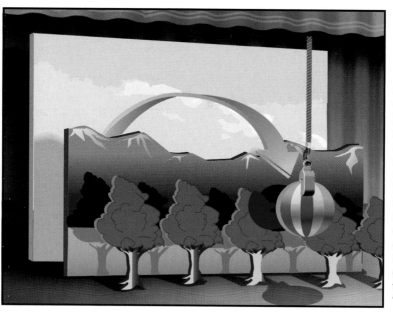

Stacking only works with grouped objects. Flash places grouped objects — whether the group consists of several objects or just one — on the overlay level, which means that they always appear stacked on top of objects that are located on the stage level. To learn more about grouping objects, see the previous section "Group Objects."

STACK OBJECTS

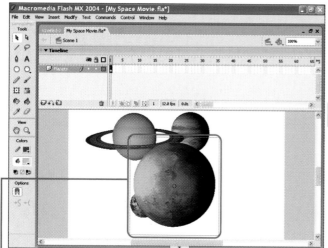

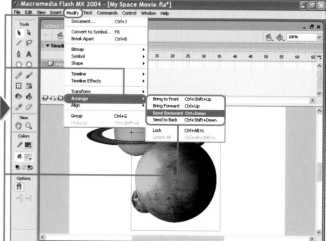

1 Select the object or group you want to reorder.

Note: See the section "Select Objects" to learn more about selecting items on the Flash Stage.

2 Click **Modify**.

3 Click **Arrange**.

4 Select whether you want to send the object to the front or back of the stack.

■ To send an object to the very back of the stack, click **Send to Back**.

■ To move an object back, click **Send Backward**.

■ To bring an object to the very front of the stack, click **Bring to Front**.

■ To bring an object forward, click **Bring Forward**.

Is there a shortcut to moving an object up or back a layer in a stack?

Yes. You can press keyboard shortcuts to quickly reposition an object in a stack. For the Mac use ⌘ instead of Ctrl.

Windows	Result
Ctrl + ↑	Moves the object up one layer
Ctrl + Shift + ↑	Moves it directly to the top of the stack
Ctrl + ↓	Moves the object back a layer
Ctrl + Shift + ↓	Moves the object directly to the back of the stack

Can I stack objects located on the stage level?

No. You cannot apply the stacking commands to objects on the stage level; if you try, they do not work. Objects you place on the stage level interact, which means if you move a shape over a line, the line is covered. If you move the shape again, the line is no longer there; it has become a part of the shape. Stacking only works on objects you place on the overlay level.

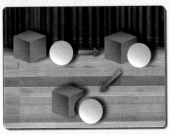

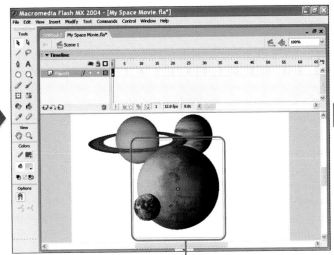

■ The object now relocates in the stacking order.

■ In this example, the selected planet moves back in the stack.

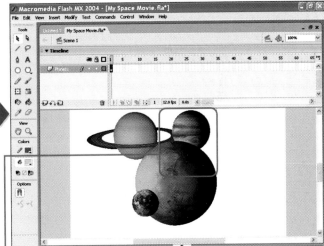

■ In this example the selected planet moves forward in the stack.

ALIGN OBJECTS

You can control the alignment of objects you add to the Stage, whether they are shapes you draw or graphics you import. You can align objects vertically and horizontally by their edges or centers. You can align objects with other objects, with the edges of the Stage, or even control the amount of space between the objects.

The alignment commands come in handy when you are trying to position several objects on the Stage, and dragging them around manually does not seem to create the results you want. Although the Flash rulers and grid can help you line things up on the Stage, applying alignment options are much faster and easier. For more on rulers and grids, see Chapter 1.

ALIGN OBJECTS

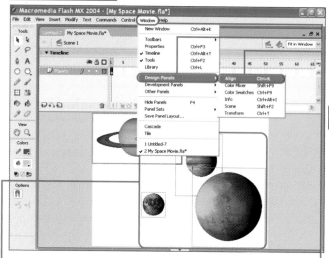

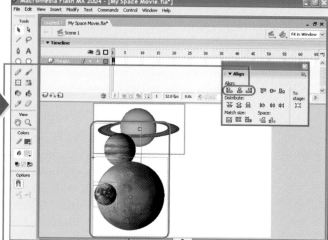

ALIGN OBJECTS WITH OTHER OBJECTS

1 Select the objects you want to align.

■ You can select multiple items by pressing and holding Shift while clicking each item.

2 Click **Window**.

3 Click **Design Panels**.

4 Click **Align**.

■ The Align panel opens.

ALIGN OBJECTS HORIZONTALLY

5 Click an alignment option.

■ Click the Align Left Edge option (🖹) to align objects to the left.

■ Click the Align Horizontal Center option (🖺) to center align the objects.

■ Click the Align Right Edge option (🖺) to align the objects to the right.

■ Flash aligns the objects horizontally.

What other options does the Align panel provide?

The Align panel also has additional alignment options you can utilize. For example, you can select from the Distribute buttons to distribute objects evenly on the Stage, either vertically or horizontally. You can select from the Match size buttons to make the selected objects all the same width or height. You can use the Space buttons to ensure each object is separated by the same amount of spacing between. Be sure to experiment with the alignment options to create just the right combination for your own objects.

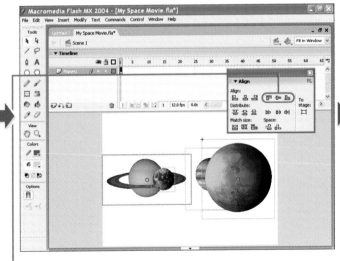

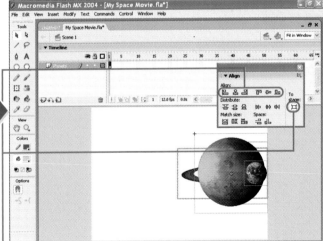

ALIGN OBJECTS VERTICALLY

■6 Click a vertical alignment.

■ Click 🗗 to align objects to the top.

■ Click 🗗 to align the objects vertically centered.

■ Click 🗗 to align the objects to the bottom.

■ In this example, the selected objects align vertically centered.

■ Flash aligns the object vertically.

ALIGN OBJECTS WITH THE STAGE

■7 Click 🗖.

■8 Click an alignment option.

■ Flash aligns the objects to the Stage.

■ In this example, the selected objects line up on the far left edge of the Stage.

CHAPTER 4

Working with Imported Graphics and Videos

Do you want to use artwork from a non-Flash program? Follow the steps in these tasks to import art from other programs to work with in Flash.

IMPORT GRAPHICS

You can import graphics, including vector or bitmap graphics, from other sources to use in Flash. You can manipulate imported images with Flash commands. In addition to importing graphics, you can also use the Paste command to paste graphics you cut or copy from other programs.

Bitmap graphics, also called *raster* graphics, are comprised of thousands of pixels. While bitmaps offer a great deal of detail, their file sizes are often large. Vector graphics use mathematical equations, or *vectors*, to define the image, making for smaller file sizes.

IMPORT GRAPHICS

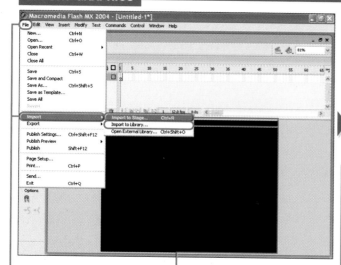

IMPORT A GRAPHIC FILE

1 Click **File**.

2 Click **Import**.

3 Click **Import to Stage**.

■ To import a graphic directly to the file's library to use later, select **Import to Library** instead.

■ The Import dialog box opens.

4 Click the file you want to import.

■ You may need to specify a file type to locate the file you want.

5 Click **Open**.

■ Flash places the graphic on the Stage as a grouped object.

78

What graphic file types does Flash support?

Flash MX supports GIF, animated GIF, JPEG, PNG, BMP, DIB, TGA, TIF, QTIF, WMF, EMF, PDF, PICT, PCT, PNTG, Freehand and Illustrator files, Flash Player files (SWF and SPL), QuickTime Movie (MOV), and AutoCAD (DXF) file types. If you have QuickTime 4 or later installed, Flash also supports PNTG, PCT, PIC, SGI, TGA, TIF, QuickTime image files (QTIF), and Photoshop files (PSD).

Can I reuse the bitmap graphic?

When you import a bitmap graphic, Flash immediately adds it to the Flash Library for use in other frames in your movie. To view the Library, click **Window**, and then **Library,** or press Ctrl + L (⌘ + L) on the keyboard. See Chapter 7 to learn more about using the Flash Library.

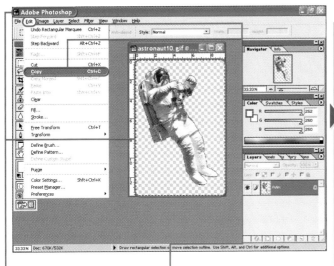

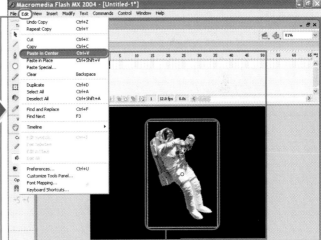

COPY AND PASTE A GRAPHIC

1 Open the program and file containing the graphic you want to copy.

2 Select the graphic.

■ In most programs, selection handles surround the selected object.

3 Click **Edit**.

4 Click **Copy**.

5 Switch back to Flash.

6 Click **Edit**.

7 Click **Paste in Center**.

■ Flash pastes the graphic onto the Stage area.

CONVERT BITMAPS INTO VECTOR GRAPHICS

You can use the Trace Bitmap command to convert a bitmap graphic. Turning a bitmap graphic into a vector graphic can minimize the file size and enable you to utilize the Flash tools to manipulate the graphic. See the previous task to learn how to import graphics.

When you apply the Trace Bitmap command, you can adjust several parameters that define the rendering of the image, including how Flash handles the color variances, pixel size translation, and the smoothness of curves or sharpness of corners.

CONVERT BITMAPS INTO VECTOR GRAPHICS

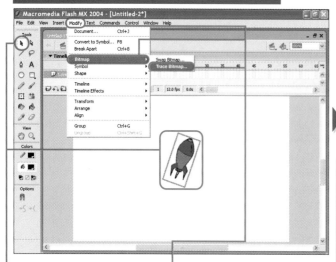

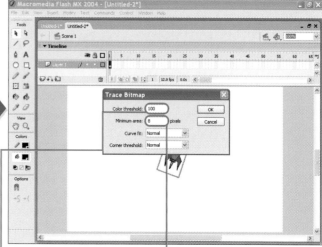

1 Using the Selection tool (▶), select the bitmap graphic you want to convert.

Note: For more on selecting objects on the Stage, see Chapter 3.

2 Click **Modify**.

3 Click **Bitmap**.

4 Click **Trace Bitmap**.

■ The Trace Bitmap dialog box opens.

5 Type a value that determines the amount of color variance between neighboring pixels.

■ A smaller value results in many vector shapes; a larger value results in fewer vectors.

6 Type a minimum pixel size for any vector shape.

What if my converted graphic does not look like the original?

When applying the Trace Bitmap controls, you might need to experiment with the settings to get the results you want. Start with the default settings. If those do not work, click **Edit**, and then **Undo,** and try again, making a few adjustments.

Does converting a bitmap reduce its file size?

Yes, if you do not set the Trace Bitmap threshold settings too low. If the bitmap is a complex drawing with lots of colors and shapes, low threshold settings may result in a larger vector file size. Try to find a balance when adjusting the threshold settings.

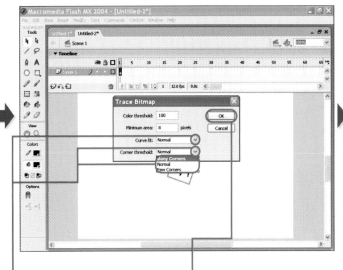

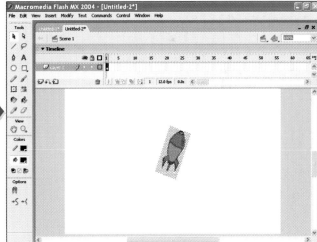

7 Click ⌄ and select how smoothly Flash traces outlines of the bitmap.

8 Click ⌄ and select how sharply Flash traces corners.

9 Click **OK**.

■ Flash traces the graphic, replacing the bitmap with vector shapes.

TURN BITMAPS INTO FILLS

You can turn a bitmap image into a fill for use with Flash tools that use fills, such as the Oval, Rectangle, or Brush. Fills are solid colors or patterns that fill a shape. Conventional fills include colors and gradient effects. You can also use a bitmap image, such as a photo, as a fill. Depending on the size of the shape, Flash repeats the image within the shape.

To prepare a bitmap image as a fill, you must utilize the Break Apart command. This command converts the image into separate pieces. Once you separate the image, you can use the Eyedropper tool to duplicate the image as a fill.

TURN BITMAPS INTO FILLS

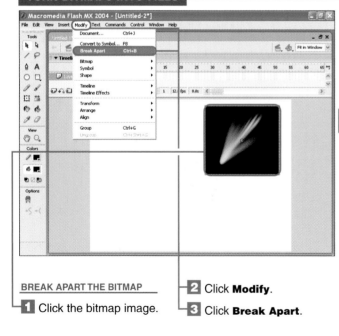

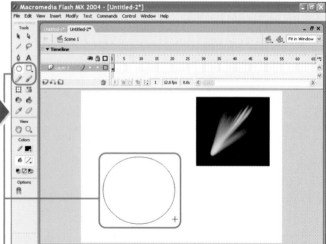

BREAK APART THE BITMAP

1 Click the bitmap image.

2 Click **Modify**.

3 Click **Break Apart**.

TURN THE BITMAP INTO A FILL

4 Select the tool of your choice to create a shape you want to fill.

5 Draw an empty shape on the Stage to contain the bitmap fill.

■ You can place the new shape on another layer to help you keep objects organized.

Note: To learn more about working with layers, see Chapter 6.

What types of edits can I perform on the bitmap fill?

You can edit a bitmap fill just as you can any other fill, including rotating the image and scaling it to another size. See Chapter 3 to learn more about editing fills in Flash.

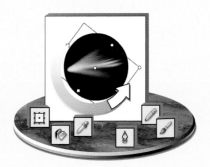

How do I use a bitmap fill with the Brush tool?

Turn the bitmap into a fill following the steps in this task. Click the Brush tool ( ), select a brush size or shape, and then draw brush strokes on the Stage. Everywhere you draw, Flash uses the bitmap image as your paint color. To learn more about the Brush tool and its options, see Chapter 2.

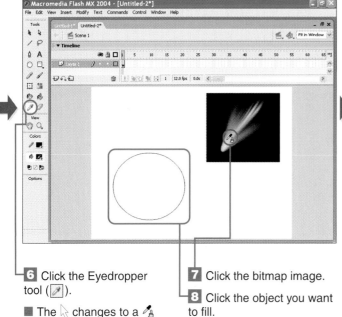

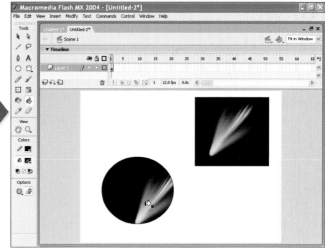

6 Click the Eyedropper tool ( ).

■ The ⟍ changes to a ⟍ when you move the mouse over the bitmap image.

7 Click the bitmap image.

8 Click the object you want to fill.

■ The bitmap image appears as a fill.

IMPORT VIDEO CLIPS

You can import video clips from other sources into your Flash projects. For example, you can embed a video clip into a Flash movie, making the clip a part of the movie much like an imported graphic. As soon as you import a video clip, Flash adds it to the Stage and to the Library. You can use multiple instances of the video clip throughout your project.

Flash supports Windows Media (ASF or WMV), Digital Video (DVI or DV), MPEG (MPG), Video for Windows (AVI), and QuickTime (MOV) video file formats.

IMPORT VIDEO CLIPS

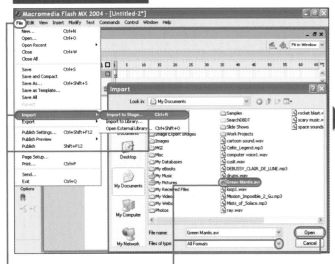

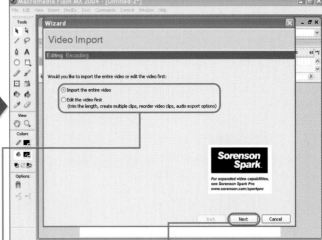

1 Click **File**.

2 Click **Import**.

3 Click **Import to Stage**.

■ The Import dialog box opens.

4 Select the movie clip you want to import.

■ If needed, click ⌄ and then **All Formats** to locate the file.

5 Click **Open**.

■ The Video Import Wizard opens.

6 Select how you want to import the video (○ changes to ◉).

■ Click **Import the entire video** to import the clip without editing it first.

■ Click **Edit the video first** if you want to trim the clip length before importing the clip.

7 Click **Next**.

Why does Flash increase the frames in my Timeline for the video?

A video object requires the same number of frames equal to its length when you add the video clip to a Flash frame. For example, if you have a 500-frame clip, it requires 500 Timeline frames in Flash.

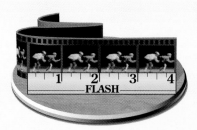

Can I edit my video clip first?

Yes. If you select the **Edit the video first** option in the first Video Import Wizard dialog box that appears, you can make rudimentary edits to the clip using tools in the Wizard. For example, you can trim the clip to reduce its length. See the Flash Help files to learn more about this wizard. When you finish editing the clip, click the Next button to continue.

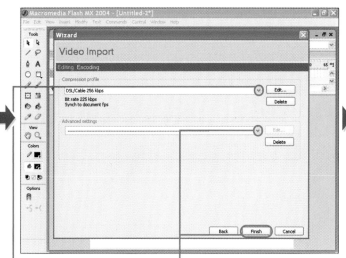

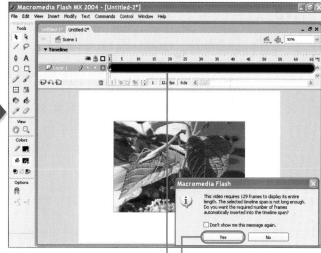

8 Click the Compression profile ⌄ and select another bandwidth compression option for the clip.

■ You can click the Advanced settings ⌄ and create a new profile to change the encoding for the clip, including color, dimensions, and tracking options.

9 Click **Finish**.

■ A prompt box appears if the imported clip contains more frames than you are currently using in the Flash Timeline.

10 Click **Yes**.

■ Flash adds the clip to the Stage and as an embedded video in the file's Library.

CHAPTER 5

Working with Text

Does your Flash project need some text? Learn how to add text elements to your drawings with the Flash text tools.

ADD TEXT WITH THE TEXT TOOL

You can use the Text tool to add animated text to a Flash movie. You can use three types of text elements: *static, dynamic,* or *input* text. Static text, the default text property, does not change—you edit the text the way you want it and it appears the same way in your Flash movie.

You use dynamic text for text fields that you insert into your movie to change and update values. Input text is text that a user enters into a field. You often use dynamic and input text with Flash ActionScript.

You can either add text using a single-line text box, or you can use multiple-line text boxes to enter lines of text that you want to wrap to other lines.

ADD TEXT WITH THE TEXT TOOL

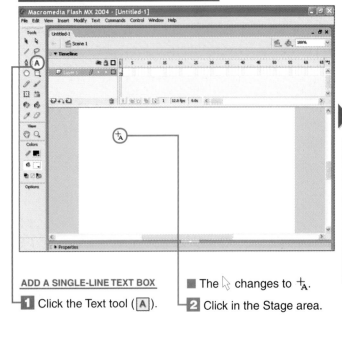

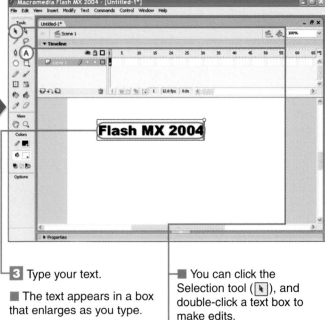

ADD A SINGLE-LINE TEXT BOX

1 Click the Text tool (A).

■ The ↕ changes to +_A.

2 Click in the Stage area.

3 Type your text.

■ The text appears in a box that enlarges as you type.

■ You can click the Selection tool (▶), and double-click a text box to make edits.

■ You can click A, and then the text box to make edits.

What is the difference between single-line and multiple-line text boxes?

When you type text into a *single-line* text box, text does not wrap. The width of the text box keeps expanding as you type characters. With a *multiple-line* text box, you specify a width, and when the text reaches the end of the block, it wraps to start a new line, increasing the depth of the text box. To visually discern between the two text box types, look at the icon in the upper-right corner of the text box. Single-line text boxes display a tiny circle icon (○), and multiple-line text boxes have a tiny square icon (□).

How do I turn a single-line text box into a multiple-line text box?

Select the text box and move the mouse pointer over ○ in the upper-right corner of the text box. Drag ←→ to the right and release the mouse button. The single-line text box is now a multiple-line text box. Note that you cannot turn multiple-line text boxes into single-line text boxes.

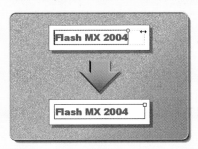

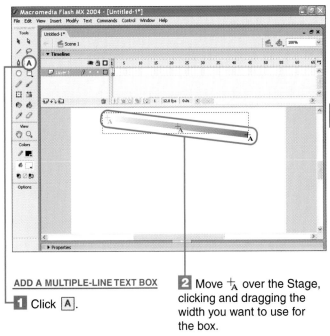

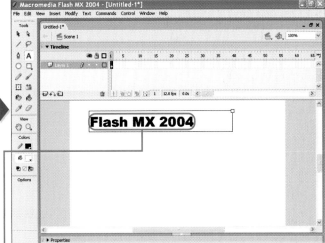

ADD A MULTIPLE-LINE TEXT BOX

1 Click A.

2 Move ⁺ₐ over the Stage, clicking and dragging the width you want to use for the box.

3 Type the text.

■ The text appears in a box.

Note: See the next section, "Format Text" to learn how to assign text attributes.

FORMAT TEXT

You can format text to change the impact or appearance of words and characters. The Properties inspector has all the controls for changing text attributes located in one convenient mini-window. You can quickly change the font, font size, font color, and spacing.

The Properties inspector offers many of the same formatting controls you find in word processing programs. For example, you can click the Bold button to make your text boldface. See Chapter 1 to learn more about opening and using the Properties inspector. See Chapter 10 to learn more about using dynamic and input text with Flash Actions.

FORMAT TEXT

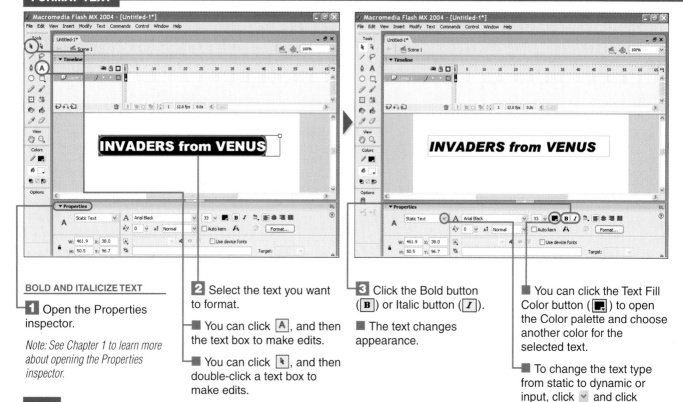

BOLD AND ITALICIZE TEXT

1 Open the Properties inspector.

Note: See Chapter 1 to learn more about opening the Properties inspector.

2 Select the text you want to format.

■ You can click A, and then the text box to make edits.

■ You can click ▸, and then double-click a text box to make edits.

3 Click the Bold button (B) or Italic button (I).

■ The text changes appearance.

■ You can click the Text Fill Color button (■) to open the Color palette and choose another color for the selected text.

■ To change the text type from static to dynamic or input, click ▾ and click another text type.

Do I have to use the Properties inspector to format text?

No. You can also find text formatting controls in the Text menu. For example, to change the font, click **Text** and then **Font**, and then click a font from the menu list that appears.

_sans
_serif
_typewriter
Abadi MT Condensed
Abadi MT Condensed Extra Bold
Abadi MT Condensed Light
Agency FB
Albertus Extra Bold
Albertus Medium
Algerian
Almanac MT
American Uncial
Andale Mono IPA
Andy
Antique Olive
Arial
Arial Alternative
Arial Alternative Symbol
Arial Baltic
Arial Black
Arial CE
Arial CYR
Arial Greek
Arial Narrow
Arial Rounded MT Bold
Arial TUR
Arial Unicode MS
Augsburger Initials
AvantGarde Bk BT
Baskerville Old Face
Bauhaus 93
Beesknees ITC
Bell MT

When do I use dynamic or input text?

You can use dynamic and input text boxes to display dynamically updating text in your Flash project, such as user input boxes, text retrieved from a database, or a variable value obtained from a function within your movie or an external script. You commonly use dynamic and input text with Flash actions. See Chapter 10 to learn more about actions and ActionScript.

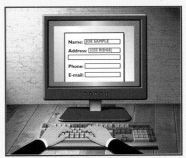

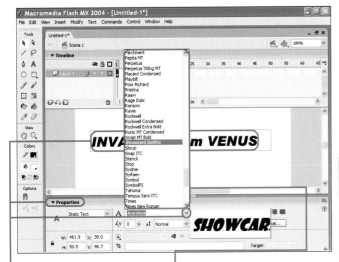

CHANGE TEXT FONT

1 Open the Properties inspector.

2 Select the text you want to format.

3 Click the Font ⌄.

■ A list of available fonts appears, along with a sample box.

4 Click a font name.

■ The text changes font type.

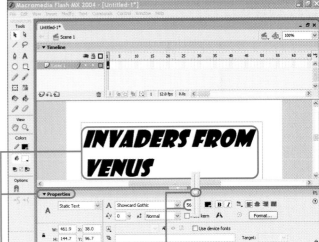

CHANGE THE FONT SIZE

1 Open the Properties inspector.

2 Select the text you want to format.

3 Click the Size ⌄.

4 Click and drag the slider (⬤) to select a new size.

■ You can also type the exact size in the Size box.

■ The text changes size.

ALIGN AND KERN TEXT

You can control the position of text within a text box using the alignment options in the Properties inspector or on the Text menu. Alignment options include setting horizontal controls for the positioning of text, such as left, center, right, or fully justified.

Another way to control the positioning of text is with kerning. *Kerning* refers to the spacing of characters. By changing the kerning setting, you can create text effects such as word characters condensed together or pulled apart.

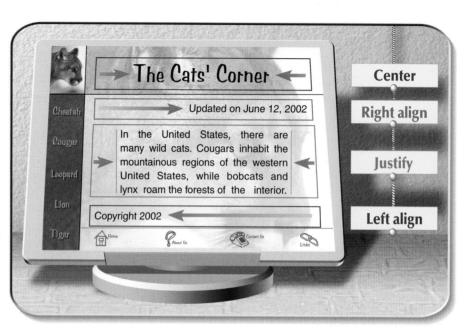

ALIGN TEXT

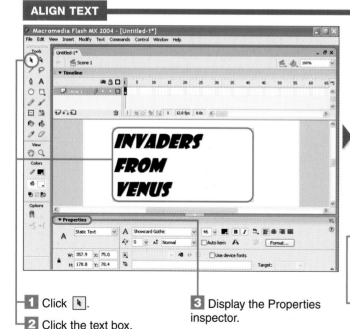

■1 Click [ ].

■2 Click the text box.

■3 Display the Properties inspector.

Note: See Chapter 1 to learn how to display or hide the Properties inspector.

■4 Click an alignment button.

■ You can click [≡] for left-aligned text, [≡] for center, [≡] for right, or [≡] for fully justified.

■ You can also click **Text**, **Align**, and then an alignment option.

■ The text aligns immediately in the text box.

How do I copy attributes from one text box to another?

1 Click the Selection tool (▶).

2 Click the text box containing the text to which you want to copy attributes.

3 Click the Eyedropper tool (🖊).

4 Click the text box containing the attributes you want to copy.

■ Flash immediately copies your attributes.

KERN TEXT

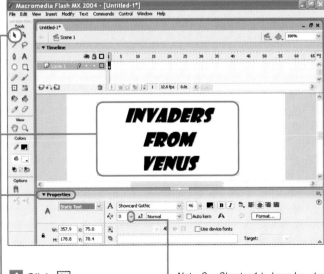

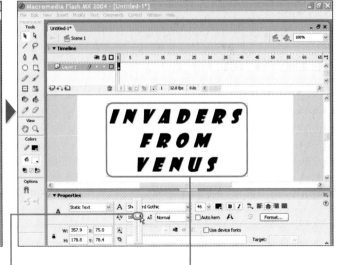

1 Click ▶.

2 Click the text box.

3 Open the Properties inspector.

Note: See Chapter 1 to learn how to display or hide the Properties inspector.

4 Click the Kerning ▾.

5 Click and drag ⬆ up to add space between characters or down to remove space.

■ Flash immediately kerns the characters in the text box.

SET TEXT BOX MARGINS AND INDENTS

You set margins and indents within text boxes for greater control of text positioning. *Margins* define the distance between the edge of the text box and the text inside. You use *indents* to control where a line of text sits within the margins. You can find margin and indent commands in the Format Options dialog box, which you can only access through the Properties inspector panel.

In addition to margin and indent controls, the Paragraph panel also has controls for line spacing. *Line spacing* is the distance between lines of text.

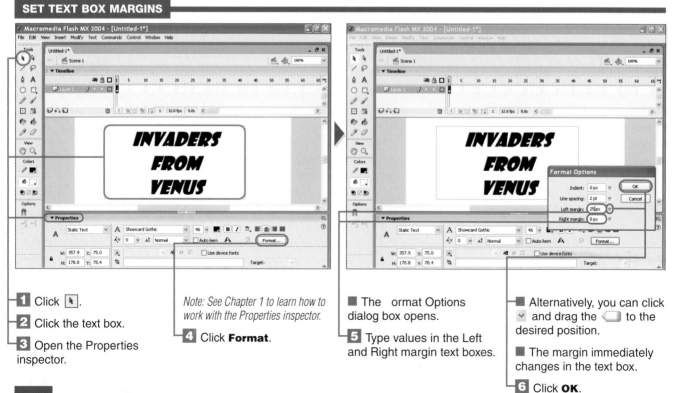

1 Click ▶.

2 Click the text box.

3 Open the Properties inspector.

Note: See Chapter 1 to learn how to work with the Properties inspector.

4 Click **Format**.

■ The ormat Options dialog box opens.

5 Type values in the Left and Right margin text boxes.

■ Alternatively, you can click ⌄ and drag the ▭ to the desired position.

■ The margin immediately changes in the text box.

6 Click **OK**.

The margin's unit of measurement is pixels. How do I change this?

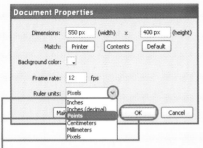

1 Press **Ctrl** + **J** (**⌘** + **J**).

2 In the Document Properties dialog box, click here and select the appropriate units.

3 Click **OK**.

■ The margin values reflect the new unit of measure in the Properties inspector.

Can I use the Line Spacing slider to set superscript or subscript characters?

No. The ⬤ only works on entire lines, not individual characters.

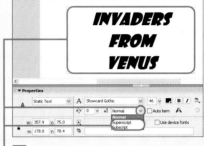

1 Select the text.

2 In the Properties inspector, click here and then click **Superscript** or **Subscript**.

■ Flash immediately applies the attribute.

SET TEXT BOX INDENTS

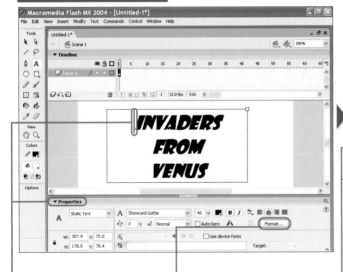

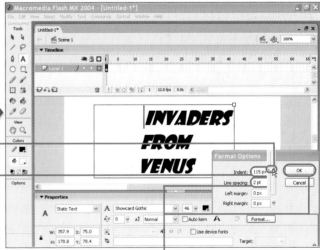

1 Click in front of the text line you want to indent.

2 Open the Properties inspector panel.

Note: See Chapter 1 to learn how to work with the Properties inspector.

3 Click **Format**.

■ The Format Options dialog box opens.

4 Type an indent value in the indent text box.

■ Alternatively, you can click the Indentation ⌄ and drag the ⬤ to change the number.

■ The indent immediately appears in the text box.

■ You can control the spacing between lines by clicking and dragging the Line Spacing ⬤.

5 Click **OK**.

95

MOVE AND RESIZE TEXT BOXES

You can move text boxes around on the Flash Stage or resize them as needed. Text boxes are as mobile and scalable as other objects you add to the Stage.

You can resize the text inside depending on the direction you select to scale the box. Flash overrides any font sizes you have set for the text. If you want the text set at a certain size, you must manually change the font size again after you scale the text box.

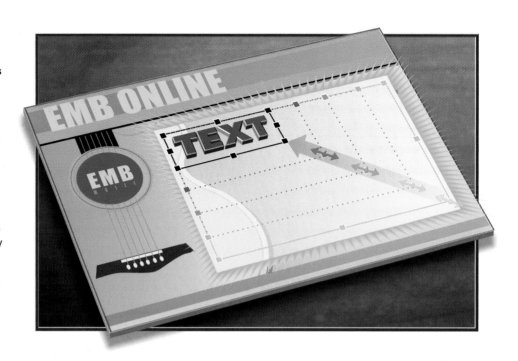

MOVE AND RESIZE TEXT BOXES

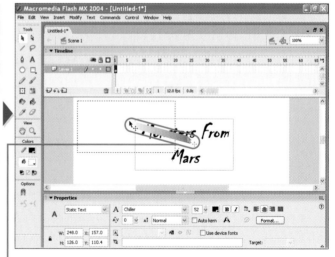

MOVE A TEXT BOX

1 Click ![cursor].

2 Click the text box you want to move.

■ You can also double-click the text box to select it.

3 Move ![cursor] near a text box border or center of the box (![cursor] changes to ![move cursor]).

4 Click and drag the box to a new location and release the mouse button.

■ The text box moves to its new location.

How can I rotate or scale a text box?

You can easily rotate or scale a text box by using the Free Transform tool (◫) with either the Rotate and Skew (⬚) or Scale tool (⬚). For more on rotating or resizing objects, see Chapter 3.

How can I change the text direction?

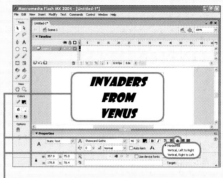

1 Select the text box.

2 Click the Change Orientation of Text button (⬚).

3 Click a text direction.

■ Flash immediately applies the new setting.

RESIZE A TEXT BOX

1 Double-click the text box you want to resize.

2 Move the mouse pointer over the text box handle (↘ changes to ↔).

3 Click and drag left or right to resize the text box width.

■ The text box resizes.

BREAK APART TEXT

You can use the Break Apart command to turn text into graphics, and then manipulate the text with the various Flash drawing and editing tools. For example, you can break text apart into separate blocks and distribute them to different layers in your animation, or you can break text apart to make modifications on each character in a word.

Once you apply the Break Apart command to a text block, you can no longer edit the text, such as change the font or font size. For that reason, be sure you apply all the text formatting you want to use before applying the Break Apart command.

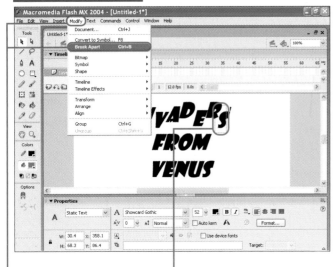

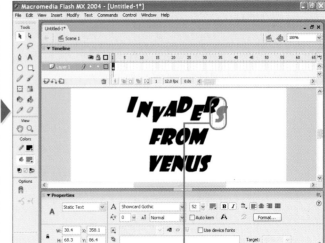

■ **1** Click the text box you want to edit.

■ **2** Click **Modify**.

■ **3** Click **Break Apart**.

■ Flash breaks apart the text block into mini-character blocks.

■ You can reposition each character as an object on the Stage.

■ Repeat steps **2** and **3** to turn the text into a shape.

■ In this example, the text becomes a shape, and you can assign a fill color to one of the letters.

Note: See Chapter 3 for more on applying a fill color.

You can use the Free Transform tool's Envelope modifier to distort the appearance of text in a Flash project. For example, you can make the text appear as a wave or exaggerate the size of some letters while keeping the other letters the same, or you can make the text seem to follow a path.

In order to use the Envelope modifier, you must apply the Break Apart command to your text box. See the preceding page to learn more about this command. Once you apply the Break Apart command to a text block, you cannot edit the text formatting again.

DISTORT TEXT

1 Apply the Break Apart command twice to the text box you want to edit.

Note: See the preceding page to learn how to use the Break Apart command.

2 Click the Free Transform tool (▦).

3 Click the Envelope modifier (▨).

■ Edit points appear around the text shape.

4 Click and drag an edit point to change the text shape (⬚ changes to ▷).

■ An outline of the change appears as you drag.

5 Release the mouse button.

■ Flash modifies the text shape.

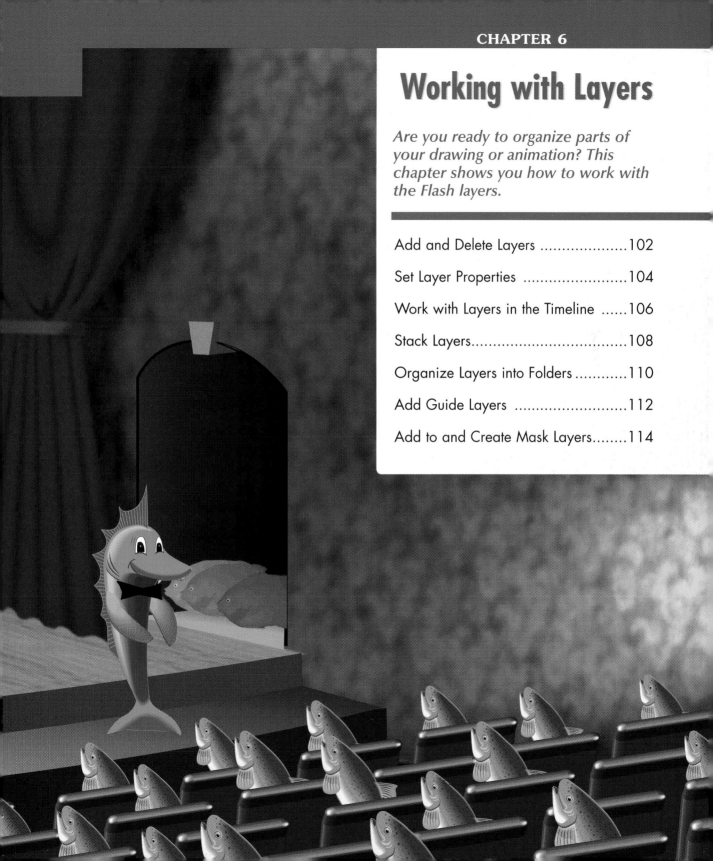

CHAPTER 6

Working with Layers

Are you ready to organize parts of your drawing or animation? This chapter shows you how to work with the Flash layers.

ADD AND DELETE LAYERS

When you create a new movie or scene, Flash starts you out with a single layer and a Timeline. You can add layers to the Timeline, or delete layers you no longer need. Additional layers do not affect the file size, so you can add and delete as many layers as your project requires.

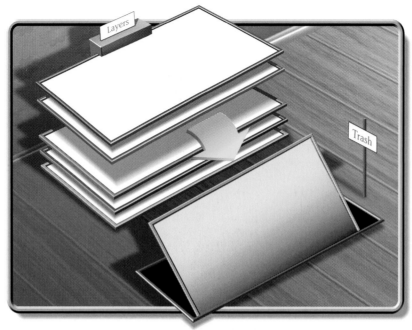

Layers can help you keep track of related items in your movie. For example, you might want to place all the objects you use for a logo on a single layer, and all the objects for a product illustration on another layer.

ADD AND DELETE LAYERS

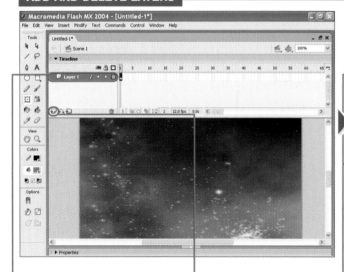

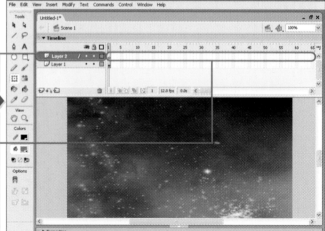

ADD A LAYER

■1 Click the layer that you want to appear below the new layer.

■2 Click the Insert Layer button (⤵).

■ A new layer immediately appears.

■ Flash adds the same amount of frames to the new layer to match the layer with the longest frame sequence.

Note: See Chapter 8 to learn more about frames.

102

Why would I use layers?

Layers Can Organize

The bigger your project, the more elements it is likely to contain. Rather than placing all of these elements in a single layer, which makes them more difficult to locate and edit, you can insert them into separate layers and name each layer with a descriptive name that tells what is in the layer.

Add Depth

Layers act similarly to transparent sheets of paper when you stack one on top of another. Flash stacks layers from top to bottom. Each layer lets you see through to the layer below. As you add more layers, existing layers move down in the stack to appear behind new layers. For example, you might place a background on the bottom layer, and add other objects to subsequent layers to create a feeling of depth.

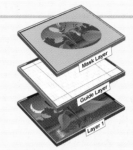

Create Guides and Masks

Guide layers can assist you with the layout and positioning of objects on other layers. Mask layers enable you to hide elements in underlying layers from view. You create a hole, as it were, in the mask layer that lets you view layers below.

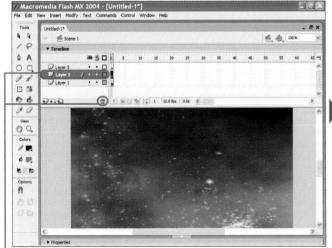

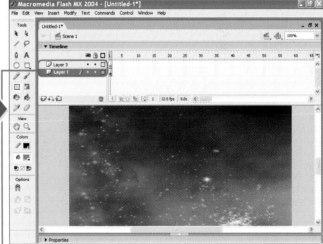

DELETE A LAYER

1 Click the layer you want to delete.

2 Click the Delete Layer button (🗑).

■ You can delete more than one layer by clicking the first layer you want to remove, and then pressing `Ctrl` (⌘) while clicking other layers and then clicking 🗑 .

■ The layer disappears from the Timeline.

Note: If you accidentally delete the wrong layer, you can click the Edit menu and click Undo.

SET LAYER PROPERTIES

You can define the aspects of any given layer through the Layer Properties dialog box, a one-stop shop for controlling a layer's name, function, and appearance. The more you work with layers in Flash, the more necessary it is to change layer properties.

By naming layers you can more easily keep track of their contents and position. You also have the option of hiding the layer to get its contents out of the way. To keep the layer's contents safe from editing, you can lock the layer.

SET LAYER PROPERTIES

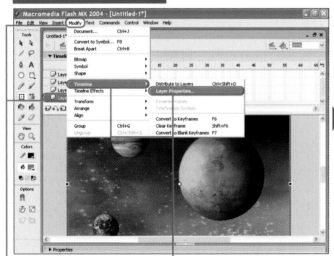

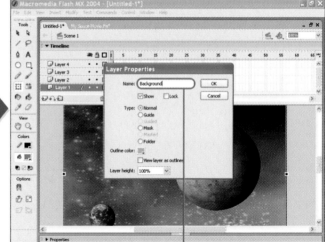

1 Click the layer for which you want to set controls.

Note: Flash automatically selects all objects associated with the selected layer.

2 Click **Modify**.

3 Click **Timeline**.

4 Click **Layer Properties**.

■ You can also right-click over the layer and click **Properties** to open the Layer Properties dialog box.

■ The Layer Properties dialog box opens.

5 Type a distinctive name for the layer in the Name text box.

What are layer types?

By default, all layers you add to
the Timeline are *normal,* which
means all the objects on the layer
appear in the movie. A *guided*
layer is a layer linked to a regular
guide layer. Objects you place on
guide layers do not appear in the
movie. You can use a regular
guide layer for reference points
and alignment. A *mask* layer hides
any layers linked to it. To change
the layer type, click a type in
the Layer Properties dialog
box (○ changes to ◉).

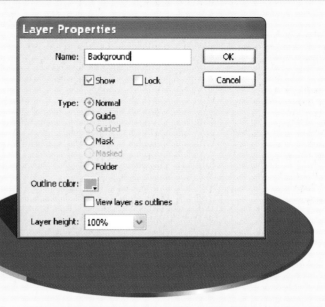

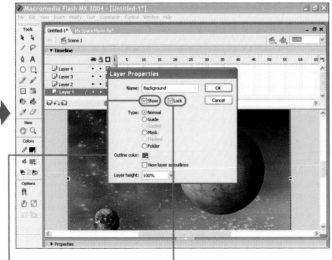

6 Change the desired layer
property.

■ To make the layer visible
in the Timeline, you can
leave the **Show** option
selected (☐ changes to ☑).

■ To lock the layer to
prevent changes, you can
click the **Lock** option
(☐ changes to ☑).

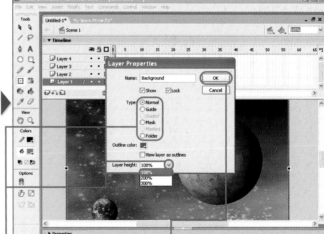

■ You can select a layer
type (○ changes to ◉).

■ To enlarge the layer
height, you can click ☑ and
select a percentage.

■ An enlarged height is
useful for viewing sound
waveforms in the layer.

7 Click **OK**.

■ The layer properties
change to your
specifications.

WORK WITH LAYERS IN THE TIMELINE

Flash makes it easy to control layers in the Timeline. You can quickly rename a layer, hide a layer, or lock a layer to prevent unnecessary changes without having to open a separate dialog box. The Timeline has buttons and toggles that you can use to control a layer with a quick click.

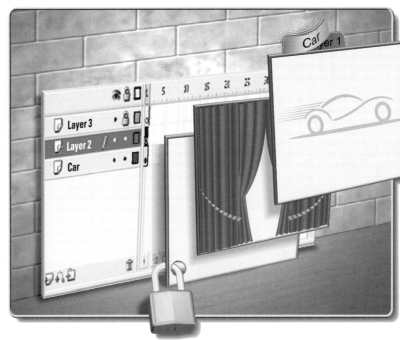

In addition to controlling layer status, you can also quickly name layers in the Timeline by entering new labels directly on the layer name list.

WORK WITH LAYERS IN THE TIMELINE

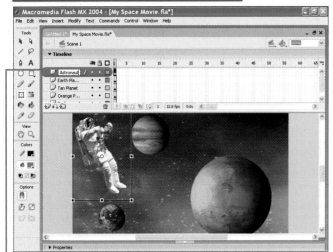

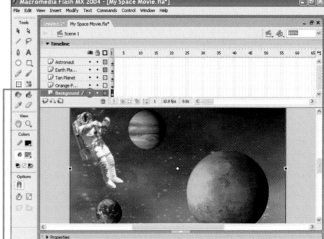

RENAME A LAYER

1 Double-click the layer name.

2 Type a new name.

3 Press Enter (Return).

■ The layer's name changes.

HIDE A LAYER

1 Click the bullet (■) beneath the eye icon column.

How can I tell which objects are on which layer?

You can choose to view layer contents as outlines, which makes it easy to distinguish the objects from other layers. Click ▢ under the square icon column (▢ changes to ▣). All objects on the layer are now outlined in the same color as the selected square.

Can I enlarge the size of a layer?

All layers you add to the Timeline use a default size; however, you can enlarge a layer to better view its contents. To enlarge the layer height:

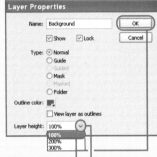

1 Open the Layer Properties dialog box.

Note: See the section "Set Layer Properties" to open this dialog box.

2 Click the Layer Height ✓.

3 Select a percentage.

4 Click **OK** to apply your changes.

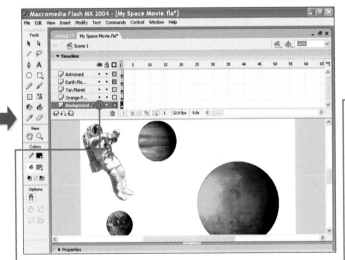

■ All the objects on the layer become invisible (● changes to ✗).

■ To make the layer objects visible again, you can click ✗ under the eye icon column (✗ changes to ●).

LOCK A LAYER

1 Under the padlock icon column, click the layer's bullet (● changes to 🔒).

■ Flash MX locks the layer and you cannot edit the contents.

■ To unlock a layer, click the layer's padlock icon (🔒 changes to ●).

STACK LAYERS

To rearrange how objects appear in your Flash movie, you can stack layers. Layers act like sheets of transparent plastic. Depending on the placement of the layers, objects can appear in front of or behind objects on other layers. Stacking layers in this manner creates the illusion of depth in your movie.

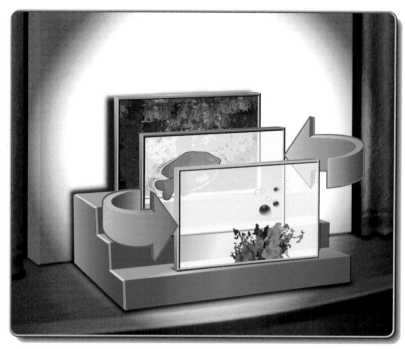

You can change the order of a layer by moving it up or down in the layer list on the Timeline. The layer at the top of the list appears at the top of the stack, while the layer at the bottom of the list appears at the bottom of the stack.

STACK LAYERS

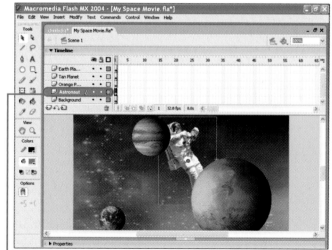

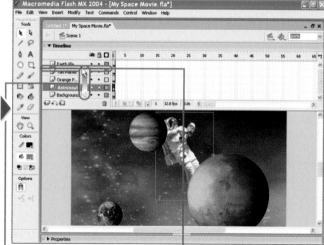

1 Click the layer you want to move.

■ Flash automatically selects all objects associated with the selected layer.

2 Drag the layer up or down to its new location in the stack.

■ An insertion point appears, showing where the dragged layer will rest.

How can I see more layers at a time in my Timeline?

You can resize the Timeline to see more of your layers. Move the 🡢 over the bottom border of the Timeline until the 🡢 becomes a ⬍. Click and drag the border down to increase the size of the Timeline. This should enable you to see more of the layers in the Timeline.

I cannot see all my layers. Why?

The more layers you add to the Timeline, the longer the list of layer names. Not all the layers stay in view. Use the scroll bar at the far right end of the Timeline to scroll up and down the layer list and view other layers. You can also use the Flash layer folders to organize layers in the Timeline. See the section "Organize Layers into Folders" to learn more.

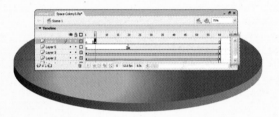

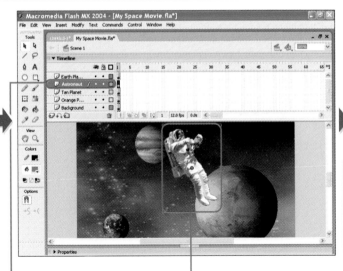

3 Release the mouse button.

■ The layer assumes its new position.

■ In this example, the layer moves up in the stacking order, and any objects on the layer now appear on top of all the other layer objects.

■ In this example, the layer moves down in the stacking order, and any objects on the layer now appear below other top layer objects.

ORGANIZE LAYERS INTO FOLDERS

You can use layer folders to further organize the numerous layers you use in a Flash movie project. Layer folders act just like the folders found on your computer's hard disk drive. For example, you can place related layers into one layer folder on the Timeline. This makes it much easier to find a layer for editing later. Flash identifies layer folders in the Timeline by the tiny folder icons next to the folder names.

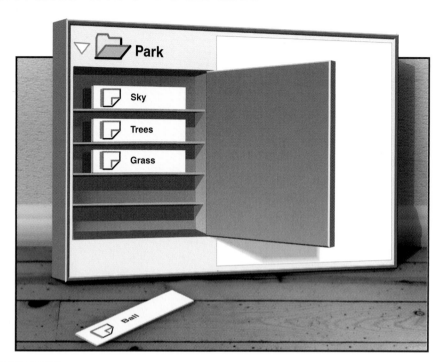

ORGANIZE LAYERS INTO FOLDERS

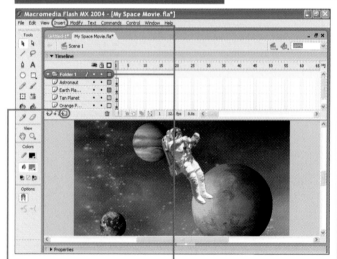

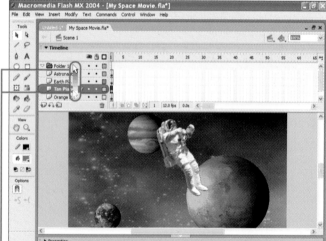

CREATE A FOLDER

1 Click the Insert Layer Folder button ().

■ Flash adds a layer folder to the Timeline.

■ You can also click the **Insert** menu and click **Timeline**, **Layer Folder**.

ADD A LAYER TO A FOLDER

1 Click the layer you want to move into a folder.

2 Drag the layer over the folder.

3 Release the mouse button.

■ The layer moves to the layer folder.

How do I remove a layer from a folder?

Display the layer folder's contents, then drag the layer you want to remove from the folder. To remover the layer completely from the Timeline, click the layer name and click the Delete Layer icon (🗑).

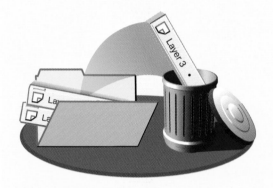

Can I lock a layer folder?

Yes. You can lock and hide layer folders just as you can lock and hide layers. Locking a folder locks all the layers included within the folder. Click the folder layer's bullet (● changes to 🔒). Flash locks the folder and any layers associated with the folder.

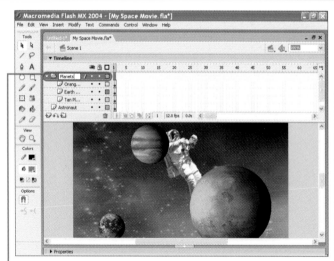

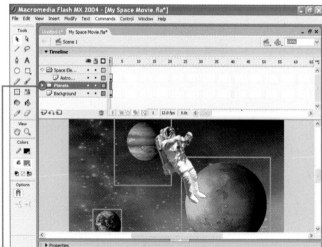

RENAME A FOLDER

1 Double-click the layer folder name you want to rename.

2 Type a new name.

3 Press Enter.

■ Flash renames the layer folder.

COLLAPSE A FOLDER

1 Click the layer folder's Expand icon (▽). (▽ changes to ▷).

■ Flash hides layers associated with the folder.

■ Click the layer folder's Collapse icon (▷) to view the folder's contents again (▷ changes to ▽).

111

ADD GUIDE LAYERS

Guide layers help you position objects. There are two types of guide layers in Flash: *plain* and *motion*. A plain guide layer can help you position objects on the Stage, but it does not appear in your final movie. Use plain guide layers to assist you in lining things up.

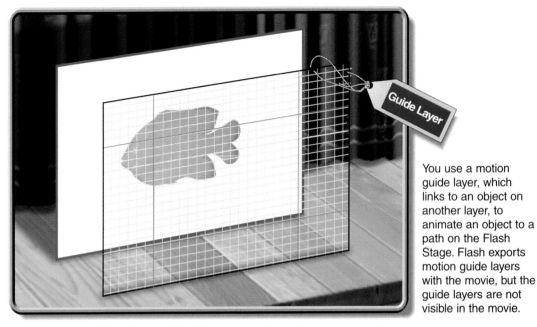

Guide Layer

You use a motion guide layer, which links to an object on another layer, to animate an object to a path on the Flash Stage. Flash exports motion guide layers with the movie, but the guide layers are not visible in the movie.

ADD GUIDE LAYERS

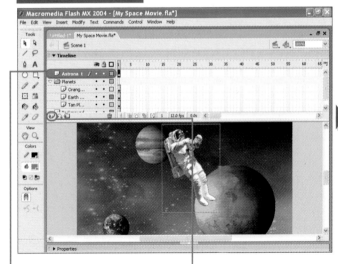

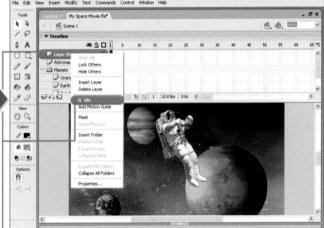

ADD A PLAIN GUIDE LAYER

1 Click the layer that you want to appear below the new guide layer.

2 Click 🛂.

■ Flash adds a new layer to the Timeline.

3 Right-click the new layer name.

4 Click **Guide**.

■ The layer becomes a guide layer.

■ You can distinguish a plain guide layer by its unique icon (◁).

■ You can place objects on the layer or use it to create a layout.

How exactly does a motion guide layer work?

Flash links motion guide layers to layers containing objects you want to animate along a given path. The motion guide layer contains the path, and you can link it to one or more layers. The motion guide layer always appears directly above the layer (or layers) to which it links. To learn more about animating in Flash, see Chapter 8.

Can I lock my guide layer in place?

Yes. In fact, it is a good idea to always lock guide layers and motion guide layers in place so you do not accidentally move anything on them. To lock a layer, click the 🔒 column for the layer. To unlock the layer again, click the 🔒 again. See the section "Work with Layers in the Timeline" to learn more about using the layer toggles.

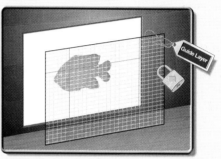

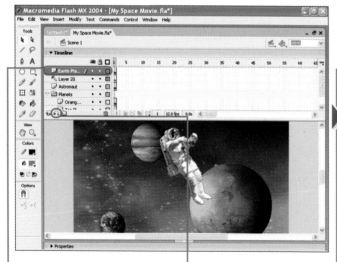

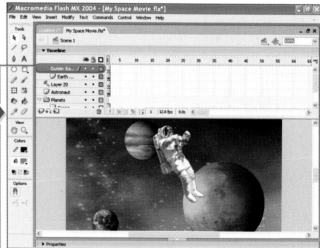

ADD A MOTION GUIDE LAYER

1 Click the layer that you want to link to a motion guide layer.

2 Click the Add Motion Guide icon (⊞).

■ Flash adds the motion guide layer to the Timeline and links it to the layer you selected.

■ You can distinguish a motion guide layer by its unique icon (▣).

ADD TO AND CREATE MASK LAYERS

You can use mask layers to hide various elements on underlying layers. A mask is much like a stencil you tape to a wall. Only certain portions of the underlying layer appear through the mask design, while other parts of the layer are hidden, or *masked*. Flash links masked layers to the layer to which you associate them, and exports them in the final movie file.

Mask layers appear with a unique icon on the Timeline. You can only link a mask layer to the layer directly below it. Mask layers can only contain one fill shape, symbol, or object to use as a window.

ADD TO AND CREATE MASK LAYERS

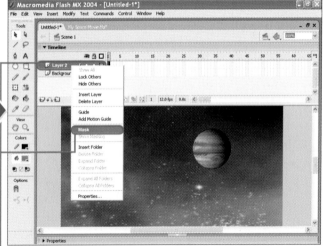

ADD A MASK LAYER

1 Click the layer to which you want to add a mask.

2 Click [icon].

■ A new layer appears.

3 Right-click the new layer's name.

4 Click **Mask**.

■ Flash marks the layer as a mask layer, locks it against any changes, and links it to the layer below.

I cannot see the mask effect. Why not?

Probably because you unlocked the layer. You must first lock the mask layer in order to see the mask effect. You can also see the effect if you run the movie in test mode; click the **Control** menu and click **Test Movie**. The Flash Player window opens and runs the movie. Click the window's ☒ to return to the Flash program window.

What sort of fill should I draw for my mask shape?

You can use any kind of fill color or pattern to create the mask shape. Regardless of what makes up your fill, Flash treats the shape as a window to the linked layer, or layers, below. For that reason, you might consider using a transparent fill rather than a solid so you can see through the fill to the layer below and position it correctly on the Stage.

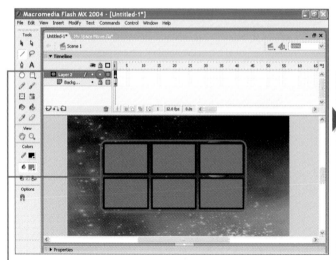

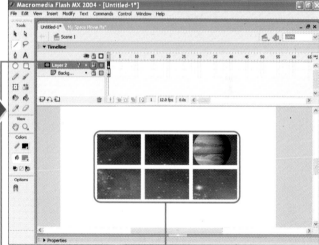

CREATE A MASK

1 Unlock the mask layer (🔒 changes to ●).

2 Draw a fill shape on the Stage over the area you want to view in the layer below.

■ In this example, several rectangle fill shapes are used as a window-like mask.

Note: See Chapter 2 to create a fill shape.

3 Lock the mask layer.

Note: To lock or unlock a layer, see the section "Work with Layers in the Timeline."

■ You can now see the masking effect.

■ Flash masks out anything appearing outside the fill shape.

CHAPTER 7

Working with Flash Symbols and Instances

Are you ready to start using drawn objects or imported artwork in your Flash movie? This chapter teaches you how to use Flash symbols and store them in the Library.

UNDERSTANDING SYMBOLS AND INSTANCES

In Flash, a *symbol* is a reusable element you can store in the Flash Library. You can repeatedly use a symbol throughout your movie by inserting an instance of the symbol in the frame in which you want it to appear. An *instance* is merely a copy of the original symbol.

Flash Symbol

A *symbol* is any element you store in the Flash Library. A symbol can be an object you draw with the Flash drawing tools, a movie clip, or a graphic created in another program. Symbols can also be sound clips or buttons.

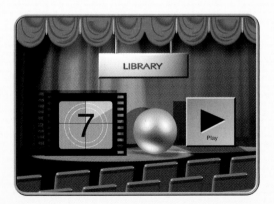

Flash Instances

Anytime you insert a copy of the symbol into your project, you are inserting an *instance*. The instance references the original so the file size is not greatly affected by how many times you reuse a symbol.

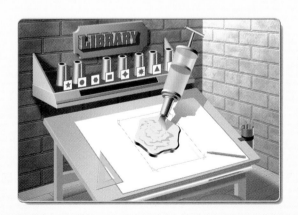

You can reuse symbols to create animations in your Flash movies. Every time you reuse a symbol, you must specify how you want the symbol to behave. Flash classifies symbols, or *behaviors*, into three types: graphics, buttons, or movie clips.

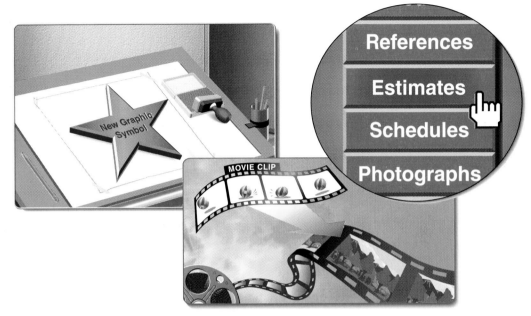

Graphic Symbols

You can reuse graphic objects, such as those you create in Flash with the drawing tools, for creating animation in the Flash Timeline.

Button Symbols

You can save interactive buttons, also called rollover buttons, as symbols and reuse them by associating different actions to the same button.

Movie Clips

Movie clip symbols are simply mini-movies that reside inside the main Flash movie file. Movie clips utilize timelines that are independent of the main movie's Timeline.

USING THE FLASH LIBRARY

A Flash project can contain hundreds of graphics, sounds, interactive buttons, video and movie clips. The Flash Library can help you organize these elements. For example, you can store related symbols in the same folder, create new folders, or delete folders and symbols you no longer need.

Every time you import a graphic image into a Flash file, convert a graphic element into a symbol, or add a new sound to a frame, Flash adds it to the file's Library. In effect, the Library is a compendium of your movie's contents

USING THE FLASH LIBRARY

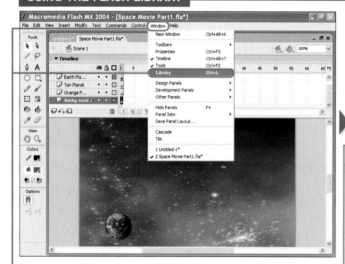

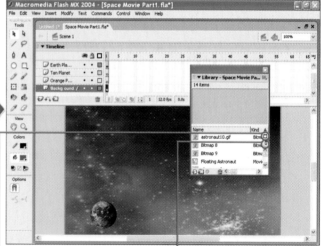

OPEN THE LIBRARY PANEL

1 Click **Window**.

2 Click **Library**.

■ You can also press **F11** to quickly open the Library panel.

■ The Library panel appears.

■ You can click the Wide Library View button (□) to display the full Library panel.

■ You can return the panel to Narrow state by clicking the Narrow Library View button (□).

Can I use symbols from another movie's Library?

You can easily insert symbols into your current project from another file's library.

■1 Click **File**.

■2 Click **Import**.

■3 Click **Open as External Library**.

■4 In the Open as Library dialog box, click the filename.

■5 Click **Open**.

■ The Library panel opens listing the other file's symbols.

■6 Drag the symbol you want to use onto the Stage.

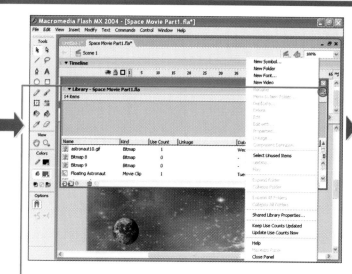 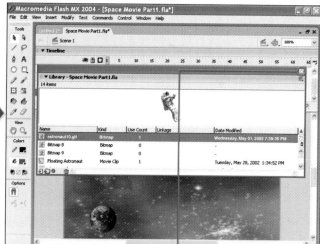

■ You can click the Options menu (📋) to display a menu of commands related to Library tasks and items.

■ You can preview an item in the Library by clicking the item.

Note: You can manipulate the Library panel just like you can any other panel in Flash by dragging it around the program window to move it out of the way. See Chapter 1 to learn how to work with panels.

■3 Click ⊠.

■ Flash closes the Library panel.

Note: See the section "Insert an Instance" to learn how to place a symbol on the Stage.

CONTINUED ▶ 121

USING THE FLASH LIBRARY

To organize all of your symbols, you can store them in folders. A Library folder displays like any other folder on your computer system. Open the folder to view its contents or hide the contents and view only the folder name. When you open a folder, you can see every symbol it contains. The icons next to the symbol name in the Library panel indicate the symbol type.

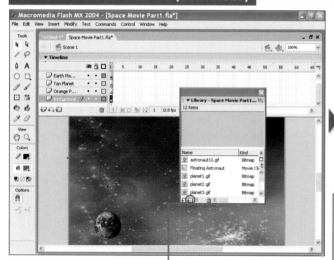

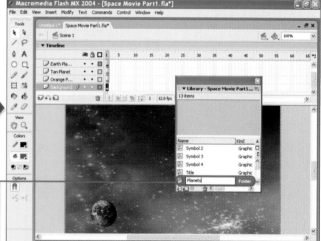

CREATE A NEW FOLDER

1 Open the Library panel.

Note: See the previous page to learn how to open the Library.

2 Click the New Folder button (▢).

3 Type a name for the folder.

4 Press [Enter] ([Return]).

■ Flash creates a new folder

122

How do I rename a folder?

Double-click the folder name in the Library panel to highlight it. Type a new name, press **Enter** (**Return**) and Flash applies the new name. You can use this technique to rename symbols in the Library window.

Can I delete a folder I no longer need?

Yes, but make sure it does not contain any symbols you want to keep or are currently using in the file. Once you delete a folder, Flash deletes its contents, along with any instances you use in your animation. To delete a folder, click it, and then click the Delete icon (🗑) at the bottom of the Library panel. Flash warns you that you are about to permanently delete the folder and its contents. Click **Yes** and Flash removes the folder.

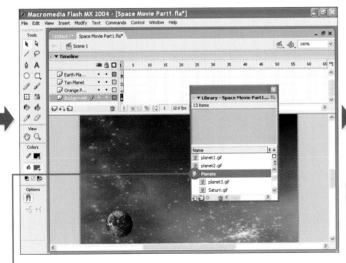

■ To view a folder's contents, you can double-click the Folder icon (📁).

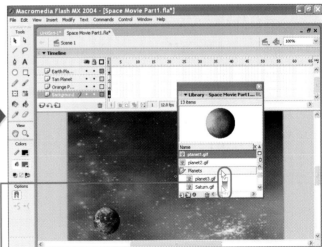

MOVE A SYMBOL TO ANOTHER FOLDER

5 Click and drag the symbol over 📁.

6 Release the mouse button.

■ The symbol moves into the folder.

CREATE A SYMBOL

You can easily turn any object you draw on the Flash Stage into a symbol you can reuse throughout your project. You can also convert any existing drawing or graphical element into a symbol. When you save an item as a symbol, Flash stores it in the file's Library. When you reuse the symbol, you are using an *instance* or copy of the original symbol.

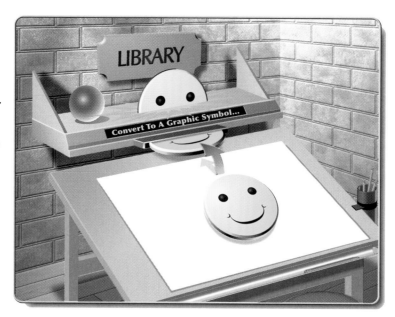

There are three types of behaviors you can assign to a symbol: graphic, movie clip, or button. The behavior you assign depends on what you want to do with the symbol.

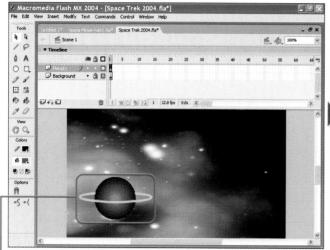

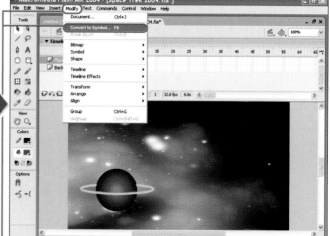

CONVERT AN OBJECT TO A SYMBOL

1 On the Stage, select all the objects you want to convert into symbols.

Note: To select objects, see Chapter 3.

■ To select multiple objects, you can hold down **Shift** while clicking each object.

2 Click **Modify**.

3 Click **Convert to Symbol**.

■ You can also press **F8** to quickly convert a symbol.

How do I create a symbol from scratch?

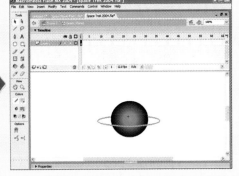

■1 Click **Insert**.

■2 Click **New Symbol**.

■3 In the Create New Symbol dialog box, type a name for the symbol.

■4 Assign a behavior to the symbol.

■5 Click **OK**.

■ Flash switches to symbol-edit mode where you can use drawing tools to create a new symbol.

■ To save the symbol and exit symbol-edit mode, click the Scene name link to the left of the symbol name.

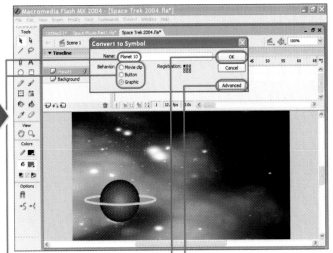

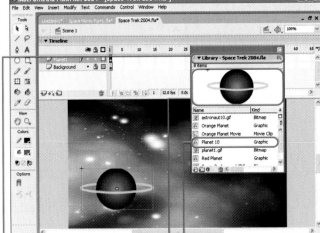

■ The Convert to Symbol dialog box opens.

■4 Type a unique name for the symbol.

■5 Click a behavior to assign to the symbol (○ changes to ◉).

■ You can click **Advanced** to see additional options.

■6 Click **OK**.

■ Flash adds the symbol to the file's Library.

PREVIEW THE SYMBOL

■1 Open the Library panel.

Note: See the section "Using the Flash Library" to learn how to open the Library panel.

■2 Click the symbol name.

■ The symbol appears in the top section of the Library panel.

125

INSERT AN INSTANCE

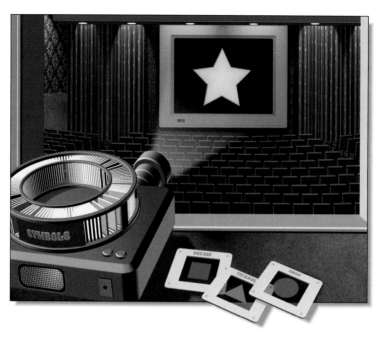

To reuse a symbol in your Flash project, you can place an *instance* of it on the Stage. An instance is a copy of the original symbol. The copy references the original instead of redrawing the object completely. Referencing a vector object for reuse is much more efficient than copying an object repeatedly in a file.

Ordinarily, copying an object means you copy the entire set of instructions that tells the computer how to draw the object. With the Flash method, the symbol instance merely points to the original symbol without needing a complete set of instructions for re-creating the object. This greatly decreases the movie's file size.

INSERT AN INSTANCE

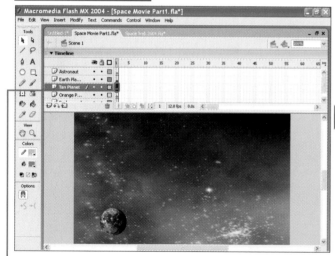

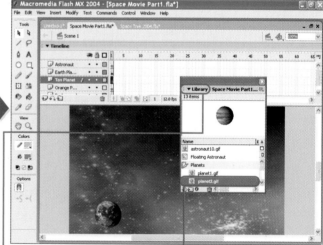

1 Click the frame and layer where you want to insert the instance.

Note: To learn more about frames, see Chapter 8. To learn more about layers, turn to Chapter 6.

2 Open the Library panel.

Note: See the section "Using the Flash Library" to learn how to open the Library panel.

3 Click the symbol's name.

How do I replace one instance with another?

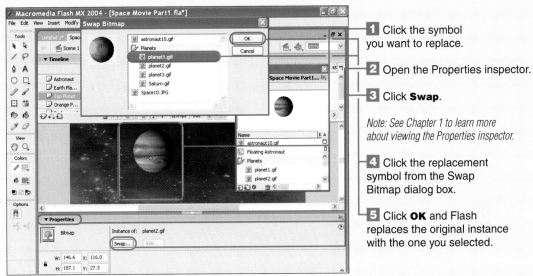

1 Click the symbol
you want to replace.

2 Open the Properties inspector.

3 Click **Swap**.

*Note: See Chapter 1 to learn more
about viewing the Properties inspector.*

4 Click the replacement
symbol from the Swap
Bitmap dialog box.

5 Click **OK** and Flash
replaces the original instance
with the one you selected.

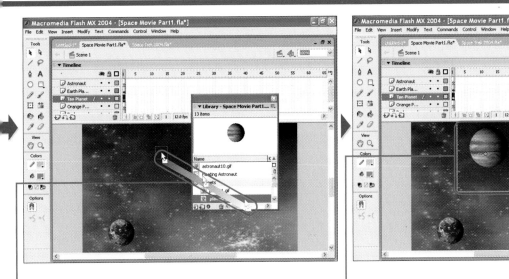

4 Click and drag the
symbol from the Library
panel.

5 Release the instance on
the Stage.

■ An instance of the symbol
now appears on the Stage.

MODIFY AN INSTANCE

After you place a symbol instance on the Stage, you can change the way it appears without changing the original symbol. For example, you can change its color or make it appear transparent.

When you make changes to an instance in the Properties inspector, you use several tools to modify its properties. You can change the object's behavior by turning a graphic symbol into a movie clip, or into a button. You can also experiment by fine-tuning an instance's color effects.

MODIFY AN INSTANCE

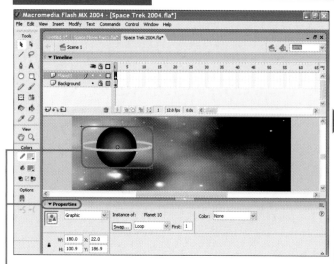

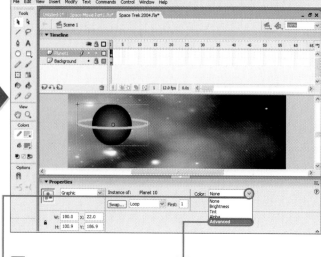

1 Click the instance you want to modify.

2 Open the Properties inspector.

Note: See Chapter 1 to learn more about using the Properties inspector.

3 Click the Color ⌄.

4 Click **Advanced**.

How do I make the instance transparent?

To make an instance appear transparent, change its Alpha setting.

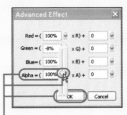

1 Follow steps **1** to **5** in this section.

2 Click the **Alpha** setting.

3 Click and drag the Alpha slider.

4 Click **OK**.

■ Flash changes the transparency.

Can I name an instance?

You can name a movie clip instance and use the name in your action variables. Click inside the Name text box in the Properties inspector and type a name. This only works for movie clip instances. See Chapter 10 to learn more about Flash actions.

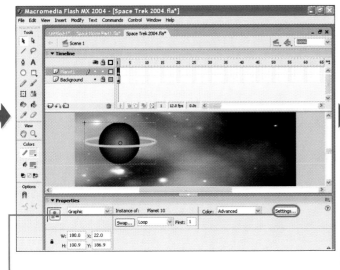

5 Click **Settings**.

■ The Advanced Effect dialog box opens.

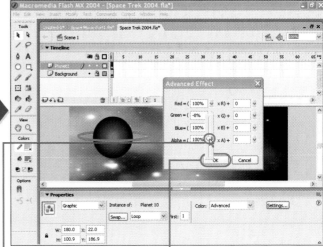

6 Click ☑ next to a color.

■ A slider bar appears.

7 Drag the slider (▭) to a new color setting.

■ The selected object changes color as you drag the slider.

8 Click **OK**.

■ Flash applies the new settings.

EDIT SYMBOLS

You can edit symbols you have in the Library. For example, you can change a symbol slightly by adjusting a line or shape. You can save considerable time and effort by making changes to the original symbol because Flash automatically updates all instances of it in your movie.

You can edit symbols in symbol-edit mode or in a new window. In symbol-edit mode, Flash locks the other objects on the Stage to prevent accidental changes. When you edit in a new window, only the symbol you want to edit appears.

Depending on the complexity of the symbol, you may need to first apply the Break Apart or Ungroup command, both in the Modify menu, to place the symbol into an editable form. See Chapter 3 to learn more about using these commands.

EDIT SYMBOLS

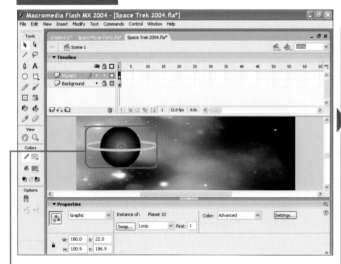

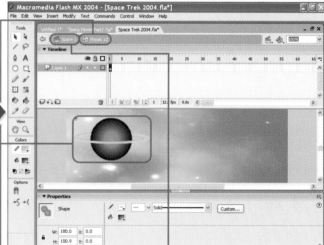

EDIT A SYMBOL IN SYMBOL-EDIT MODE

■1 Double-click the symbol you want to edit.

■ Flash switches you to symbol-edit mode.

■ If the symbol name appears at the top of the Stage, you know you are in symbol-edit mode.

■2 Edit the symbol using the Flash drawing tools to change object properties, such as the fill color, or to adjust a line segment.

Note: See Chapter 3 to learn more about editing objects.

■3 Click the scene name.

■ Flash returns to Movie-Edit mode.

How do I remove a symbol I no longer want?

First, make sure you do not use the symbol anywhere in your Flash movie. When you delete a symbol, Flash removes any instances of the symbol, and you cannot undo the action.

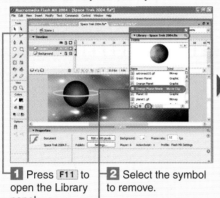

1 Press **F11** to open the Library panel.

2 Select the symbol to remove.

3 Click 🗑.

■ When a warning prompt box appears, click **Yes**.

■ Flash permanently removes the symbol from the file's Library.

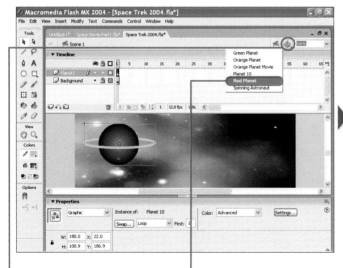
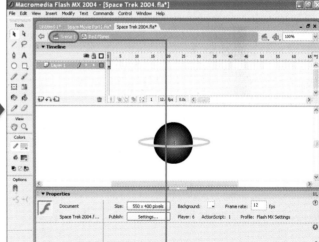

**EDIT A SYMBOL
IN A NEW WINDOW**

1 Click the Edit Symbols button (🔲).

2 Click the symbol you want to edit.

■ Flash opens a new window for editing the symbol.

3 Edit the symbol using the Flash drawing tools to change object properties, such as the fill color, or to adjust a line segment.

Note: See Chapter 3 to learn more about editing objects.

4 Click the scene name.

■ Flash returns to Movie-Edit mode, closes the window, and returns to the main movie.

131

CHAPTER 8

Creating Animation in Flash

Are you ready to start animating? This chapter shows you how to use frames and create simple animations.

INTRODUCING FLASH ANIMATION

One of the most
exciting aspects of
Flash is its animation
features. You can
animate objects,
synchronize the
animation with
sounds, add
backgrounds, animate
buttons, and much
more. After you
complete a Flash
animation, you can
place it on a
Web page or
distribute it
for others to
view.

How Do I Use Animations?

You can use Flash animations to present a lively
message or to simply entertain. Animations you create
in Flash can make a Web site come to life. For
example, you can create a cartoon to play in your
site's banner, or animate buttons for the user to click.
With the Flash animation tools, you have complete
control over your movies.

How Do Animations Work?

Animation is simply a change that occurs between two or
more frames in a movie. You can make the change the
placement of an object that moves slightly from one area
on the screen to another, or a change in color, intensity,
size, or shape of an object. Any change you make to an
object makes the object appear animated when you play
back your movie.

Animation History

Back in the early days of animating, cartoonists and other animators painted objects and scenes on transparent *cels*. They stacked the cels to create an image. A movie camera then took a snapshot of that image to create a single frame. The animators reused some of the *cels* for the next frame, such as backgrounds, and changed other cels to create an object's movement across the foreground.

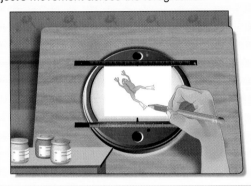

Animation in Flash

Flash uses similar principles to create animations today. Instead of transparent cels, you add content to frames and layers, and then stack the layers to create depth. Anytime you want the content to change, you can add keyframes to the Timeline and vary the position or appearance of the content. When you play back the animation, or movie, the content appears to move.

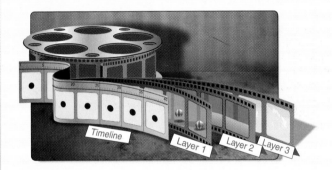

Frame-by-Frame Animation

Frame-by-frame animation is just as its name implies—you create the effect of movement by subtly changing the content's appearance from frame to frame. This type of animation method gives you a great deal of control over how the content changes across the Flash Timeline. You determine how much of a change appears from one frame to the next. However, frame-by-frame animations increase the overall file size.

Tweened Animation

The other method of animating in Flash is called *tweened animation*. With tweened animation, you tell Flash to calculate the in-between frames from one keyframe to the content change in the next keyframe. Flash then draws the in-between phases of change to get from the first keyframe to the next. This in-between framing is where the term *tweened* comes from. Tweened animation is faster, easier to edit, and consumes less file size.

Tweened Frames

UNDERSTANDING FRAMES

Frames, the backbone of your animation effects, hold the content of your movie. When you start a new Flash file, it opens with a single layer and hundreds of placeholder frames in the Timeline. Before you start animating objects, you need to understand how frames work.

Frame Rates

The number of frames you use in your Flash movie combined with the speed at which they play determines the length of the movie. By default, newly created Flash files use a frame rate of 12 frames per second, or 12 fps. You can set a frame rate higher or lower than the default, if needed.

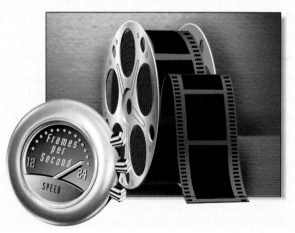

Frame Types

You can work with several different types of frames in the Flash Timeline: placeholder frames, keyframes, static frames, and tweened frames. Frames appear as tiny boxes in the Timeline. By default, the frames appear in Normal size; however, you can use the Timeline Options menu to change the appearance of frames in your Timeline.

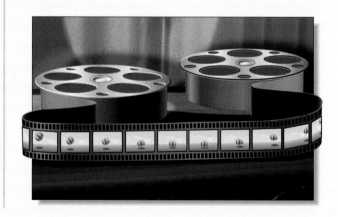

Placeholder Frames

A placeholder frame is merely an empty frame. It has no content. When your movie reaches an empty frame, it stops playing. With the exception of the first frame in a new layer, the remaining frames are all placeholders until you assign another frame type.

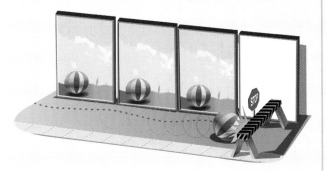

Keyframes

A keyframe defines a change in animation, such as an object moving or taking on a new appearance. By default, Flash inserts a blank keyframe for you in the first frame of every new layer you add to the Timeline. When you add a keyframe, it duplicates the content from the previous keyframe. This technique makes it easy to tweak the contents slightly to create the illusion of movement between frames.

Static Frames

Static, or regular frames, display the same content as the previous frame in the Timeline. You must precede static frames with a keyframe. Flash uses static frames to hold content that you want to remain visible until you add another keyframe in the layer.

Tweened Frames

One way to create animation in a movie is to allow Flash to calculate the number of frames between two keyframes to create movement. Called *tweening*, Flash determines the in-between positions of the animated object from one keyframe to the next and spaces out the changes in the tweened frames between the two keyframes. See Chapter 9 to find out more about tweening effects.

Tweened Frames

SET MOVIE DIMENSIONS AND SPEED

You can specify the size and speed of a movie before you begin building the animation. A movie's dimensions refer to its vertical and horizontal size on the Flash Stage. The movie's play speed determines the number of frames per second, or *fps*, that the animation occurs. Taking time to set the movie dimensions and speed now saves you time and prevents headaches later.

SET MOVIE DIMENSIONS AND SPEED

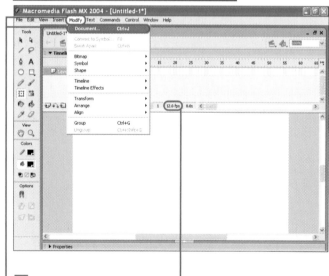

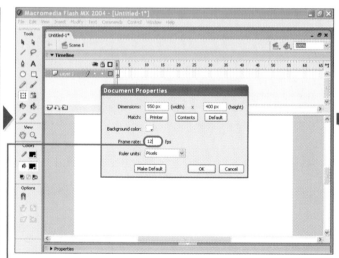

■1 Click **Modify**.

■2 Click **Document**.

■ You can also double-click the frame rate on the Timeline to open the Document Properties dialog box.

■ The Document Properties dialog box opens.

■3 Type the number of frames per second you want the movie to play in the Frame rate text box.

Note: If you use a higher fps setting, slower computers may not be able to play back your movie properly.

What is a good frame rate for my movie?

The default frame rate of 12 fps works well for most projects. The maximum rate you should set is 24 fps, unless you are exporting your movie as a QuickTime or Windows AVI video file, which can handle higher rates without consuming computer processor power. If you set a higher frame rate, slower computers struggle to play at such speeds.

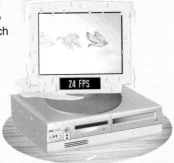

Can I vary the frame rate throughout my movie?

No. Once you set a frame rate, that rate is in effect for the entire movie. You can, however, vary the speed of animation sequences by adding or removing frames. If a sequence seems to go too fast, you can add regular frames between the keyframes to slow it down. See the next section, "Add Frames," to learn more.

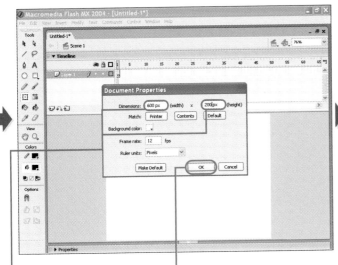

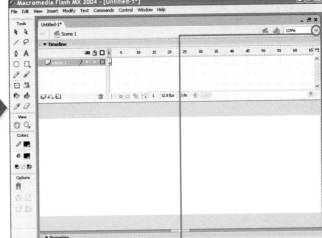

■ **4** Type a width value in the (width) text box.

■ **5** Type a height value in the (height) text box.

■ The allowable dimensions in Flash are 1 to 2,880 pixels in size.

■ **6** Click **OK**.

■ The Flash Stage adjusts to the new dimensions you assigned.

■ You can click the Magnification ∨ to choose another view to see the new dimensions you set.

ADD FRAMES

You can add frames to give your movie content and length. When you add a new layer or start a new file, Flash starts you out with one keyframe in the Timeline and a lot of placeholder frames. Adding more frames is as easy as adding pages to a document.

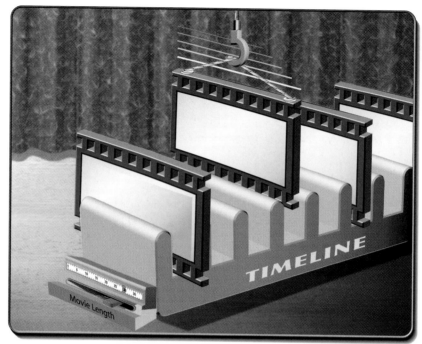

You can add regular frames, keyframes, blank keyframes, and you can add more than one at a time. You add keyframes to define changes in the animation's appearance. You add regular frames to repeat the content of the keyframe preceding them.

ADD FRAMES

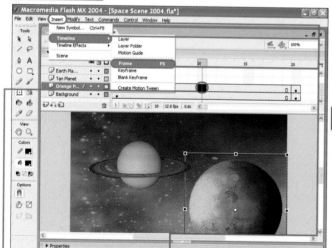

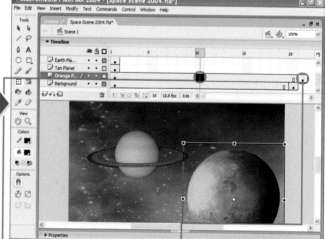

ADD A REGULAR FRAME

1 Click a frame on the Timeline where you want to insert a new frame.

Note: See Chapter 1 to learn more about the Flash Timeline.

2 Click **Insert**.

3 Click **Timeline**.

4 Click **Frame**.

■ You can also right-click over a frame and select which type of frame you want to add from the pop-up menu.

■ Flash inserts a regular frame.

■ If you add a regular frame in the midst of existing regular frames, all the frames to the right of the insertion move over to make room for the new frame.

■ This example adds a regular frame to increase the number of frames for the range Planet layer to 21.

How can I tell which frames are which in the Timeline?

You can identify Flash frames by the following characteristics:

- Keyframes with content appear with a solid bullet (●) in the Timeline.
- In-between frames that contain content appear tinted or grayed on the Timeline.
- Flash places a hollow box (▯) preceding a keyframe.
- Blank keyframes—keyframes which have no content added yet—appear as hollow bullets (○).
- Flash highlights selected frames in black.
- Empty frames appear white.

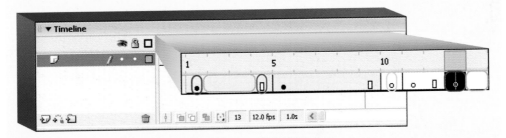

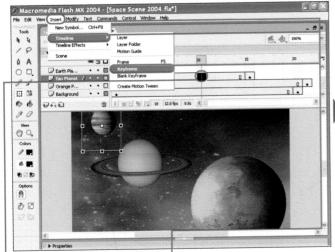

ADD A KEYFRAME

1 Click the frame on the Timeline that you want to turn into a keyframe.

Note: If you are having trouble selecting a single frame within a group of frames, press **Ctrl** *(⌘) while clicking the frame.*

2 Click **Insert**.

3 Click **Timeline**.

4 Click **Keyframe**.

■ You can also right-click over a frame and select which type of frame you want to add from the pop-up menu.

■ Flash inserts a keyframe, marked by a solid bullet (●) in the Timeline.

■ If the frame you selected in step **1** is a regular frame, Flash converts it to a keyframe.

■ If the frame is an empty frame, Flash inserts regular frames in between the last regular frame or keyframe up to the frame you clicked in step **1**.

CONTINUED

ADD FRAMES

You can add a blank keyframe when you want to start brand new content in your movie. Unlike a default keyframe, which copies the content from the previous keyframe in the sequence, a blank keyframe is completely without content.

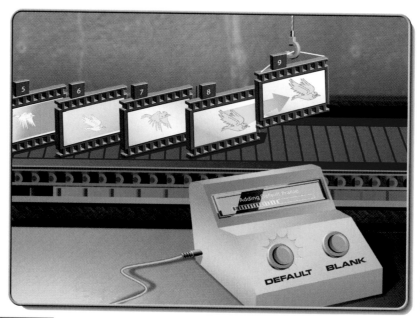

You can also add multiple frames. For example, perhaps you are creating an animation sequence that you need to extend a bit in the Timeline in order to play more slowly in playback. Rather than insert one regular frame at a time, you can insert multiple frames, such as five frames at once.

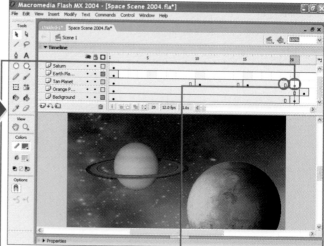

ADD A BLANK KEYFRAME

1 Click a frame on the Timeline.

■ If you are having trouble selecting a single frame within a group of frames, press **Ctrl** (⌘) while clicking the frame.

2 Click **Insert**.

3 Click **Timeline**.

4 Click **Blank Keyframe**.

■ You can also right-click over a frame and select which type of frame you want to add from the pop-up menu.

■ Flash inserts a blank keyframe with a hollow bullet (○).

■ A hollow box (▯) precedes the blank keyframe.

■ In this example, a blank keyframe is inserted into frame 20.

Can I change the size of the Timeline frames?

Yes. By default, the frames appear in **Normal** size. You can change them to **Tiny** or **Small** to fit more frames in the Timeline view, or try **Medium** or **Large** to make the frames easier to see. The Preview options let you see thumbnails of frame content in the timeline. Click the Timeline Options menu button ([⊞]), then click a frame size.

Tiny
Small
Normal
Medium
✓ Large
Short
✓ Tinted Frames
Preview
Preview In Context

Can I resize the Timeline to view more layers?

Yes. You can drag the bottom border of the docked Timeline to increase its size. To learn more about using the Flash Timeline, see Chapter 1.

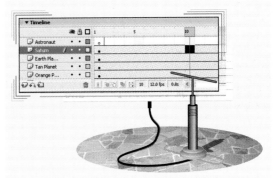

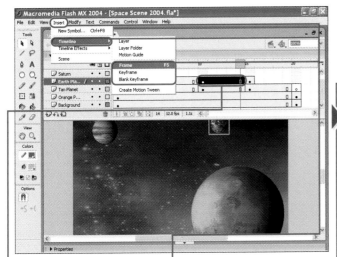

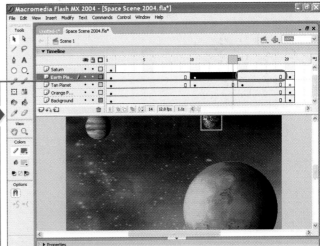

ADD MULTIPLE FRAMES

1 Select two or more frames by clicking them.

Note: See the section "Select Frames" to find out more about selecting frames.

2 Click **Insert**.

3 Click **Timeline**.

4 Click **Frame** to insert regular frames, or click **Keyframe** or **Blank Keyframe** to make the new frames all keyframes.

■ Flash inserts the new frames, lengthening the Timeline by the selected number of frames.

SELECT FRAMES

You can select frames in the Flash Timeline in order to add content or to edit the frames. You must also select frames in order to remove them from the Timeline. You can use a couple of selection techniques when working with frames.

When you select a single frame, it appears highlighted in the Timeline and the frame number appears in the Timeline's status bar. The playhead also appears directly above the selected frame.

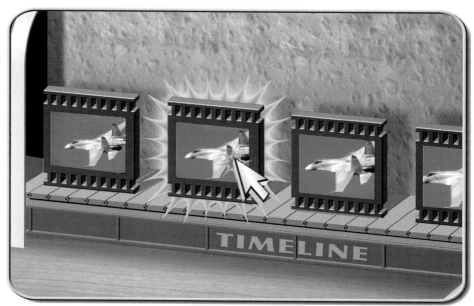

SELECT FRAMES

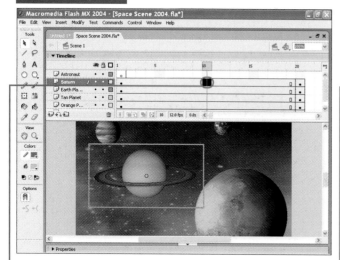

SELECT A SINGLE FRAME

1 Click the frame to select it.

■ Flash highlights the frame in the Timeline.

Note: See the section "Understand Frames" in this chapter to find out more about frame types.

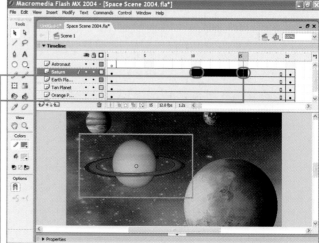

SELECT MULTIPLE FRAMES

1 Click the first frame in the range of frames you want to select.

2 Press and hold **Shift**.

3 Click the last frame in the range.

■ Flash selects all the frames in-between.

■ To select multiple frames between two keyframes, click anywhere between the two keyframes.

You can use the
Properties inspector to
define properties for
frames, such as labels
and tweening status.
Frame labels, for
example, help you
immediately recognize
a frame's contents. You
can also use labels to
organize frames with
actions, animation
effects, sounds,
and so on.

When you select a
tweening status, additional
options appear in the
Properties inspector. See
Chapter 9 to learn more
about creating tweened
animations.

MODIFY FRAME PROPERTIES

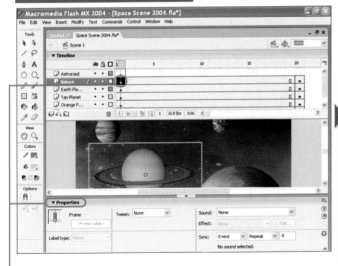

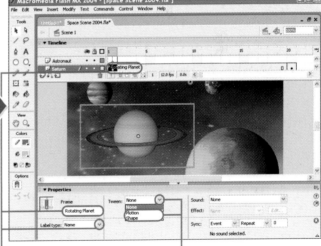

1 Click the frame you want
to modify.

2 Open the Properties
inspector.

■ You can press **Ctrl** + **F3**
to open the panel.

*Note: See Chapter 1 to learn how to
display the Properties inspector.*

3 Type a label for the
frame.

■ The label appears in the
Timeline.

■ To specify another type of
label, such as a comment,
click here and select a type.

4 Click the Tween ∨ and
select the frame type, such
as assigning a tweening
status.

■ Flash assigns the new
frame type.

*Note: See Chapter 9 to learn more
about tweening and frame types.*

DELETE OR CHANGE THE STATUS OF FRAMES

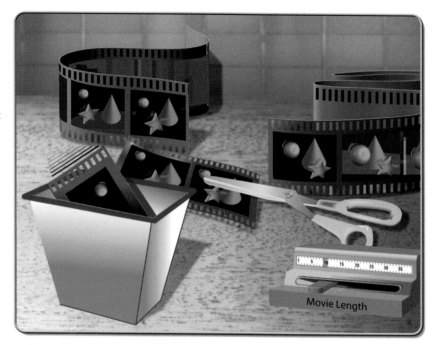

You can remove frames you no longer need or change them to a type of frame that you do need. You can remove regular frames to speed up an animation sequence. Or you might make a drastic change in your animation and decide you no longer need a particular keyframe in the sequence.

Instead of removing a keyframe completely, you can turn it into a regular frame. Using the Clear Keyframe command you can remove the frame's keyframe status and demote it to a regular frame. If you change a keyframe's status, Flash alters all in-between frames as well.

DELETE OR CHANGE THE STATUS OF FRAMES

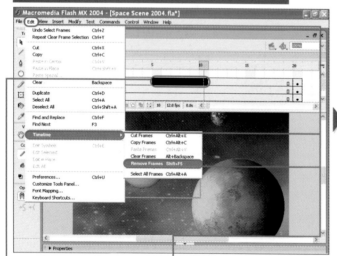

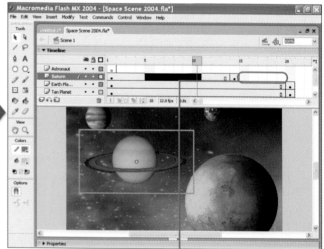

DELETE FRAMES

1 Click the frame, or range of frames, you want to delete.

2 Click **Edit**.

3 Click **Timeline**.

4 Click **Remove Frames**.

Note: See the section "Select Frames" to learn more about selecting frames in the Timeline.

■ To select multiple frames within a group of frames, press `Ctrl` + `Shift` (`⌘` + `Shift`) while clicking the frames.

■ Flash removes the frame and any existing frames to the right move over to fill the void.

Can I delete a keyframe?

To delete a keyframe completely from the Timeline, you must select both the keyframe and all the in-between frames associated with it; otherwise, the **Remove Frames** command does not work properly to remove the keyframe.

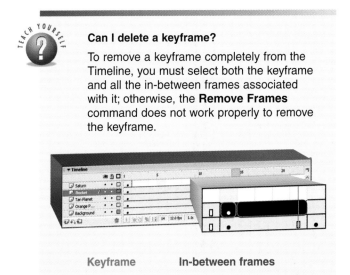

Keyframe   In-between frames

If I delete a frame, is the frame label removed as well?

Yes. Any time you remove a frame from the Timeline, any associated frame labels are removed as well. See the section "Modify Frame Properties" to learn more about frame labels.

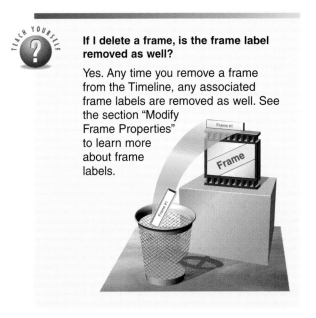

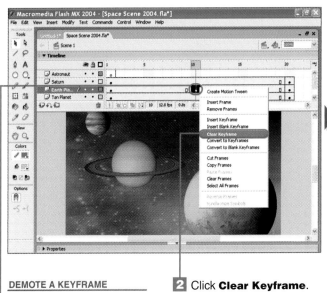

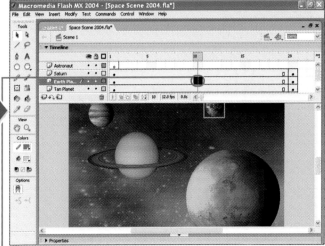

DEMOTE A KEYFRAME

1 Right-click the keyframe you want to change.

2 Click **Clear Keyframe**.

■ Flash converts the frame to a regular frame, and changes the frame to match the previous keyframe's contents.

Note: You cannot change the status of the first keyframe in a layer.

CREATE FRAME-BY-FRAME ANIMATION

You can create the illusion of movement in a Flash movie by changing the placement or appearance of the Stage content from keyframe to keyframe in the Flash Timeline. This type of animation is called, appropriately, *frame-by-frame animation*.

You can add an animation sequence to any layer in your movie, and you can use one sequence right after another. For example, you may start your movie with a fade-in animation of your company logo, then jump to a completely different animation detailing a new product or service.

CREATE FRAME-BY-FRAME ANIMATION

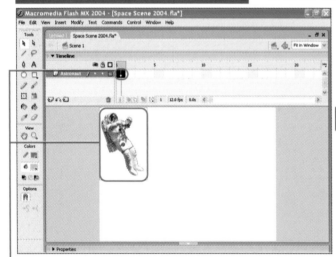

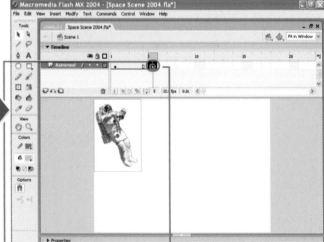

1 Click the first keyframe in the layer you want to animate.

2 Place the object you want to animate on the Flash Stage.

■ You can add an instance of a symbol from the Library to animate, or you can use the drawing tools to create an object.

3 Click the next frame in the Timeline where you want to continue the animation.

■ You can continue the animation in the very next frame, or space the animation out with a few regular frames in between.

4 Press F6.

■ Flash inserts a keyframe that duplicates the previous keyframe's contents.

Can I add in-between frames to the animation?

Yes. To slow down the animation sequence, especially if the changes between keyframes are happening too fast to see very well, just add regular frames between keyframes in your frame-by-frame animation. To add in-between frames, first click a keyframe and press **F5**. Flash adds a regular frame behind the keyframe. You can keep adding more regular frames to achieve the effect you want. When you play back the movie, the animation appears to slow down a bit in its movement.

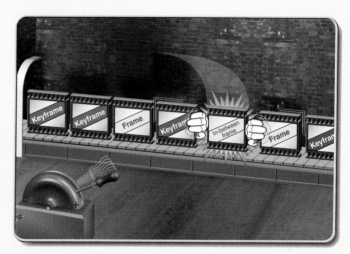

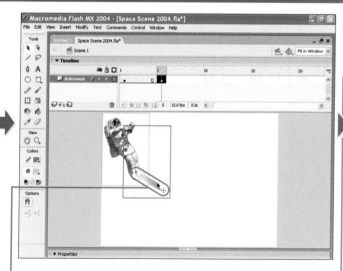

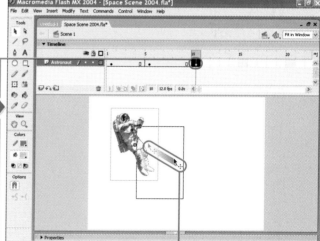

5 Change the object slightly to animate.

■ You can click and drag the object to move it a bit on the Stage, or change the object's appearance, such as color or size.

Note: See Chapter 3 to learn more about editing objects.

6 Click the next frame in the layer and add a keyframe.

■ Flash inserts a keyframe that duplicates the previous keyframe's contents.

7 Change the object slightly again.

■ You can move the object a bit more on the Stage, or change the object's appearance.

CONTINUED ►

CREATE FRAME-BY-FRAME ANIMATION

You can create all kinds of animation effects using frame-by-frame animation techniques. For example, a simple circle shape can become a bouncing ball, if you move the ball strategically around the Stage in each frame of the movie.

The example in this section shows how to create the illusion of a floating astronaut by moving the astronaut slightly down the Stage in each keyframe. By the last keyframe, the astronaut reaches the bottom. During playback, the astronaut appears to drop from the top-right corner to the bottom-left corner.

CREATE FRAME-BY-FRAME ANIMATION (CONTINUED)

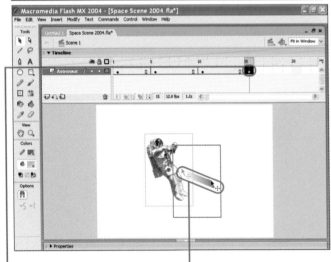

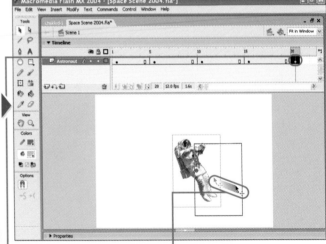

■8 Click the next frame in the layer to which you want to change the animation and add a keyframe.

■ Flash inserts a keyframe that duplicates the previous keyframe's contents.

■9 Change the object again so it varies from the previous keyframe.

■10 Click the next frame in the layer and add a keyframe.

■ Flash inserts a keyframe that duplicates the previous keyframe's contents.

■11 Change the object again.

How do I edit a symbol as I create the animation?

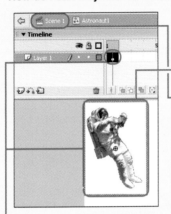

■ This opens the symbol in symbol-edit mode,

3 Make your edits.

4 Click the Scene name to return to movie-edit mode.

■ You can switch back and forth between edit modes as needed when creating your animation sequence.

1 Click the keyframe where you want to introduce a change.

2 Double-click the symbol.

How do I know where to reposition an object on the Stage?

To help you control how an object moves around the Stage, turn on the gridlines by clicking **View Grid**, and then **Show Grid**. With the grid turned on, you can more clearly see the placement of objects on the Stage. To turn off the grid marks again, click **View**, **Grid**, and then **Show Grid**. See Chapter 1 to learn more about rulers and grids.

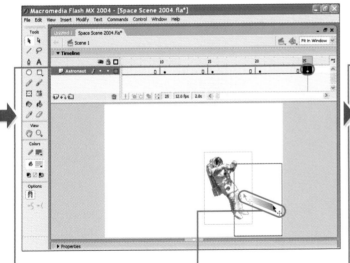

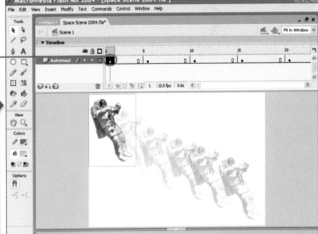

12 Click the next frame in the layer and add a final keyframe.

■ Flash inserts a keyframe that duplicates the previous keyframe's contents.

13 Change the object again for the final keyframe in the animation sequence.

14 Click the first keyframe in the layer.

Note: You can also drag the playhead to the first frame of any layer to play the movie.

15 Press [Enter]([Return]).

■ Flash plays the entire animation sequence.

ONION SKINNING AN ANIMATION

You can use the onion skinning feature to quickly assess the positioning of objects in surrounding frames in your movie. By viewing the placement of objects in other frames, you can more clearly determine how you want to position the object in the frame in which you are working.

The name *onion skinning* refers to the effect of seeing the contents of other frames as shaded layers — like the translucent layers of an onion — in context to the current frame. Onion skinning offers two modes of display: dimmed content or outlined content.

Dimmed content mode shows dimmed versions of the surrounding frame's content. Use dimmed mode to view more details of surrounding frames. Outline mode shows the content outlines instead of the entire object. Use outline mode to view less details of surrounding frames.

ONION SKINNING AN ANIMATION

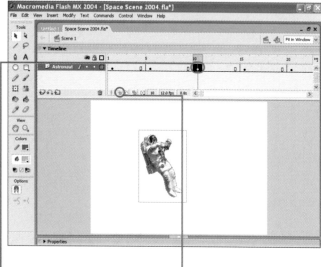

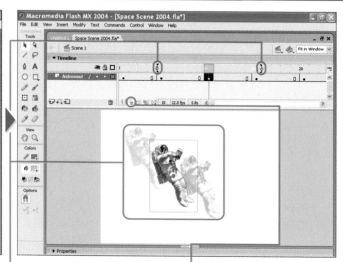

TURN ON DIMMED ONION SKINNING

1 Click a frame.

2 Click the Onion Skin button at the bottom of the Flash Timeline.

■ Flash displays dimmed images from the surrounding frames.

■ Flash also places onion skin markers ( ) at the top of the Timeline.

■ To turn off onion skinning, you can click again.

Can I edit the onion skinned frames?

No. You cannot edit the onion skin frames unless you click ▣. When you make the other frames editable, you can select and move the onion skinned objects to fine-tune the animation sequence.

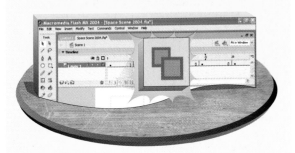

Can I play back my movie with the onion skin feature on?

Yes. However, the onion skinning turns off while the movie plays. Click the first frame of your movie and then press `Enter` (`Return`). Flash plays the movie on the Stage. When it reaches the last frame, the onion skin feature resumes its active state again.

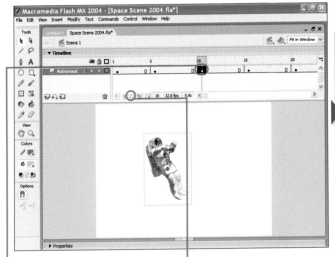

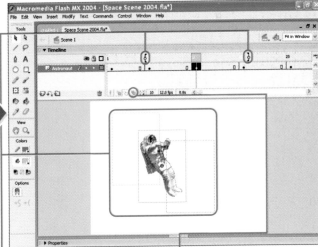

TURN ON ONION SKINNING OUTLINES

1 Click a frame.

2 Click the Onion Skinning Outline button (▣) on the Flash Timeline.

■ Flash displays outlines of the images from the surrounding frames.

■ Flash also places onion skin markers at the top of the Timeline.

■ To make the content of the onion skin frames editable, click ▣.

CONTINUED

LONION SKINNING AN ANIMATION

The onion skinning features can help you better gauge the changes you need to make to create your animations. You can control which frames appear in onion skin mode using the onion skin markers that appear on the Timeline. You can also opt to control the markers using the Modify Onion Markers menu.

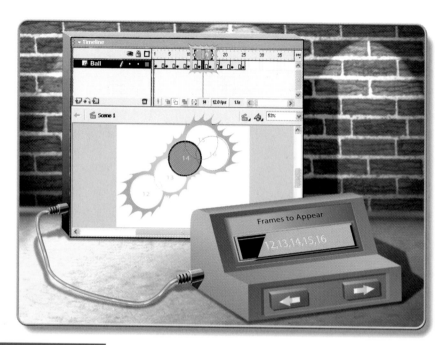

When you activate the Modify Onion Markers button, the menu displays several choices for controlling markers on the Timeline.

ONION SKINNING AN ANIMATION (CONTINUED)

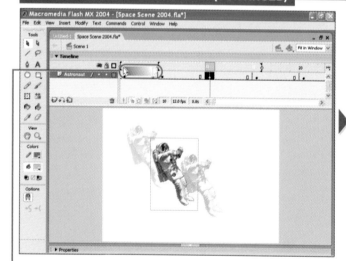

MOVE THE ONION SKIN MARKERS

1 Click and drag an onion skin marker left or right.

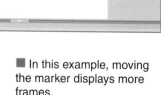

■ Flash adds or subtracts the additional frames from the view.

■ In this example, moving the marker displays more frames.

What are my options for modifying the onion-skin markers?

When you click 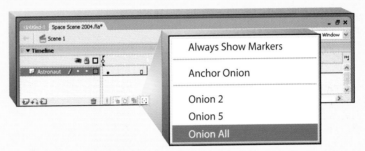, the menu displays several choices for controlling markers on the Timeline.

■ Click **Always Show Markers** to leave the markers on even when onion-skinning is turned off.

■ Click **Anchor Onion** to lock the markers in place, even as you view frames at the other end of the Timeline.

■ Click **Onion 2** or **Onion 5** to display the corresponding number of frames before and after the current frame.

■ Click **Onion All** to onion-skin all the frames.

Always Show Markers

Anchor Onion

Onion 2

Onion 5

Onion All

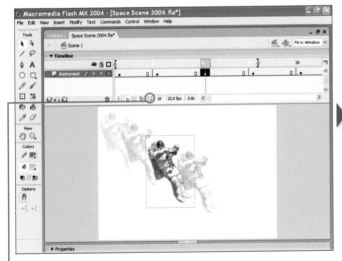

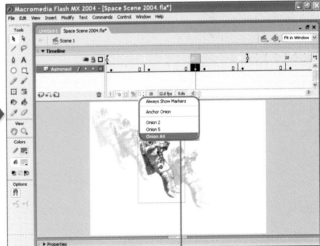

CHANGE THE MARKER DISPLAY

1 Click the Modify Onion Marker icon (▣).

■ The Modify menu appears with options for changing the marker display.

2 Click the marker setting you want to apply.

■ Flash applies the new setting.

PREVIEW A FLASH ANIMATION

You can click an animation sequence one frame at a time to see each frame's contents, but a faster way to check the sequence is to play the movie. You can use the built-in Flash Player window to see the movie without all the surrounding Flash tools. Test Movie mode lets you see the movie as your audience will see it.

PREVIEW A FLASH ANIMATION

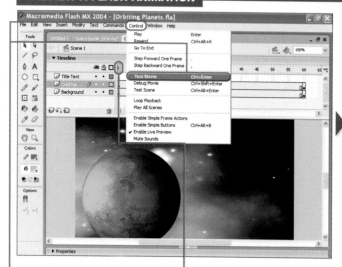

■1 Click **Control**.

■2 Click **Test Movie**.

■ Another quick way to test the movie by playing it directly on the Stage is to move the playhead to the first frame and press **Enter**.

■ Flash exports your movie to the Flash Player and plays the animation.

■ To stop the animation from playing, press **Esc**.

■ To resume playing, press **Enter** (**Return**).

■3 To return to the Flash Editor window, click ☒.

ADJUST THE ANIMATION SPEED

You can use regular frames in your movie to adjust the speed of an animation sequence. Although a movie's frame rate is constant throughout the movie, you can slow or speed up an animation by adding or subtracting frames. Adding regular frames to an animation sequence extends the length of time the sequence plays back.

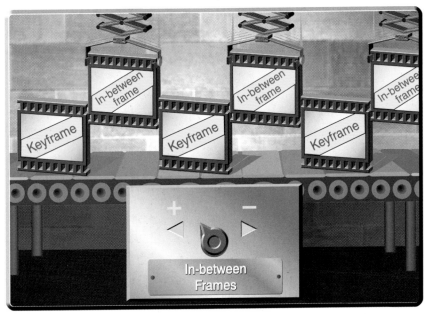

If a particular section of your animation seems to happen too quickly during playback, you can slow it down a bit if you insert regular frames between two keyframes. By adding in-between frames rather than keyframes, you do not increase the movie's file size.

ADJUST THE ANIMATION SPEED

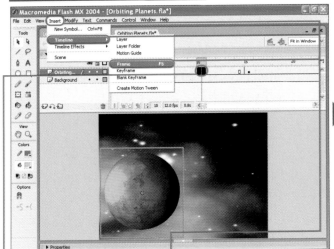

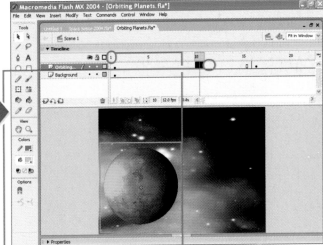

1 Click the keyframe to which you want to add frames, or click a regular frame from between two keyframes.

2 Click **Insert**.

3 Click **Timeline**.

4 Click **Frame**.

■ You can also press F5 to add a regular frame.

■ Flash adds a regular frame.

■ Because adding just one regular frame is not always enough, repeat steps **2** to **4** as needed to add more frames to the sequence.

■ To test the animation, click the first frame in the Timeline and press Enter (Return).

MOVE AND COPY FRAMES

You can move and
copy frames in your
animation sequence
to change the way
in which it plays.
For example, you
may want to move
a keyframe up
or back in the
Timeline, or copy
multiple regular
frames to place
between two
keyframes.

You cannot copy
frames like you
copy other objects
in Flash; you must
use the Copy
Frames and Paste
Frames commands
in the Edit menu.
Using the standard
Copy and Paste
commands do
not work.

MOVE AND COPY FRAMES

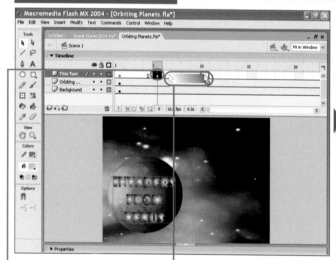

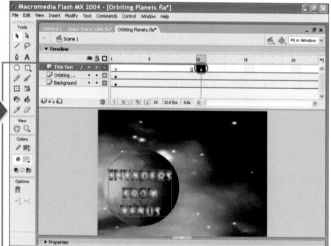

MOVE A FRAME

1 Click the frame to
select it.

■ Flash highlights the frame
in the Timeline.

2 Drag the frame to a new
location in the Timeline.

3 Release the mouse to
drop the frame in place.

■ The frame moves.

Can I use the drag-and-drop technique to copy frames?

Yes. First select the frame or frames you want to copy. Press and hold Alt (option) and then drag the frame or frames and drop into the new location on the Timeline. Flash duplicates the frames.

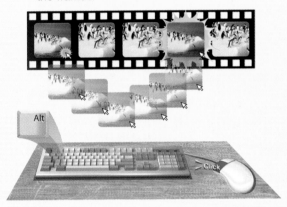

Alt
Click

Can I drag an end keyframe to extend an animation?

Yes. Dragging an end keyframe in your animation sequence can quickly lengthen or shorten an animation, depending on which direction you drag. For example, you can drag a keyframe to the right a couple of frames and Flash automatically adds in-between frames for you. This extends your animation sequence.

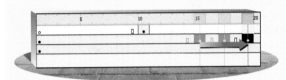

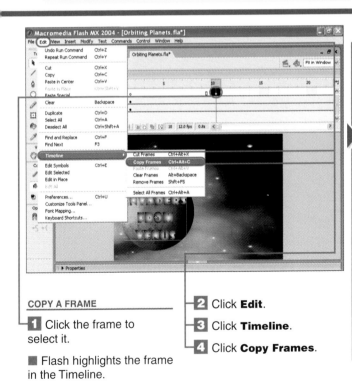

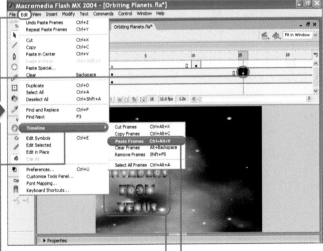

COPY A FRAME

1 Click the frame to select it.

■ Flash highlights the frame in the Timeline.

2 Click **Edit**.

3 Click **Timeline**.

4 Click **Copy Frames**.

5 Click a frame where you want to place the copy.

6 Click **Edit**.

7 Click **Timeline**.

8 Click **Paste Frames**.

■ Flash pastes the copied frame into the selected frame and any copied frame content appears on the stage.

CREATE SCENES

You can create scenes in your movie to organize your animation sequences. Scenes are blocks of the animation frames turned into their own independent Timelines. Rather than scrolling around long Timelines and trying to keep track of where you are, you can break your movie into smaller, manageable scenes that you can work with individually.

The current scene's name appears at the top of the Timeline. During playback, Flash plays the scenes in the order in which you list them in the Scene panel.

CREATE SCENES

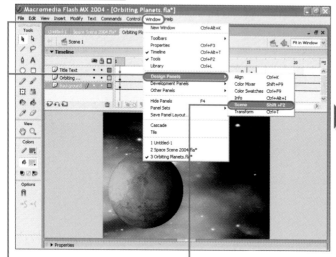

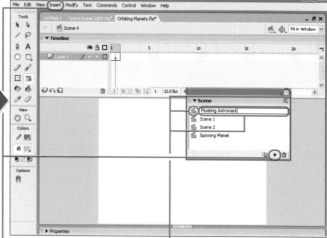

OPEN THE SCENE PANEL

1 Click **Window**.

2 Click **Design Panels**.

3 Click **Scene**.

■ The Scene panel opens.

ADD A NEW SCENE

4 Click the Add Scene button (+).

■ You can also click **Insert** and then select **Scene** to add a scene.

■ Flash adds a scene to the panel, and the Timeline switches to the new scene.

■ To rename the scene, double-click the scene name, type another name, and then press Enter (Return).

■ You can click ☒ to close the panel.

How do I rearrange the scene order?

You can move scenes around using the Scene panel:

1 Follow steps **1** to **3** in the "Open the Scene Panel" section to open the Scene panel.

2 Click the scene you want to move.

3 Drag the scene to a new location in the list and release the mouse button.

■ Flash reorders the scenes.

How do I delete a scene?

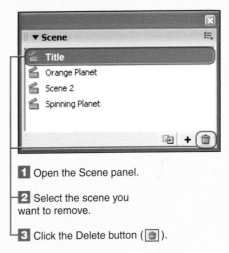

1 Open the Scene panel.

2 Select the scene you want to remove.

3 Click the Delete button (🗑).

■ Flash deletes the scene.

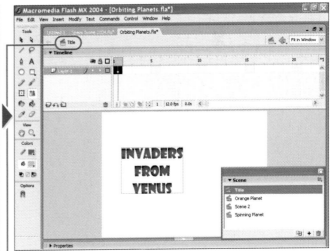

SWITCH BETWEEN SCENES

1 Click the Edit Scene button (📄).

■ Flash displays a pop-up menu listing all the available scenes.

2 Click the scene you want to view.

■ If the Scene panel is open, you can also click on the scene name you want to view.

■ Flash switches to the scene you selected.

■ Scene names always appear above the Timeline.

SAVE AN ANIMATION AS A MOVIE CLIP

You can save an animation sequence as a movie clip that you can use again elsewhere in your movie. When you save an animation sequence, Flash saves it as a movie clip symbol. Movie clip symbols are just one of the three symbol types you can create in Flash. Movie clips utilize their own timelines apart from the main movie Timeline.

As with graphic and button symbols, you can place a movie clip symbol on the Stage for any frame. When Flash reaches that frame during playback, it plays the movie clip animation.

SAVE AN ANIMATION AS A MOVIE CLIP

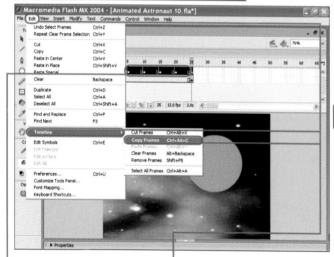

1 Select all the frames included in the animation sequence.

Note: See the section "Select Frames" to learn how to select frames in the Timeline.

2 Click **Edit**.

3 Click **Timeline**.

4 Click **Copy Frames**.

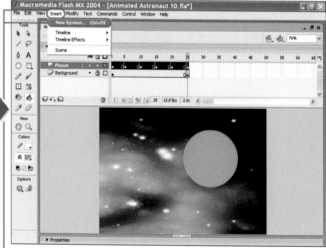

5 Click **Insert**.

6 Click **New Symbol**.

■ Flash opens the Create New Symbol dialog box.

How do I place a movie clip in my movie?

You can place movie clips into your movie just as you place any other item saved in the Flash Library. Click the frame where you want to insert the clip, open the Library panel and drag the movie clip onto the Stage. You can turn any animation effect, including frame-by-frame motion and shape tweens, into movie clips.

How do I save an existing clip as a new clip?

You can use the Convert to Symbol command. You may do this if you want to alter the clip slightly and use it again elsewhere.

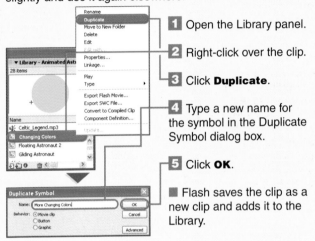

1 Open the Library panel.

2 Right-click over the clip.

3 Click **Duplicate**.

4 Type a new name for the symbol in the Duplicate Symbol dialog box.

5 Click **OK**.

■ Flash saves the clip as a new clip and adds it to the Library.

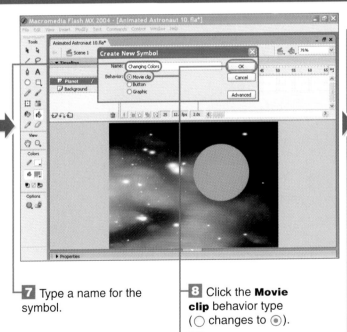

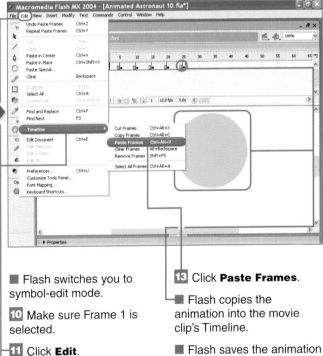

7 Type a name for the symbol.

8 Click the **Movie clip** behavior type (○ changes to ◉).

9 Click **OK**.

■ Flash switches you to symbol-edit mode.

10 Make sure Frame 1 is selected.

11 Click **Edit**.

12 Click **Timeline**.

13 Click **Paste Frames**.

■ Flash copies the animation into the movie clip's Timeline.

■ Flash saves the animation in the Flash Library as a movie clip.

163

ADD A TIMELINE EFFECT

You can add pre-built animation effects to your movies. New to Flash, Timeline effects enable you to animate text, graphics, and buttons without any effort. Flash sets up the animation for you. The Timeline effects include animated transitions, blurring, drop shadows, and more.

When you assign a Timeline effect, Flash creates a new layer with the selected object and automatically adjusts the number of frames you need to display the effect.

ADD A TIMELINE EFFECT

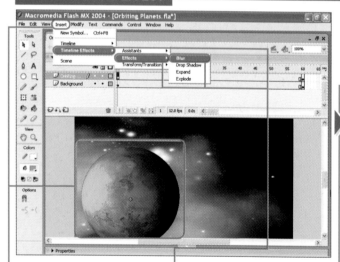

1 Select the object to which you want to assign an effect.

2 Click **Insert**.

3 Click **Timeline Effects**.

4 Click **Effects**.

5 Click the effect you want to assign.

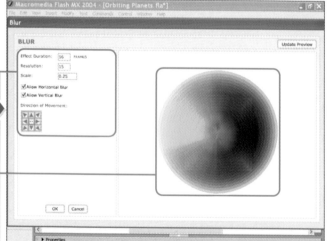

■ Flash creates the effect, opens the effect's dialog box and previews the effect.

Note: Flash may take a few moments to process the effect before displaying the preview.

6 Change any effect parameters you want to edit.

■ You can adjust the length of the effect, the resolution of the blur, the scale and direction.

■ In this example, the Blur effect is assigned.

How do I edit or remove an effect at a later time?

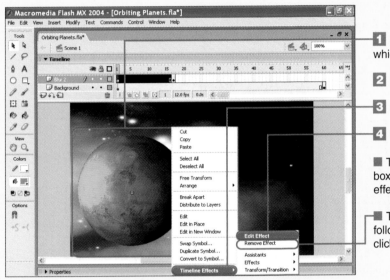

1 Select the object to which an effect is assigned.

2 Right-click over the object.

3 Click **Timeline Effects**.

4 Click **Edit Effect**.

■ This reopens the effect's dialog box where you can fine-tune the effect parameters as needed.

■ To remove an effect, follow steps **1** to **3**, but click **Remove Effect**.

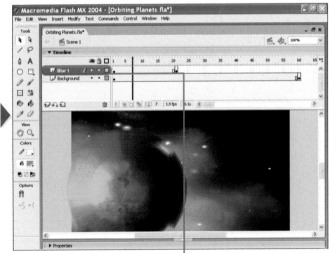

7 Click **Update Preview** to preview the changes.

Note: Flash may take a few moments to process the changes before displaying the preview.

8 When you finish adjusting the effect, click **OK**.

■ Flash closes the effect dialog box.

■ Flash also changes the layer name and number of frames to reflect the Timeline effect.

Creating Animation by Tweening

Flash includes built-in animating techniques. This chapter shows you how to create animation using motion and shape tweening.

CREATE A MOTION TWEEN

Flash can help you animate moving objects when you apply a motion tween. A *motion tween* is when you define two points of movement in the Timeline with two keyframes, and then let Flash calculate all the in-between frames necessary to get from point A to point B.

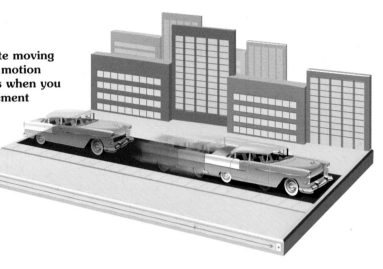

Motion-tweened animations take up much less file space than frame-by-frame animations. You can motion tween only symbols or grouped objects, and you can tween only one symbol per layer.

CREATE A MOTION TWEEN

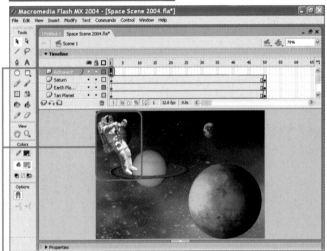

ADD KEYFRAMES AND SYMBOL

■1 Insert a keyframe where you want to start the motion tween.

Note: See Chapter 8 to learn about adding frames.

■2 Place the symbol you want to animate on the Stage.

■ You should make the symbol's position the starting point of the animation effect, such as a corner or side of the movie area.

Note: Chapter 7 explains how to work with symbols.

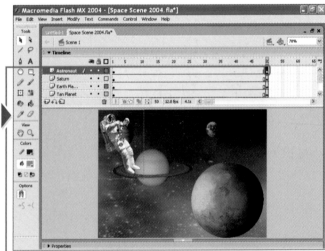

■3 Click the last frame you want to include in the motion tween.

■4 Insert a keyframe.

■ You can press **F6** to quickly insert a keyframe.

Note: See Chapter 8 to learn more about keyframes.

When do I use a frame-by-frame animation as opposed to a motion tween?

Use a motion tween when you want Flash to calculate the changes between frames. You use a frame-by-frame animation when you want complete control over the changes between keyframes. However, creating a manual animation sequence results in a larger file size than the same sequence with a motion tween.

What is the difference between a shape tween and a motion tween?

You can create two types of tweened animations in Flash: motion tween or shape tween. Use motion tweening to make Flash calculate the changes for an object moving around the Stage. You use shape tweening to have Flash calculate the changes between an object that morphs into another object.

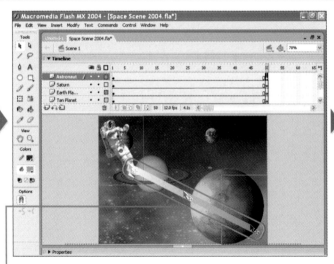

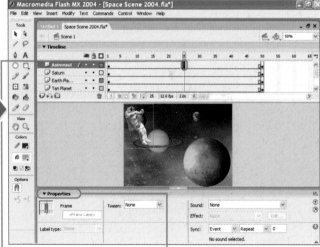

5 Click and drag the symbol to the position on which you want the motion tween to end, for example, the other side of the Stage.

6 Click a frame between the two keyframes that make up your motion tween to select the frames.

■ You can also double-click a frame to select all the frames between two keyframes.

7 Open the Properties inspector.

■ You can press Ctrl + F3 (Shift + F3) to quickly open the Properties inspector.

CONTINUED

CREATE A MOTION TWEEN

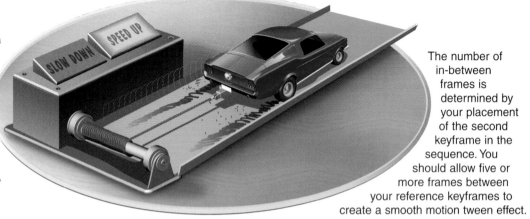

You can assign as many motion tween segments as you like throughout your movie, or you can make your animation one long motion tween. Motion tweening works best for objects you want to move around the Flash Stage.

The number of in-between frames is determined by your placement of the second keyframe in the sequence. You should allow five or more frames between your reference keyframes to create a smooth motion tween effect.

CREATE A MOTION TWEEN (CONTINUED)

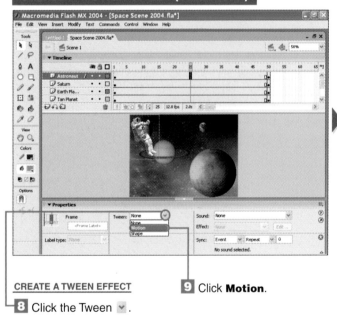

CREATE A TWEEN EFFECT

8 Click the Tween ☑.

9 Click **Motion**.

■ Flash calculates the in-between changes the symbol must undergo to move from the first keyframe to the next keyframe.

■ Flash adds a motion tween arrow (⟩—➔) from the first keyframe in the tween effect to the last keyframe in the tween effect.

Can I create a motion tween as I go?

Yes. You can start a motion tween without defining the end keyframe in the sequence and add an end keyframe when you are ready. Flash inserts a dotted line in the frames to indicate a motion tween in the making, but not yet complete. Any new frames you add to the sequence also appear with a dotted line in the frames. When you do finally complete the motion tween sequence with an end keyframe, Flash changes the dotted line marking the in-between frames to a motion tween arrow to show the tween is complete.

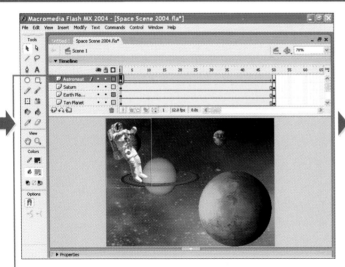

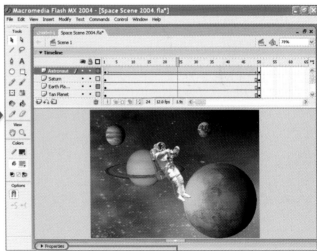

TEST THE TWEEN EFFECT

10 Click in the first frame of the motion tween.

11 Press Enter (Return).

■ Flash plays the animation sequence.

■ You can click the title bar of the panel to hide the Properties inspector.

ANIMATE BY ROTATING A SYMBOL

You can turn a regular symbol from your Library into an animated object that rotates in your movie. This method requires a series of keyframes in which you control how much rotation occurs in each keyframe. By assigning the sequence motion tween status, Flash calculates the in-between frames to create the effect.

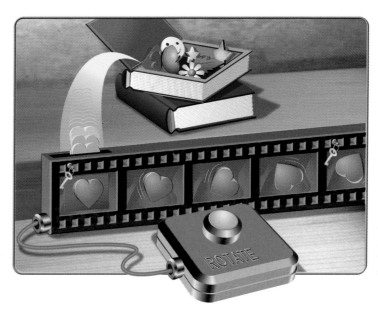

Shapes, lines, and text boxes all make good candidates for rotating. For example, you can make your corporate logo rotate at the top of your movie screen. The steps in this section show how to rotate a text box, but you can apply the same steps to rotate any symbol on the Stage.

ANIMATE BY ROTATING A SYMBOL

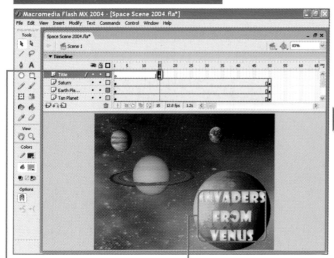

ASSIGN MOTION TWEEN STATUS

1 Insert a keyframe where you want to start the motion tween.

Note: See Chapter 8 to learn more about adding frames to the Timeline.

2 Place the symbol you want to animate on the Stage.

Note: It is a good idea to place animations on a separate layer from the movie background. See Chapter 6 to learn more about working with layers.

3 Open the Properties inspector.

■ You can press **Ctrl** + **F3** (**Shift** + **F3**) to quickly open the Properties inspector.

4 Click the Tween ⦿ to view tweening types.

5 Click **Motion**.

Can I rotate an object I draw on the Stage?

The motion tween effect does not work with items you draw on the Stage. It does work with objects that you turn into symbols or that you group together. You can also motion tween text blocks. To learn more about using symbols, see Chapter 7. To learn how to group objects, see Chapter 3.

SYMBOLS
&
GROUPS
ONLY

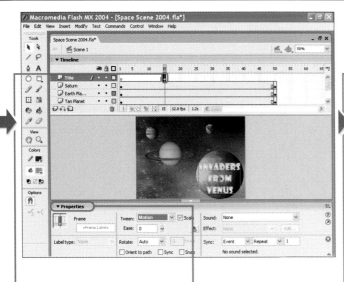

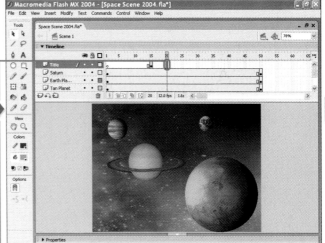

■ Flash assigns motion tween status to the current frame, as well as to subsequent frames you add to the sequence.

■ You can click the title bar of the panel to hide the Properties inspector.

6 Click the next frame you want to include in the motion tween.

■ For example, you can start the rotation five frames later.

CONTINUED

ANIMATE BY ROTATING A SYMBOL

You can add keyframes at key points of the animation to rotate your symbol. For example, you can change the rotation's progress by stretching it out over four keyframes, rotating the symbol 90 degrees each time. Then, add regular frames between the keyframes to lengthen the animation.

Creating a rotating motion tween requires more than two keyframes. Remember, you use keyframes to indicate a change in the animation, such as a position on the Stage. Flash cannot calculate the between frames without key spots that change the direction of the object in the rotation.

ANIMATE BY ROTATING A SYMBOL (CONTINUED)

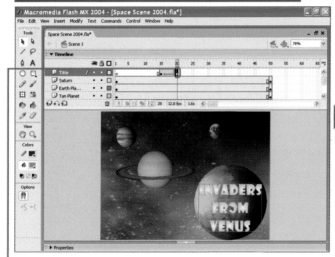

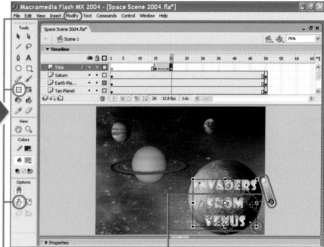

■7 Insert a keyframe.

■ You can press **F6** to quickly insert a keyframe.

■ Flash copies the contents from the previous keyframe.

ROTATE THE OBJECT

■8 Click the Free Transform tool (⊞).

■9 Click the Rotate and Skew tool (⚗).

■ You can also click **Modify**, **Transform**, and then **Rotate and Skew**.

■ Flash surrounds the selected symbol with rotation handles.

■10 Click and drag a rotation handle and rotate the symbol in the direction you want it to go.

Does it matter which direction I rotate the object?

No. You can drag a rotation handle in any direction to start rotating the object. The direction you drag determines the direction of the rotation. For example, you may want your object to rotate counterclockwise. To do this, drag a rotation handle to the left. The rotation feature works best if you drag a corner handle.

How do I make the object seem to keep rotating?

Repeat the animation sequence in your movie by copying the rotation sequence and adding it to the end of the movie as many times as needed, or set the sequence to loop with the **goto** and **play** actions. To learn more about assigning actions in Flash, see Chapter 10.

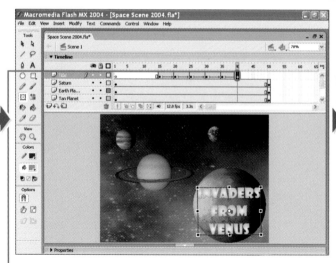

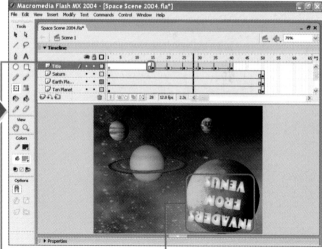

11 Repeat steps **6** to **10** to continue adding keyframes and rotating the symbol.

■ You can make the symbol complete a full rotation.

Note: To ensure the motion tween stays in effect with additional keyframes you add, be sure to select both the start and end keyframes in the tween before applying Motion tween status.

VIEW THE ROTATING EFFECT

12 Click in the first frame of the motion tween.

13 Press Enter (Return).

■ Flash plays the animation sequence.

SPIN A SYMBOL AUTOMATICALLY

You can create an animation effect that makes a symbol appear to spin. Using two identical keyframes, you can tell Flash to rotate the symbol in the in-between frames to create a spinning effect during playback.

The spinning object starts and ends up at the same spot, so the two keyframes that begin and end the effect remain the same. You specify which direction to spin the object and Flash calculates all the incremental changes that must occur in the in-between frames to create the spinning effect.

SPIN A SYMBOL AUTOMATICALLY

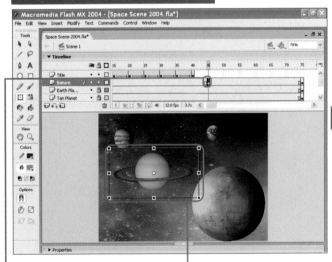

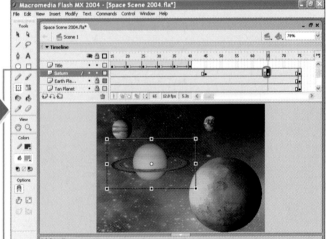

CREATE THE TWEEN EFFECT

1 Insert a keyframe where you want to start the spin motion tween in the Timeline.

■ You can press **F6** to insert a keyframe.

2 Place the symbol you want to animate on the Stage.

Note: It is a good idea to place animations on a separate layer from the movie background. See Chapter 6 to learn more about working with layers.

3 Click the end frame in which you want to conclude the motion tween.

■ For example, you can complete the spin effect 20 frames later.

4 Insert a keyframe.

■ You can press **F6** to insert a keyframe.

Does it matter in which direction the symbol spins?

No. You can set a rotation direction in the Property inspector, or you can tell Flash to set a direction for you. If you let Flash pick a direction, it chooses the rotation that involves the least amount of change from frame to frame creating a smoother animation. To instruct Flash to handle the rotation, leave the **Auto** option selected.

How do I continue a motion tween into new frames I add to the movie?

If you plan to continue the motion tween, make sure you select the end keyframe along with the start keyframe and in-between frames. See Chapter 8 to learn how to select frames. To stop a motion tween, click the last keyframe in the sequence, then assign **None** using the Tween setting in the Properties inspector.

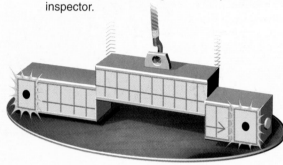

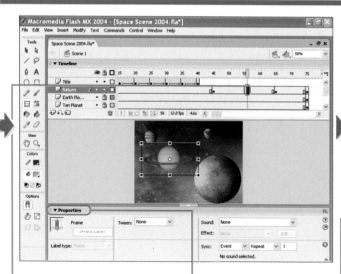

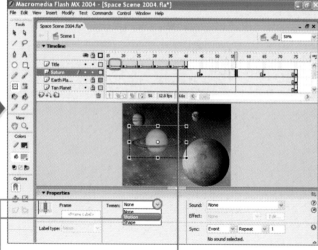

5 Double-click a frame between the two keyframes that make up your motion tween to select the frames.

Note: See Chapter 8 to learn how to select frames.

6 Open the Properties inspector.

■ You can press Ctrl + F3 (Shift + F3) to quickly open the Properties inspector.

7 Click the Tween ⌄ to view tweening types.

8 Click **Motion**.

■ Flash adds a motion tween arrow (⇒) to the selected frames.

CONTINUED

SPIN A SYMBOL AUTOMATICALLY

You can use the Rotation controls to spin items. By assigning a motion tween effect, Flash takes care of the hard work of differing each frame in the sequence for you. You can specify how many times the symbol spins between the two keyframes, and exactly which direction it goes.

The steps in this section show an example of a ringed planet as a spinning object. You can apply the same principles to other objects you create or add to the Flash Stage.

SPIN A SYMBOL AUTOMATICALLY (CONTINUED)

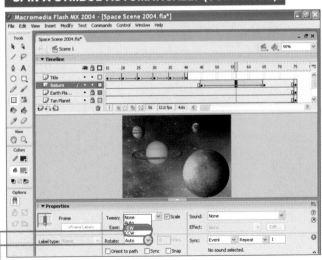

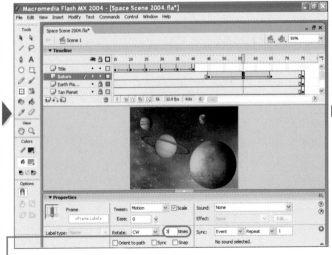

SELECT A SPIN ROTATION

9 Click the Rotate ∨ to view rotation types.

10 Click a rotation direction for the spin.

■ You can select **CW** to spin the symbol clockwise.

■ You can select **CCW** to spin the symbol counterclockwise.

11 Type the number of times you want the rotation to occur.

■ Flash calculates the in-between changes the symbol must undergo to move from the first keyframe to the next keyframe.

■ You can click the panel's title bar to hide the Properties inspector.

What does the Auto rotate setting in the Properties panel do?

You can select **Auto** from the **Rotate** menu in the Properties inspector to have Flash determine the rotation for you. The Auto selection rotates the selected object in the direction using the least amount of motion.

Can I control how quickly the object starts spinning?

Yes. Use the Ease setting in the Properties inspector panel to speed up the start of your motion tween's spinning effect. You can drag the Ease slider (⬛) up to accelerate the spin or down to slow it down.

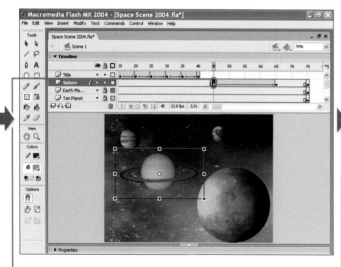

VIEW THE SPIN

12 Click in the first frame of the motion tween.

13 Press **Enter** (**Return**).

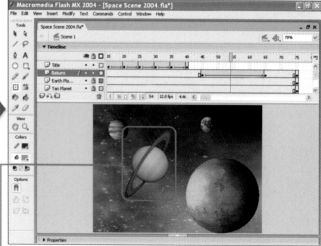

■ Flash plays the animation sequence.

ANIMATE BY CHANGING THE SYMBOL SIZE

You can use the motion tween technique to create an animation that changes size. For example, you can make a symbol seem to grow or shrink in size. You define two keyframes, one of which includes the symbol scaled to a new size. Flash fills in all the in-between frames with the incremental changes needed to create the illusion of growth or shrinkage.

You can use the same scaling tools from the Flash drawing tools to resize symbols for animation effects.

ANIMATE BY CHANGING THE SYMBOL SIZE

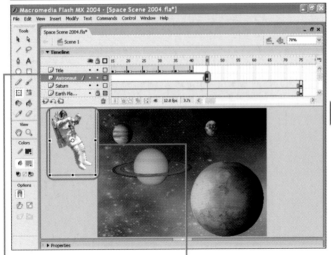

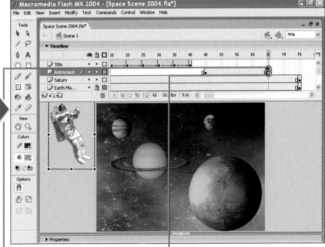

CREATE THE TWEEN EFFECT

1 Insert a keyframe where you want to start the motion tween.

■ You can press **F6** to insert a keyframe.

2 Place the symbol you want to animate on the Stage.

■ In this example, the animation starts off-screen in the work area before appearing on the Stage.

3 Click the end frame in which you want to conclude the motion tween.

■ In this example, the astronaut seems to shrink in the course of 15 frames.

4 Insert a keyframe.

How can I tell what size changes take place in my motion tween?

You can use the Onion Skin tool to see the changes in the frames that surround the current frame. Click 🔳 at the bottom of the Timeline. Drag the onion skin markers left or right to include other frames in the view. See Chapter 8 to learn more about how to use this feature.

Which Scale edit point should I drag?

When resizing an object on the Stage, you can use any of the edit points, also called *selection handles*, to drag the object to a new size. Depending on the point you drag, the object resizes in different directions. For best results, drag a corner edit point. You can press and hold down the Shift key to keep the scaling proportional.

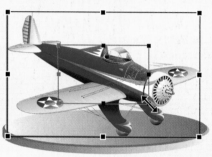

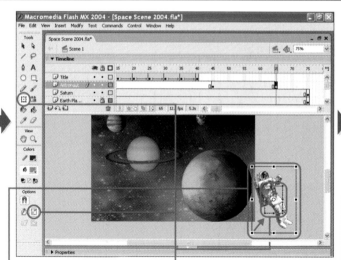

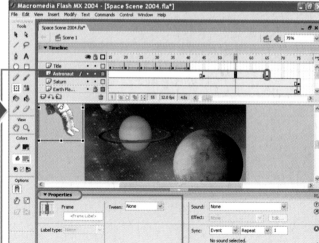

RESIZE THE SYMBOL

5 Select the symbol, and if necessary, place it where you want it to appear.

■ In this example, the animation ends offscreen in the work area after appearing on the Stage.

6 Click 🔳.

7 Click the Scale tool (🔲).

■ Flash surrounds the object with edit points, also called handles.

8 Click and drag a handle to resize the symbol.

9 Double-click a frame between the two keyframes that make up your motion tween.

Note: Select both the start and end keyframes in the tween before applying Motion tween status to continue the tween status.

10 Open the Properties inspector by pressing Ctrl + F3 (Shift + F3)

CONTINUED ▶

You can use the Scale option in the Property inspector to make symbols seem to grow or shrink. The speed at which this occurs depends on how many frames you insert between the two defining keyframes.

You can experiment with the number of regular frames to create just the right animation speed. For example, if your motion tween uses five in-between frames, adding five more slows down the tween effect. This means the object seems to grow or shrink at a slower pace.

ANIMATE BY CHANGING THE SYMBOL SIZE (CONTINUED)

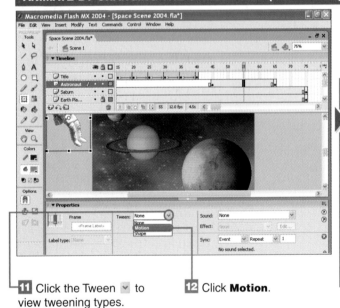

11 Click the Tween ⌄ to view tweening types.

12 Click **Motion**.

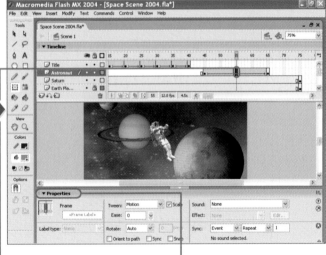

■ Flash adds a motion tween arrow (>——→) from the first keyframe in the tween effect to the last keyframe in the tween effect.

■ You can click the panel's title bar to hide the Properties inspector.

My symbol does not grow or shrink very much. Why not?

For a maximum tween effect, you need to make the final symbol in the tween sequence much smaller or larger than the symbol shown in the first keyframe. You should also allow plenty of regular keyframes in between the two anchor keyframes. See Chapter 8 to learn more about adding frames to the Timeline.

How do I make my object shrink back again to its original size?

You can copy the entire sequence and apply the **Reverse Frames** command to make the object seem to shrink again after growing. You can access this command by clicking **Modify**, and then **Timeline**. See the section "Using Reverse Frames" later in this chapter to learn how to apply this command to your motion tweens.

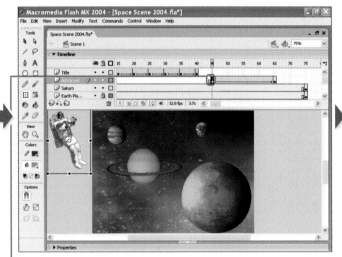

VIEW THE ANIMATION

13 Click the first frame of the motion tween.

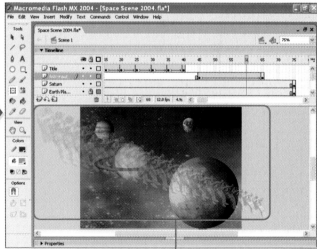

14 Press Enter (Return).

■ Flash plays the animation sequence.

You can make a symbol follow a path in your Flash movie. Using the motion tween technique and a *motion guide layer,* you define points A and B in the sequence, draw a line that tells Flash exactly where you want the symbol to move, and then Flash calculates all the in-between frames for you.

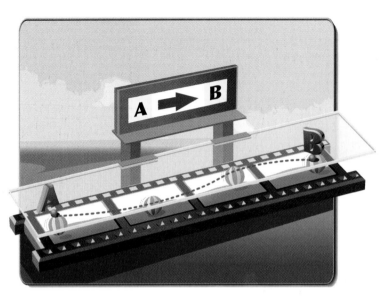

A *motion guide layer* is a special layer that defines the motion tween path. Using the drawing tools, you draw on the Stage exactly where you want the symbol to go. The symbol follows your path. The motion guide layer is not visible when you export the movie.

ANIMATE SYMBOLS ALONG A PATH

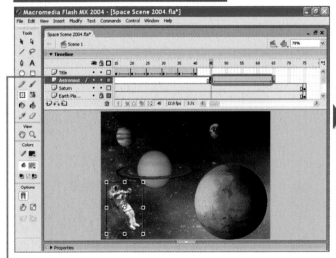

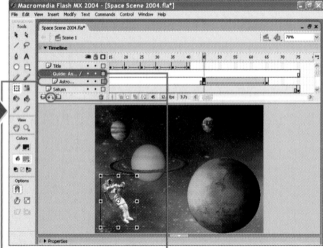

CREATE AND SELECT A TWEEN LAYER

1 Create a motion tween animation.

Note: See the section "Create a Motion Tween" earlier in this chapter to learn how to make a motion tween animation sequence.

2 Select the layer containing the motion tween.

Note: See Chapter 6 to learn more about working with layers.

3 Click the Add Motion Guide icon ( ).

■ Flash adds a motion guide layer directly above the layer containing the motion tween.

Does it matter which line color or thickness I use to draw the motion path?

No. You can use any line color or attributes for the motion path. To make the line easy to see, consider using a thicker line style in a bright color. Be sure to set the line attributes in the Properties inspector before you start drawing the path.

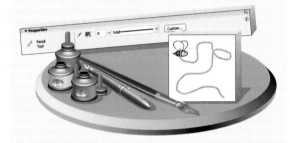

What Drawing tools can I use to define a path?

You can use any of the following Drawing tools to add a path to the motion guide layer: Pencil, Brush, Line, Oval, or Rectangle. For example, to make a symbol follow a perfect loop around the Stage, use the Oval tool to draw the motion path, creating a circular line for the path to follow. For more on using these various tools, see Chapter 2.

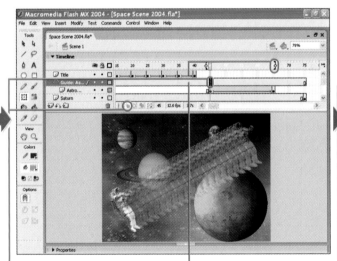

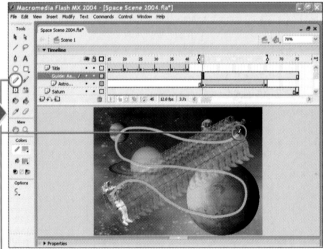

■4 Click the motion guide layer's first frame.

■5 Click 🔲.

■6 Click and drag the onion skin markers ({ }) to include all the frames in the motion tween.

Note: See Chapter 8 to learn more about the onion-skinning feature.

DRAW THE MOTION PATH

■7 Click 🖉.

■8 Drag 𝒷 to draw a path from the center of the first motion tween symbol to the center of the last motion tween symbol.

Note: If you do not draw your path from the center of the start object to the center of the end object, the symbol cannot follow the motion path.

CONTINUED ▶

ANIMATE SYMBOLS ALONG A PATH

You can make your motion tween follow any type of path, even if it falls out of the movie area's boundaries. Starting and ending your path directly in the center of the symbol you are animating is very important. Do not stop your path line when you reach the edge of the object. Continue it on to the middle of the object.

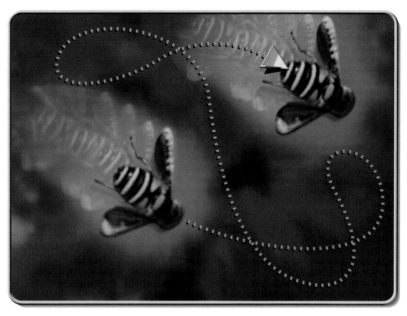

You must also make sure that you select the Snap option in the Properties inspector. This feature sticks the symbol to the path, much like a magnet. Without the Snap feature turned on, the symbol may not properly follow the established path.

ANIMATE SYMBOLS ALONG A PATH (CONTINUED)

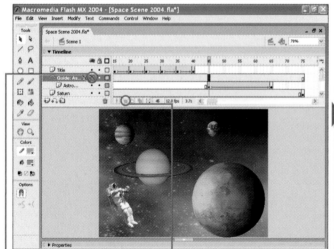

9 Hide the Motion Guide layer.

■ You can lock the layer to keep from accidentally changing the path.

Note: See Chapter 6 to learn more about hiding and locking layers.

10 Click 🔲 to turn off the onion skin feature.

11 Click the first frame of the motion tween.

12 Open the Properties inspector.

■ You can press `Ctrl` + `F3` (`Shift` + `F3`) to quickly open the Properties inspector.

What does the Orient to Path option do?

To make your symbol orient itself to the motion path you have drawn, click the **Orient to path** option (☐ changes to ☑) in the Properties inspector. This option aligns the symbol to the path, regardless of which direction the path goes. Sometimes, the effect makes the symbol's movement seem unnatural. To remedy the situation, you can insert extra keyframes in the animation sequence and rotate the symbol to where you want it on the path. Flash recalculates the in-between frames for you. To learn more about rotating objects, see Chapter 3. To learn how to rotate animated symbols, see the section "Animate by Rotating a Symbol" earlier in this chaper.

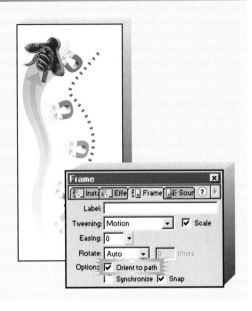

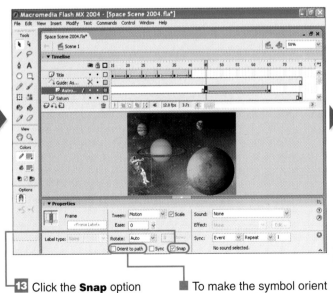

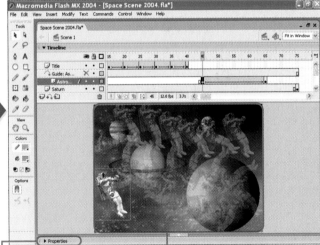

13 Click the **Snap** option (☐ changes to ☑).

■ To make the symbol orient itself to the path, you can click the **Orient to path** option (☐ changes to ☑).

VIEW THE ANIMATION

14 Hide the Properties inspector panel to view more of the Stage area.

15 Select the first frame of the motion tween.

16 Press Enter (Return).

■ Flash plays the animation sequence along the motion path.

EASE TWEEN SPEED

You can control a
tweened animation's
speed by using the Ease
control. Found in the
Properties inspector
panel, the Ease control
enables you to speed
up or slow down the
tween effect.

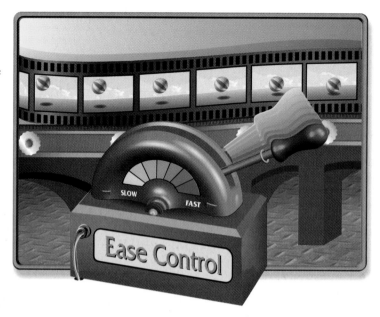

You may have learned
in some of the previous
sections that you can
slow down or speed up
an animation sequence
by subtracting or adding
frames. The addition or
subtraction of regular
frames between two
keyframes does not
affect tween speed. You
use the Ease control
when you want to make
the effect appear to
speed up or slow down
at the beginning or end
of the tween.

EASE TWEEN SPEED

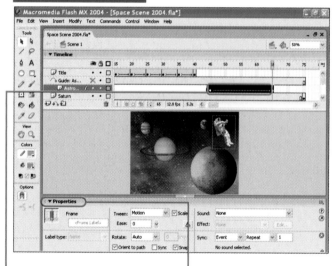

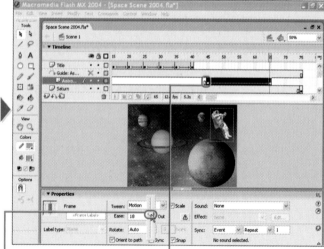

1 Select the frames
containing the motion tween
you want to adjust.

2 Open the Properties
inspector.

■ You can press `Ctrl` + `F3`
(`Shift` + `F3`) to quickly open
the Properties inspector.

3 Click and drag the Ease
slider ( ) to a new setting.

■ You can click and drag
up to accelerate the
tween speed.

■ You can click and drag
down to decelerate the
tween speed.

■ A zero value indicates a
constant rate of speed.

■ To test the new speed,
click the first frame in the
motion tween and press
`Enter`.

You can control the opacity of an animated symbol instance using the Alpha setting control. For example, you may want the symbol to appear to fade out at the end of a motion tween, or fade in at the beginning of the animation.

You can find the Alpha setting in the Properties inspector. The Alpha setting allows you to change the opacity or *alpha value* of an instance. Transparency is measured in a percentage range, with 100% being completely visible, or saturated, and 0% being completely transparent.

ADJUST SYMBOL OPACITY

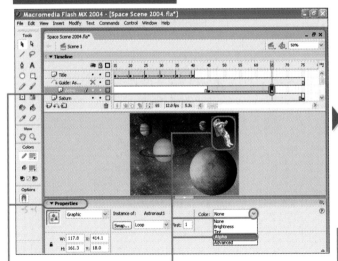

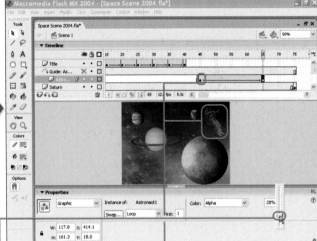

1 Click the keyframe containing the symbol you want to change.

2 Open the Properties inspector.

■ You can press Ctrl + F3 (Shift + F3) to quickly open the Properties inspector.

3 Click the symbol you want to edit.

4 Click the Color ⌄.

5 Click **Alpha**.

■ The Alpha setting option appears.

6 Click and drag the Alpha ⌒ up or down to increase or decrease symbol opacity.

■ Flash applies the changes to the symbol.

■ To test the new speed, click the first frame in the motion tween and press Enter.

CREATE A SHAPE TWEEN

You can create a shape tween to morph objects in an animation. Shape tweens enable you to create dynamic animations that change from one form to an entirely different form over the course of several frames. For example, you can morph a circle shape into a square or turn your company logo into a graphic depicting a product.

Unlike other animations you create in Flash, shape tweening does not require the use of symbols or groups. You can animate any object you draw with the Drawing tools using the shape tween effect.

CREATE A SHAPE TWEEN

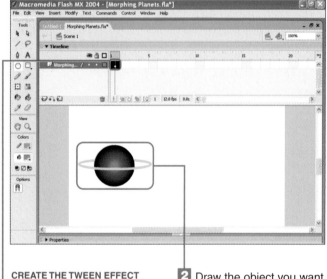

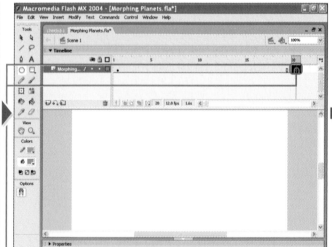

CREATE THE TWEEN EFFECT

1 Select the frame in which you want to start a shape tween.

2 Draw the object you want to animate in Frame 1.

3 Click the frame in which you want to end the shape tween effect.

4 Insert a blank keyframe.

■ You can press **F7** to insert a blank keyframe.

Note: See Chapter 8 to learn how to use Flash frames.

How is a shape tween different from a motion tween?

With a motion tween, you can animate only symbols, grouped objects, or text blocks. With a shape tween, you can animate any object you draw on the Stage. You do not have to save it as a symbol first or group it in order for Flash to create in-between frames. You cannot shape tween a symbol or group. Although a motion tween is good for moving objects from one point to another, you should use a shape tween when you want to morph the object into another object entirely.

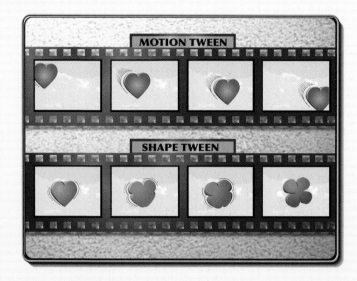

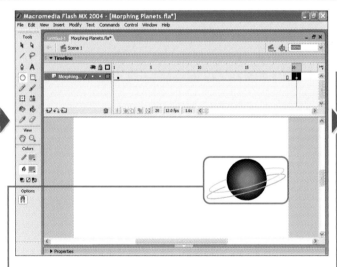

5 Draw the shape into which you want your image to morph, such as a variation of the first frame's shape, or an entirely different shape.

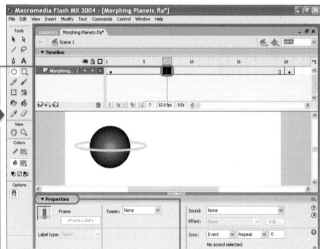

6 Click a single frame in the middle of the tween sequence, or select all the frames that make up your shape tween.

Note: See Chapter 8 to learn how to select frames.

7 Open the Properties inspector.

■ You can press `Ctrl` + `F3` (`Shift` + `F3`) to quickly open the Properties inspector.

CONTINUED

CREATE A SHAPE TWEEN

You can use as many shape tweens as you like in an animation, and you can start one right after the other in the Timeline. For best results, tween one shape at a time in your Flash movie. Doing so gives you greater control over the object and the tween effect.

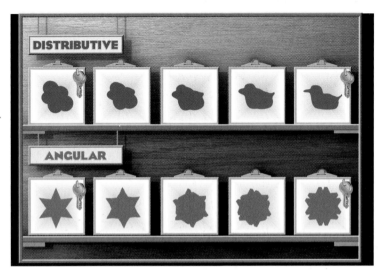

The Properties inspector offers two types of blends: Distributive or Angular. If you apply a Distributive blend, Flash smoothes out the straight lines and sharp corners as your shape morphs. If you select an Angular blend, Flash keeps all the sharp angles and lines intact during the tween.

CREATE A SHAPE TWEEN (CONTINUED)

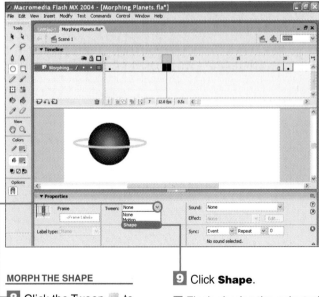

MORPH THE SHAPE

8 Click the Tween ☑ to view tweening types.

9 Click **Shape**.

■ Flash shades the selected frames green in the Timeline and adds a tween arrow from the first keyframe to the last.

10 Click the Blend ☑ to view blend types.

11 Click a blend type.

■ You can click **Distributive** to smooth out lines in the in-between frames.

■ You can click **Angular** to keep the sharp corners and straight lines that occur during the morph effect.

Can I use a symbol from my movie's Library?

Yes, but you must convert it first. You cannot shape tween symbols, but you can take a symbol and break it apart into objects that the shape tween effect can morph. To turn a symbol into an object, perform the following steps:

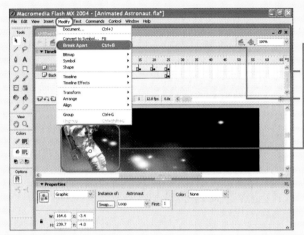

1 Place the symbol on the Stage.

2 Click **Modify**.

3 Click **Break Apart**.

■ Flash turns the symbol into an object.

■ Depending on how many groups of objects comprise the symbol, you may need to select the command several times to reach the last level of ungrouped objects.

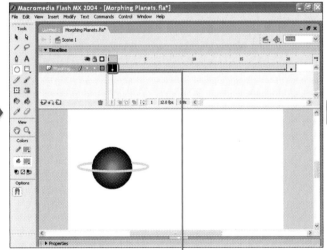

VIEW THE ANIMATION

■ You can click the Properties inspector title bar to hide the panel and view more of the Stage.

12 To view a shape tween in action, click the first frame of the shape tween.

13 Press `Enter` (`Return`).

■ Flash plays the animation sequence.

USING SHAPE HINTS

You can have more control over the morphing process during a shape tween by using shape hints. A *shape hint* is a marker that identifies areas on the original shape that match up with areas on the final shape and mark crucial points of change. Shape hints are labeled *a* through *z*, and you can use up to 26 shape hints in a shape tween.

You use shape hints when you are morphing a particularly complex shape. By assigning shape hints to the object you are morphing, you can help Flash figure out points of change

USING SHAPE HINTS

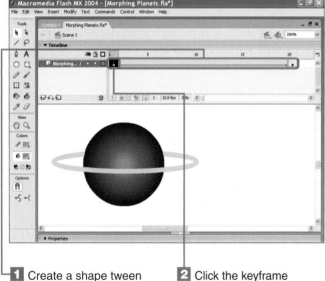

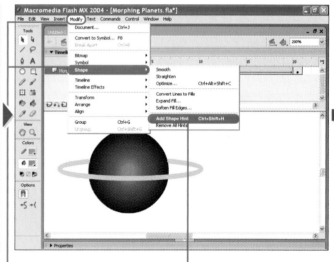

1 Create a shape tween animation.

Note: See "Create a Shape Tween" earlier in this chapter for details.

2 Click the keyframe containing the original shape you want to morph.

3 Click **Modify**.

4 Click **Shape**.

5 Click **Add Shape Hint**.

What can I do if my shape hints vary their positions between the first keyframe and the last?

Seeing exactly where you place shape hints around an object is not always easy. To help you, first make sure you have magnified your view so that you can see where you place the hints. Use the Magnification ⊡ in the upper right corner of the Timeline to set a magnification. Next, click the Onion Skin button (⬜), and click and drag the onion skin markers (⟨⟩) to show all the frames within the shape tween. Click the Onion Skinning Outline button ⬜ to turn on the outlining feature. See Chapter 8 to learn more about onion skinning.

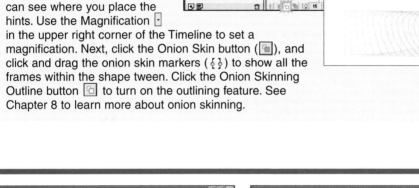

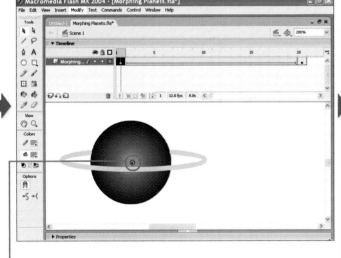

■ Flash adds a shape hint labeled with the letter ⓐ to the center of the shape.

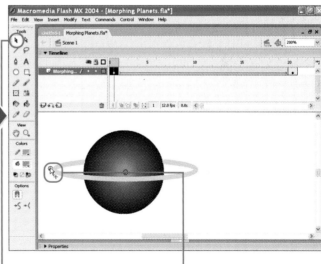

6 Click the Selection tool (▶).

7 Click and drag the shape hint to a crucial edge of the object Flash may need help with transforming.

CONTINUED ▶

USING SHAPE HINTS

The more shape hints you add to the shape tween, the smoother the morphing transformation becomes. When determining where to place your shape hints, position them at key areas of change around the edges of the shape.

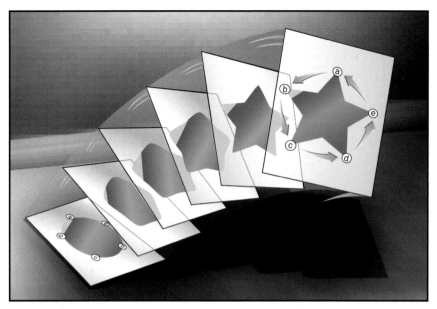

Make sure the shape hints you place around the object in the second keyframe correspond with the same order of shape hints on the object in the first keyframe.

USING SHAPE HINTS (CONTINUED)

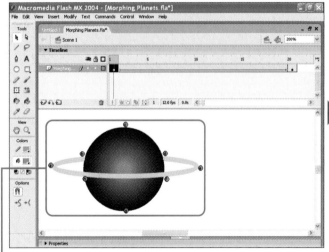

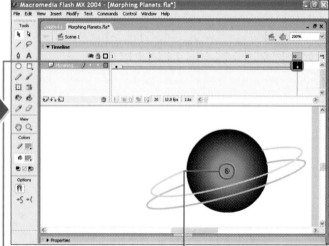

8 Repeat steps **3** to **7** to continue adding shape hints to other areas on the shape that can assist Flash with morphing the final shape design.

Note: For best results, arrange shape hints around the shape's edge in alphabetical order going clockwise or counterclockwise.

9 Click the last keyframe in the shape tween.

■ This example adds shape hints to the final shape and stacks them in the middle of the shape.

How do I remove a shape hint?

To delete a shape hint, click and drag the shape hint completely off the Stage area. To rid the keyframe of all the shape hints, click **Modify,** click **Shape**, and then click **Remove All Hints**.

Is there a quicker way to add shape hints?

Yes. Press and hold Ctrl + Shift (⌘ + Return) while pressing the H key on the keyboard. This adds a shape hint to the Stage.

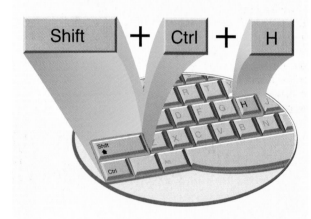

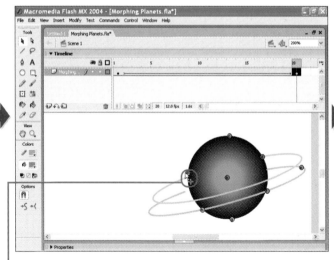

10 Click and drag each shape hint to the correct position around the final shape.

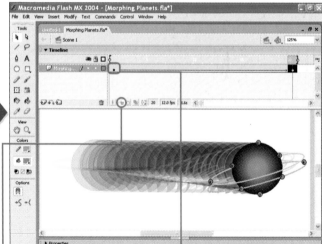

■ You can adjust the shape hints in the final frame as needed.

└ ■ Clicking 🗔 lets you see how the in-between frames morph the shape as directed by the shape hints.

■ To view the animation, click the first keyframe and press Enter (Return).

USING REVERSE FRAMES

You can reverse the order of your animation sequence with the Reverse Frames feature. The feature literally reverses the order of frames in your movie. For example, if you create a motion tween that makes a symbol grow in size, you can reverse the frame sequence to create the opposite effect in the second half of the animation.

The Reverse Frames feature allows you to save time creating an animation by reusing frames in your movie. This saves you from having to create another animation sequence for the backwards effect.

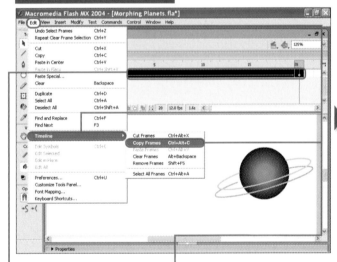

1 Select all the frames included in the animation sequence for which you want to create a reverse effect, making sure to include the end keyframe in your selection.

Note: See Chapter 8 to learn more about selecting frames.

2 Click **Edit**.

3 Click **Timeline**.

4 Click **Copy Frames**.

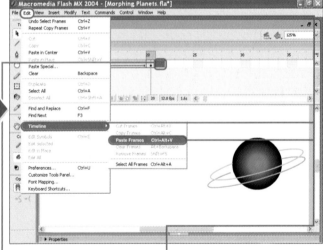

5 Click the frame where you want to insert the copied frames.

6 Click **Edit**.

7 Click **Timeline**.

8 Click **Paste Frames**.

How else can I activate the Reverse Frames command?

Right click the frames and a menu appears with frame-related commands, including the **Reverse Frames**, **Copy Frames**, and **Paste Frames** commands.

How do I reverse a reverse?

You can immediately undo the Reverse Frames command if you click **Edit**, and then **Undo**. Make sure you do this immediately after you realize you are not happy with the animation results.

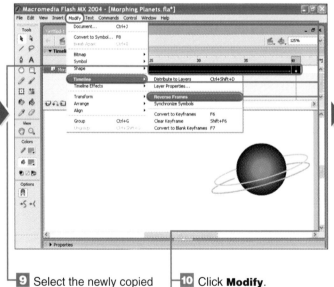

9 Select the newly copied frames.

■ If you have trouble selecting the copied frames, press and hold **Shift** + **Ctrl** (**⌘** + **Return**) while clicking the frames.

10 Click **Modify**.

11 Click **Timeline**.

12 Click **Reverse Frames**.

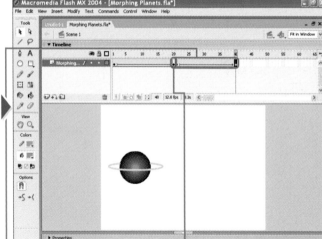

■ Flash reverses the tween effect.

■ To view the animation, click the first keyframe and press **Enter** (**Return**).

ANIMATE A MASK

You can use mask layers to hide various elements on underlying layers in your Flash movies. In addition, you can animate a mask layer using any of the Flash animation techniques, such as a motion path or shape tween.

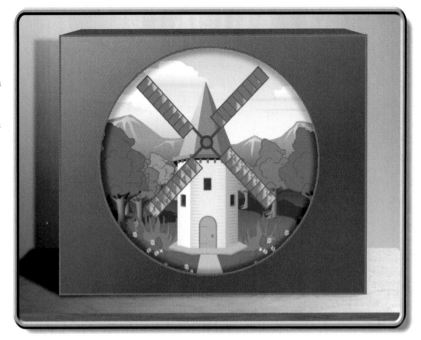

For example, you can draw an oval fill shape that acts as a peephole to the layer below the mask, and animate the peephole to move around the movie. The "hole" lets you see anything directly beneath, but the remainder of the mask layer hides anything that lies out of view of the "hole."

ANIMATE A MASK

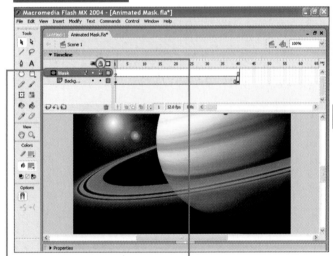

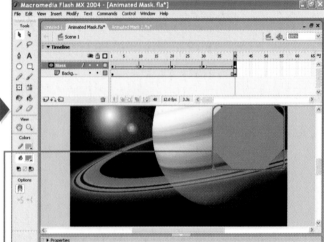

CREATE A MASK LAYER

1 Click the mask layer you want to animate.

Note: See Chapter 6 to learn how to create a mask layer.

2 Click the lock icon (🔒).

■ Flash unlocks the mask layer.

APPLY A TWEEN EFFECT

3 Apply a motion or shape tween to the mask.

■ If the mask object is a graphic symbol, you can apply a motion tween.

■ If the mask object is a fill shape, you can apply a shape tween.

Note: See the section "Create a Motion Tween" or "Create a Shape Tween" to learn how to create an animation sequence.

Flash does not let me create a motion tween in my mask layer. Why not?

You can only assign a motion tween to a mask that you create from a symbol, instance or object group. You cannot use more than one symbol as a mask. You must assign a shape tween to a fill shape. Check and make sure you know what type of object you are using as a mask and then assign the appropriate motion tween type.

Can I use the mask to mask out other layers in my movie?

Yes. Any layers placed directly under the mask layer, between the original linked layer and the mask layer, are also masked.

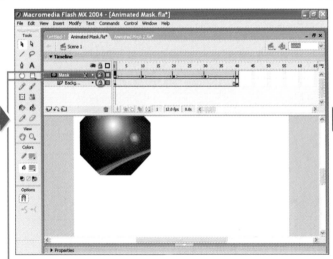

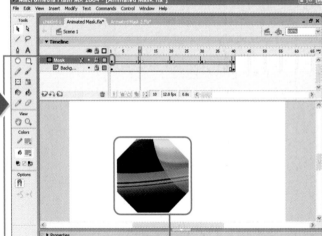

4 Click the unlock icon ( ) for the layer to lock the mask layer.

5 Click the unlock icon ( ) to lock the layer below the mask.

Note: See Chapter 6 to learn how to unlock layers.

■ Flash masks the underlying layer.

VIEW THE ANIMATION

6 To view the animated mask, click the first frame of the sequence.

7 Press **Enter** (**Return**).

■ Flash plays the animation sequence.

DISTRIBUTE OBJECTS TO LAYERS

You can use the Distribute to Layers command to quickly distribute objects to different layers in your movie and then animate each object separately. For example, you can use this technique to animate individual letters in a company logo or animate a group of graphic objects with individual motion tweens.

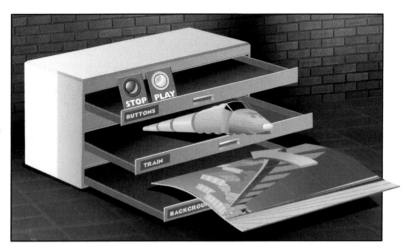

The Distribute to Layers command can help you create a variety of layered animation effects. Used in conjunction with the Break Apart command, you can create individual pieces of a whole and animate them separately. You can apply the command to objects, symbols, and grouped objects.

DISTRIBUTE OBJECTS TO LAYERS

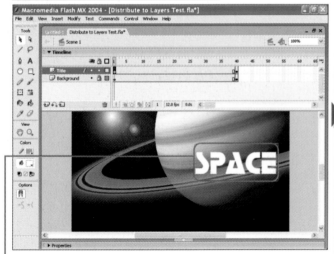

1 Click the object you want to break apart into separate layers.

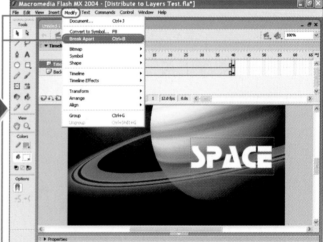

2 Click **Modify**.

3 Click **Break Apart**.

■ Flash breaks apart the object.

How do I tell which object is on which layer?

Use the Show All Layers As Outlines column for each layer to help you color coordinate what object is on what layer. Click the layer you want to identify, and then click the Outline icon (▢). Flash highlights the object in the designated color. See Chapter 6 to learn more about using layers.

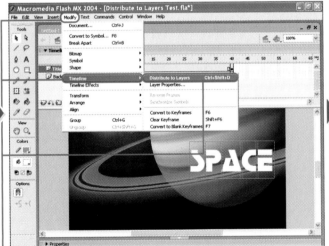

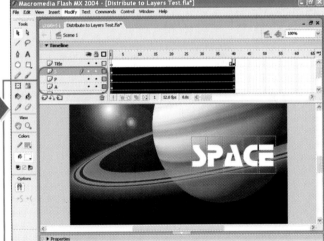

4 Click **Modify**.

5 Click **Timeline**.

6 Click **Distribute to Layers**.

Note: You must select all objects you want to distribute to layers before applying the command. If you clicked elsewhere on the Stage after using the Break Apart command, you must select all the objects again.

■ Flash distributes each object to a separate layer.

■ In this example, Flash placed each letter on a layer and named the layer accordingly.

■ You can now animate each object separately from the rest.

Go to Frame 33

Go To
Stop
Play Sounds
Load Movie
Get URL

GO TO
FRAME
27

CHAPTER 10

Adding Flash Actions

Do you need to add some user controls to your animation? In this chapter, you learn how to add interactive Flash actions to frames.

INTRODUCING FLASH ACTIONS

You can add interactivity to your Flash movies by assigning an action or behavior to a frame, a button, or movie clip instance. Actions are based on principles of cause and effect. The occurrence that triggers the action is called an *event*. An event might be a click of a button or reaching a certain frame in your movie. The result of the action is the *target*, the object that the event affects.

Actions and ActionScript

Flash actions are built on a programming language called ActionScript. This scripting language allows you to write instructions that control a movie. If you know how to write scripts, you can certainly write your own actions in Flash. However, you do not need to know a scripting language to create actions. Flash includes hundreds of prewritten scripts, or *behaviors*, you can assign.

Using Actions in Flash MX

You can use the Actions panel to add actions to frames, buttons, or movie clips—mini-movies within the main movie. You can also assign any of the built-in actions you find in the Behaviors panel. When you assign an action, Flash adds it to a list of actions for that particular frame or button. This list is called an *action list* or *script*. Flash then executes the actions in the list based on the order in which they appear.

Events

Anything that causes an action is called an *event*. In Flash terminology, an event triggers an action in your movie. Flash recognizes several types of events: mouse events, or button actions, keyboard events, clip events, and frame events, also called frame actions. A mouse event occurs when a user interacts with a button. Keyboard events occur when a user presses a keyboard key. You place frame events in keyframes in your movie. You can use clip events to control movie clips.

Targets

A *target* is the object that the action affects. You can direct targets toward the current movie (called the default target), other movies (called the Tell Target), or a browser application (called an external target). For example, you may place a button in your movie that, when clicked, opens a Web page. You direct most of your frame actions toward the current movie, which is the default target.

Types of Actions

Flash groups actions into categories in the Actions panel. The most common actions include navigational actions such as goto, play, and stop, browser actions, such as Get URL and Load Movie, and movie clip control actions. Although Flash offers hundreds of actions, this chapter focuses on the common navigations actions you can use in your own Flash movies.

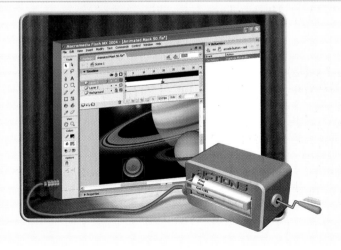

USING THE ACTIONS PANEL

You can use the Actions panel to add actions and write ActionScript for your Flash movies. Actions enable you to add interactivity to your movies. The Actions panel is part of the default panel set, appearing docked at the bottom of the screen. You can also open the panel as a floating panel.

The left pane of the Actions panel lists all the categories and actions available. Once you select an action to add, Flash lists the action in the right pane. Depending on the action, you may need to define additional parameters for the action, such as typing in a frame number or instance name.

USING THE ACTIONS PANEL

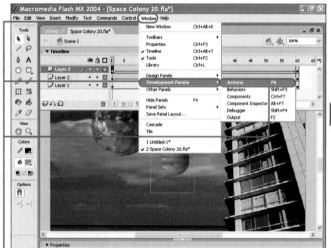

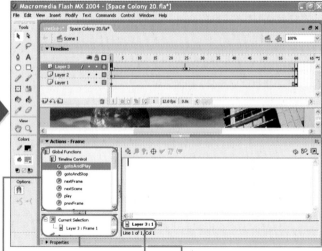

■1 Click **Window**.

■2 Click **Development Panels**.

■3 Click **Actions**.

■ If the Properties inspector is open, and you have a symbol or button selected on the Stage, you can also click the Edit ActionScript button (▣).

■ You can also press **F9** to summon the panel.

■ The Actions panel opens.

■ Flash lists the current frame or object here.

■ The toolbox lists categories, subcategories, and actions you can assign.

■ If you are using Flash Professional, the left pane also includes a Script navigator displaying a visual representation of your file structure.

Where can I find additional commands for working with the Actions panel?

You can click the Options menu button (⊞) located in the upper right corner of the Actions panel to reveal a list of related commands. An Options menu is available for every panel you use in Flash.

Can I move the panel out of the way?

You can move and resize the Actions panel just as you can with other panels available in Flash. You can also dock the panel. Click the panel's title bar to quickly hide or display the panel contents. See Chapter 1 to learn more about working with Flash panels.

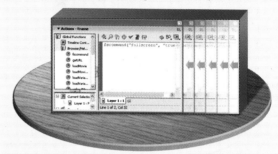

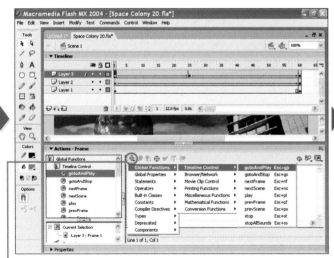

■ You can also assign actions from the list that appears when you click here.

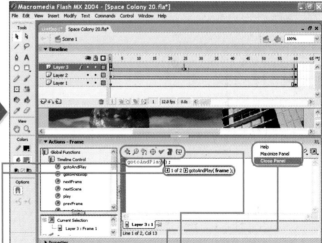

■ Flash adds assigned actions to the actions list, also called the *script pane*, where you can also type action scripts.

■ When you assign an action, a code hint tooltip appears with information about which parameters to assign.

■ You can use the buttons to help you edit and construct your ActionScript statements.

■ To close the Actions panel, right-click over the panel's title bar and click **Close Panel**.

You can use the
Actions panel to add
actions to your movie.
Frames can include
multiple actions, but
you can only assign
an action one frame
at a time. You add
actions to the frame's
action script, a list
of actions associated
with the frame. Flash
performs the actions
in the order they
appear in the list.

When you assign an
action, it appears in the
actions list on the right
side of the Actions
panel. As soon as you
assign an action to a
frame, Flash marks the
frame with a tiny icon
of the letter *a*, for
action. After assigning
an action to a frame,
you can return to the
Actions panel and
make changes to the
action as needed.

ADD ACTIONS TO FRAMES

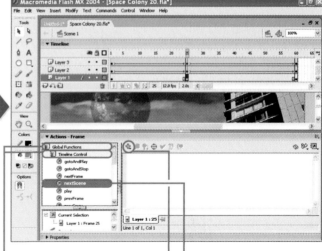

1 Select the frame to which
you want to add an action.

*Note: You can only insert actions into
keyframes, not regular frames. See
Chapter 8 to learn how to add frames.*

2 Open the Actions panel.

■ You can press **F9** to
quickly open the Actions
panel.

*Note: See the previous section,
"Using the Actions Panel," to learn
how to display the Actions panel.*

3 Click an action category.

4 Click a subcategory.

■ Most categories include
subcategories.

5 Double-click the action
you want to add or drag it
from the list and drop it in
the actions list.

■ You can also click here to
display a list of categories
and actions to assign.

How do I organize actions in my movie?

To help you clearly identify actions you assign to frames, consider creating a layer specifically for actions in your movie. This technique simplifies the process of finding the action you want to edit. See Chapter 6 to find out more about moving and positioning Flash layers.

How do I know what parame...
an action?

Click the Code Hint button (⌨) in the Actions panel to display a code hint tooltip detailing what parameters you need to type to complete the action script. Be sure to enclose each parameter with quote marks.

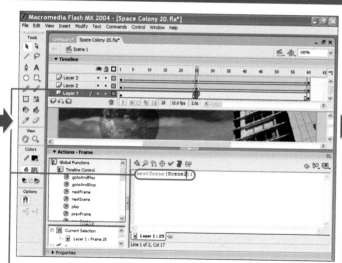

■ Flash adds the action to the actions list, also called the *script pane*.

■ Flash adds a tiny letter **α** to indicate that you have assign an action to the frame.

■ Depending on the action you select, you may need to type parameters to further define the action.

■ In this example, the action requires the name of the scene.

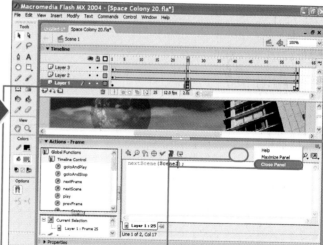

■ When you play the movie, Flash carries out the frame action you assigned.

Note: See Chapters 8 and 13 to learn how to preview and play Flash movies.

6 Right-click over the title bar.

7 Click **Close Panel**.

■ The Actions panel closes.

You can add actions to movie clip instances that appear in your main movie. For example, you may have an animation sequence of a moving car that includes movie clips for making each wheel rotate. To make the car seem to animate from parked status to moving, you can target the movie clips that comprise the wheels of the car and stop each wheel's rotation.

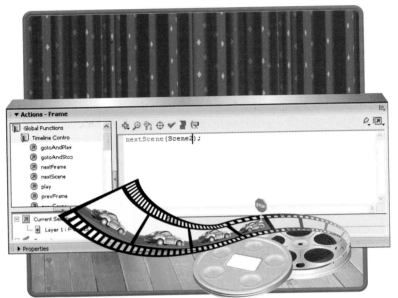

Any actions you attach to a movie clip instance apply only to that instance, not the original movie clip. Movie clip actions respond to the event much like button actions respond to on events. When assigning actions to instances, it is important to name your movie clip instances.

ADD ACTIONS TO MOVIE CLIPS

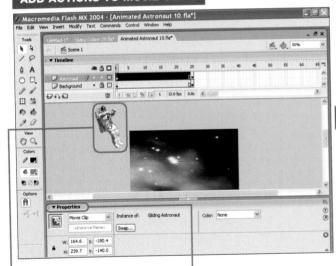

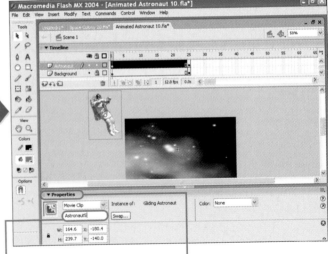

1 Click the movie clip instance to which you want to add an action.

Note: See Chapter 8 to learn how to create movie clips.

2 Display the Properties inspector.

Note: See Chapter 1 to learn how to work with the Properties inspector.

3 Click here and type a new name for the instance.

4 Press `Enter` (`Return`).

■ You can click the Properties inspector's title bar to hide the panel.

How do movie clips differ from graphic or button instances?

Movie clips are independent movies and as such, they play all their frames when you add an instance of the clip to the Stage, whether the clip is comprised of 1 frame or 100. Movie clips also loop unless you add a `stop` action to the last frame of the clip. Unlike graphic instances, movie clip instances do not play when you scrub, or drag, the Timeline's playhead. To see clips play, you must open the Flash Player window. See Chapter 13 to learn more about previewing movies.

Which category in the Actions panel lists movie clip actions?

Flash groups the majority of movie clip actions under the Movie Clip Control subcategory in the Actions panel, under the Global Functions category. You can also apply other actions to control movie clips, not just those listed under Movie Clip Control. When you select a movie clip instance on the Stage, you cannot apply grayed out actions in the panel to the clip.

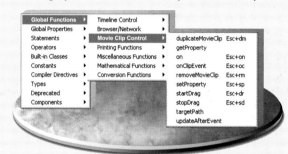

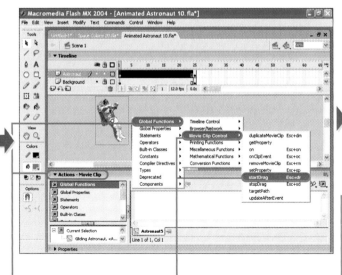

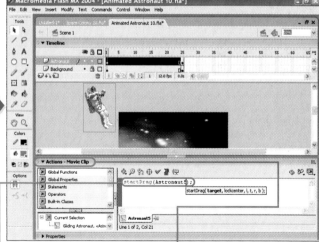

5 Press F9 to quickly open the Actions panel.

6 Click the Add button (⊞).

7 Click an action category.

8 Click a subcategory.

■ Most categories include subcategories.

9 Click the action you want to add.

■ Flash assigns the action to the clip and you can set parameters as needed.

■ You can add additional actions to the clip, if needed.

■ When finished adding actions, close or hide the Actions panel.

Note: See the section "Using the Actions Panel" to close the Action panel." See Chapter 11 to learn how to add actions to buttons.

JUMP TO A SPECIFIC FRAME OR SCENE

You can assign a `goto` action that tells Flash to start playing a particular frame in your movie. You can use the `goto` action with frames, buttons, or movie clips. When Flash follows a `goto` action, it jumps to, or goes to a specified target frame.

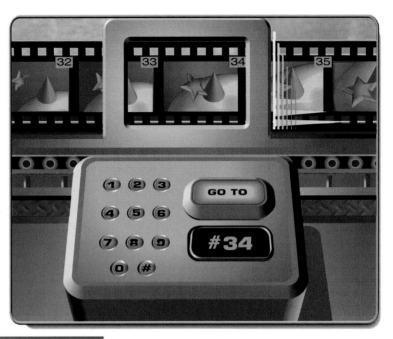

The `goto` action includes parameters you can define to play a specific frame. When you assign the `goto` action using the Actions panel, you can enter a frame number as the target frame, or if you organize your frames with labels, you can enter the label of the target frame.

JUMP TO A SPECIFIC FRAME OR SCENE

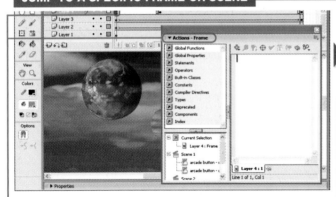

ADD A GO TO ACTION TO A FRAME

1 Select the keyframe to which you want to add the action.

2 Open the Actions panel.

■ You can press **F9** to quickly open the Actions panel, or if you have the Properties inspector open, you can also click 🗔.

3 Click the **Global Functions** category.

4 Click **Timeline Control**.

5 Double-click **gotoAndPlay**.

■ You can also drag the action from the list and drop it in the script area.

214

What is a scene?

Scenes are blocks of the animation frames that Flash turns into their own independent Timelines. You can use scenes to organize a large movie into smaller segments. You can learn more about creating scenes in Chapter 8.

If my frame has a label instead of a number, how do I define the parameter?

Instead of typing a frame number for the parameter, type the frame label. Frame labels allow you to give frames distinct titles that more readily tell you about the frame's content. Labeling frames is particularly helpful with longer Flash movies. You can use labels to tell you when a key change occurs in an animation, or to indicate a new element that appears in the movie. Labeling is an organizational tool and can help you with keeping your actions organized as well. To learn more about assigning labels to frames, see Chapter 8.

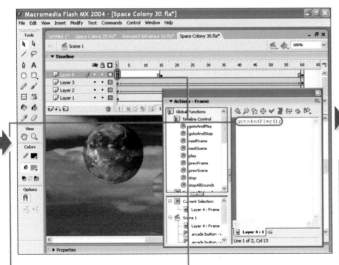

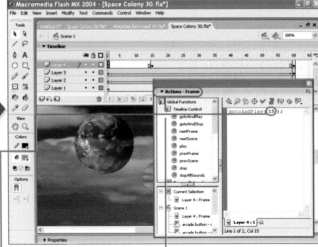

■ Flash adds the action to the actions list.

■ Flash also adds a tiny letter 🅰 to indicate that you have assigned an action to the frame.

Note: If you assign an action to a button, Flash does not display the tiny letter 🅰.

6 Type the number of the frame you want to go to in the parameter's parentheses.

■ Alternatively, you can type a frame label or scene name rather than a frame number.

■ When you play the movie, Flash follows the frame action you assigned.

Note: See Chapters 8 and 13 to learn how to preview and play Flash movies.

■ To hide the Actions panel, click the panel's title bar.

ASSIGN STOP AND PLAY ACTIONS

You can assign a `stop` action to stop a movie from playing, or you can assign a `play` action to play it again. For example, perhaps one of the keyframes in your movie is text heavy and you want to allow the user to read the text. You can create a button and assign a `stop` action that allows the user to stop the movie and assign a `play` action to another button that allows the user to play the movie again.

`Stop` and `play` actions are two of the basic Flash navigation and interaction buttons. You commonly use the `stop` and `play` actions with buttons.

ASSIGN STOP AND PLAY ACTIONS

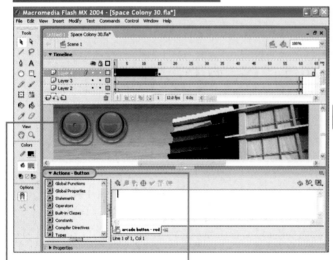

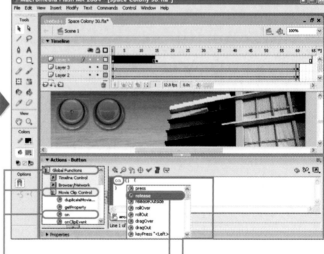

ADD A STOP ACTION

1 Click the frame or button to which you want to add a `stop` action.

Note: See Chapter 11 to learn how to create buttons.

2 Open the Actions panel.

■ You can press **F9** to quickly open the Actions panel, or if you have the Properties inspector open, you can also click 🔲.

3 Click the **Global Functions** category.

4 Click **Movie Clip Control**.

5 Double-click **on**.

■ Flash adds the `on` action to the script along with a parameter to define.

6 Double-click **release**.

What is the difference between frame actions and object actions?

You can apply actions to frames or buttons, which Flash treats as objects. You assign frame actions to frames to control how a movie plays. You assign button actions, as demonstrated in the steps below, to buttons and they require input from the user. For example, a `stop` action enables the user to stop a movie by clicking the button to which you assigned the action. You can assign `stop` and `play` actions to frames or buttons, but remember that button actions require user input in order to carry out the action.

Does Flash support a `pause` action?

No. However, a `stop` action acts like a pause action in that your movie stops playing and rests on the frame to which you assigned the `stop` action. You can place a `stop` action at the start of a movie to keep the movie from playing automatically when opened as a self-playing projector file. Do not forget to add a button with a `play` action so users can start the movie.

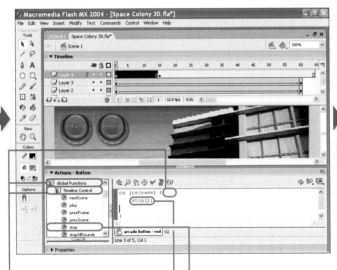

7 Click the end of the first script line and press `Enter` (`Return`).

8 Click the **Global Functions** category.

9 Click **Timeline Control**.

10 Double-click **stop**.

■ Flash adds the `stop` action, which has no parameters, to the script.

Note: If you assign an action to a button, Flash does not display the tiny letter **a** *in the Timeline.*

ADD A PLAY ACTION

11 Click the title bar to hide the Actions panel.

12 Click the frame or button to which you want to add a Play action.

Note: See Chapter 11 for more on creating buttons.

13 Click the Actions panel title bar to display the panel again.

CONTINUED

ASSIGN STOP AND PLAY ACTIONS

You assign the stop and play actions to give users control over the movie's playback. Stop and play actions act much like the controls on a VCR or CD player. In many cases, you want to use the two commands together because the stop action ceases the movie from playing while the play action starts a movie previously stopped with the stop action.

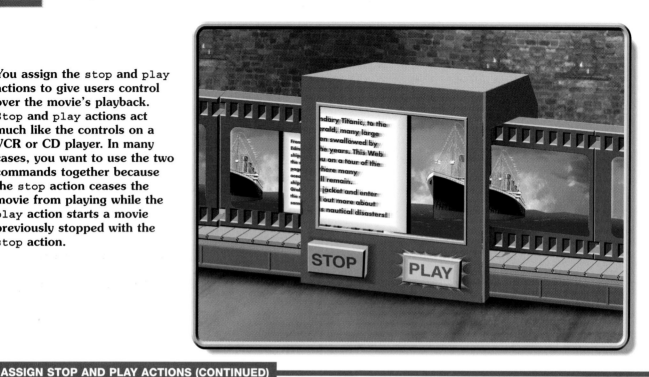

ASSIGN STOP AND PLAY ACTIONS (CONTINUED)

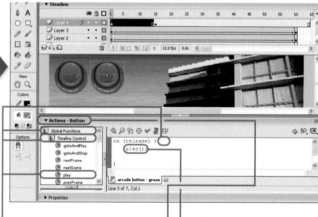

■14 Click the **Global Functions** category.

■15 Click **Movie Clip Control**.

■16 Double-click **on**.

■ Flash adds the on action to the script along with a parameter to define.

■17 Double-click **release**.

■18 Click the end of the first script line and press Enter (Return).

■19 Click the **Global Functions** category.

■20 Click **Timeline Control**.

■21 Double-click **play**.

■ Flash adds the play action to the script.

■ No parameters are available for the play action.

■22 Click the title bar to hide the Actions panel.

How can I resize the type in the actions list to make it easier to read?

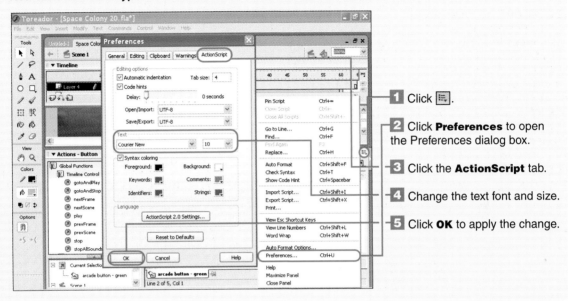

1 Click 🗐.

2 Click **Preferences** to open the Preferences dialog box.

3 Click the **ActionScript** tab.

4 Change the text font and size.

5 Click **OK** to apply the change.

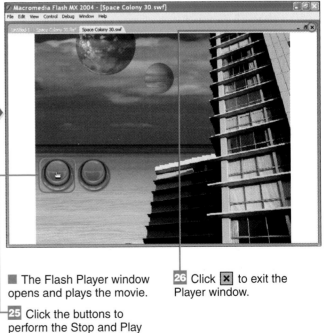

TEST THE ACTIONS

23 Click **Control**.

24 Click **Test Movie**.

■ The Flash Player window opens and plays the movie.

25 Click the buttons to perform the Stop and Play actions.

26 Click ⊠ to exit the Player window.

LOAD A NEW MOVIE INTO THE CURRENT MOVIE

You can use the `loadMovie` action to start a movie file within your current movie. Use this action to replace the current movie with another, or play the loaded movie on top of the current movie as if it were another layer.

The `loadMovie` action can help you create layered animation action. For example, you can create a movie of a wooded background. In the middle of the movie, you can load a movie of a man walking. By loading the walking man in the middle of the background movie, you combine the two movies to make it look as if the man is walking through the woods.

LOAD A NEW MOVIE INTO THE CURRENT MOVIE

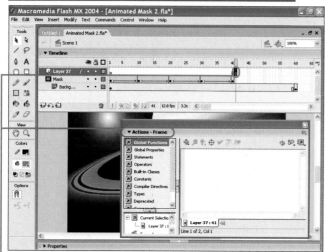

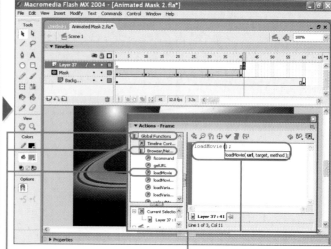

1 Select the keyframe to which you want to add the action.

2 Open the Actions panel.

■ You can press **F9** to quickly open the Actions panel, or if the Properties inspector is open, you can also click 🔘.

3 Click the **Global Functions** category.

4 Click **Browser/Network**.

5 Double-click **loadMovie**.

■ Flash adds the action to the actions list and displays a code hint tooltip demonstrating what parameters to set.

What are movie levels?

Flash handles the playing of multiple movies as levels. You can target another level using the target parameter with the `loadMovie` action. The current movie always plays at level 0. When you play a second movie with the `loadMovie` action, it plays at the level you designate, starting with level 1 or higher. Like stacking, movies play on top of the bottom level, so a movie set to play at level 2 visually appears on top of movies at levels 1 and 0. If you specify level 0 for the location level with the `loadMovie` action, the new movie replaces the existing movie. If you assign another level, the new movie plays on top of the existing movie.

LEVEL 3

LEVEL 2

LEVEL 1

LEVEL 0

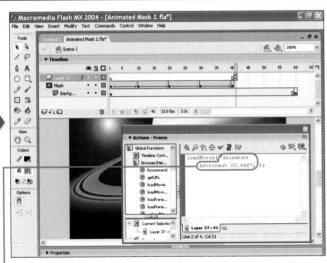

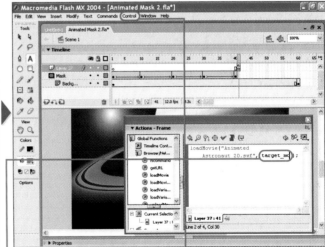

6 Click inside the parentheses and type the first parameter, which defines the name of the Flash movie file you want to load.

■ Be sure to include quote marks around the movie name.

■ The code in this example loads the Flash movie `Animated Astronaut 20.swf`.

7 Type a comma, and then the second parameter, which defines the target movie clip.

■ The code in this example targets a movie clip instance named `mc`.

■ You can test the action by clicking **Control** and then **Test Movie** to open the Flash Player window and play the movie.

CONTROL INSTANCES WITH BEHAVIORS

You can use behaviors to control instances and movie clips without writing ActionScript. Behaviors are prewritten ActionScript scripts. New to Flash, behaviors are an easy way to perform basic actions such as changing the stacking order of instances, loading other movies to play within your current movie, jumping to a specific frame, and more.

To use behaviors, you can assign an identifier name to the instance or clip. You can then use the Behaviors panel to assign behaviors.

CONTROL INSTANCES WITH BEHAVIORS

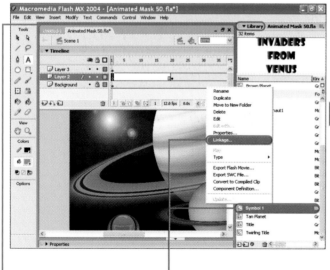

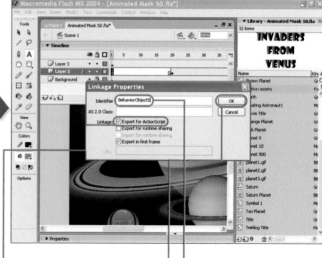

1 Open the Library panel.

■ You can press `Ctrl` + `L` (`⌘` + `L`) to open the Library.

2 Right-click over the instance or movie clip you want to use.

3 Click **Linkage**.

■ The Linkage Properties dialog box opens.

4 Click the **Export for ActionScript** option (☐ changes to ☑).

5 Type an identifier for the instance or clip.

6 Click **OK**.

■ You can press `Ctrl` + `L` (`⌘` + `L`) to close the Library panel again.

How do I undock the Behaviors panel?

The Behaviors panel works just like any other panel in Flash, which means you can move, dock, undock, minimize, and maximize the panel. To undock a docked panel or move a floating panel, simply click and drag the far left side of the panel's title bar. To dock a panel, click the same area on the title bar and drag it to the far right side of the program window. To minimize the panel to hide its contents, click the title bar.

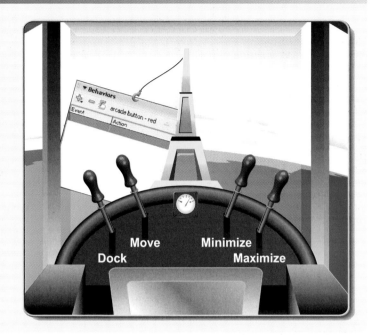

Move   Minimize

Dock   Maximize

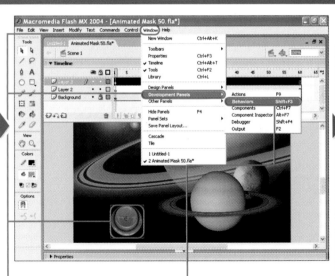

7 Select the object to which you want to assign a behavior.

8 Click **Window**.

9 Click **Development Panels**.

10 Click **Behaviors**.

■ You can also press **Shift** + **F3** to open the panel.

■ The Behaviors panel opens.

11 Click the Add button (⊞).

12 Click a behavior category.

13 Click a behavior.

■ In this example, the behavior duplicates a movie clip within the main movie.

CONTINUED ▷

CONTROL INSTANCES WITH BEHAVIORS

You can control behaviors by specifying an object to trigger the behavior and a target object that is affected by the behavior. One way to use navigational behaviors is to assign them to buttons in your movie. When assigning behaviors to buttons, Flash assigns the `On Release` event by default unless you specify another event. This means that the behavior activates when the user clicks the button and releases the mouse pointer.

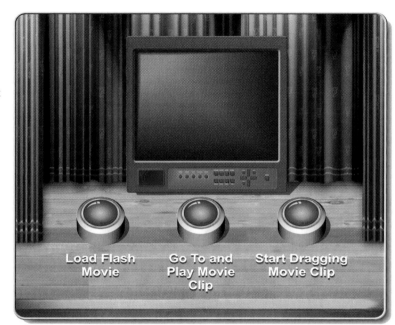

Load Flash Movie   Go To and Play Movie Clip   Start Dragging Movie Clip

CONTROL INSTANCES WITH BEHAVIORS (CONTINUED)

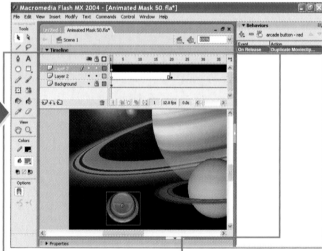

■ Depending on which behavior you select, an additional dialog box may open.

14 Type the appropriate information or select from the available options.

■ In this example, the dialog box prompts you to select a movie clip to target.

15 Click **OK**.

■ Flash assigns the behavior.

■ To change the event handler, click here and select another.

How do I delete behaviors after I assign them?

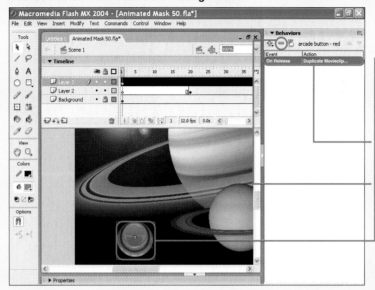

1 Select the object to which you have assigned the behavior.

2 Reopen the Behaviors panel by pressing Shift + F3 .

3 Select the behavior you want to remove.

4 Click the Delete Behavior button ( ).

■ Flash removes the behavior from the list.

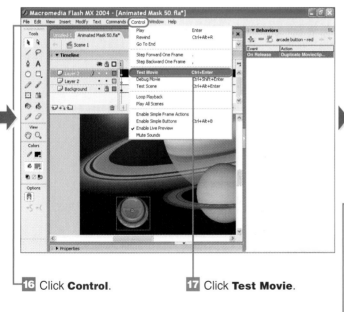

16 Click **Control**.

17 Click **Test Movie**.

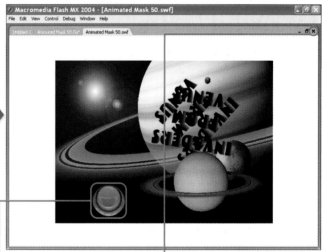

■ The Flash Player window opens.

18 Click the button or instance to test the behavior.

■ In this example, clicking the button duplicates a movie clip that is already playing, creating two playing clips.

19 Click ✕ when finished.

■ Flash returns you to the program window.

LINK A BUTTON TO A WEB PAGE

You can use the `Go to Web Page` behavior to take users to other files or Web pages. When you assign this behavior to a button or frame, it acts as an HTML hyperlink. For example, you can insert a `Go to Web Page` behavior in a standalone Flash Player projector movie, which, when activated, opens a browser window and downloads the specified HTML page.

LINK A BUTTON TO A W B PAG

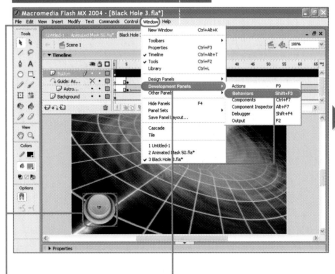

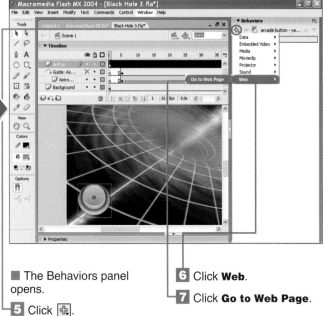

1 Select the object to which you want to assign a behavior.

Note: See Chapter 11 to learn how to create buttons.

2 Click **Window**.

3 Click **Development Panels**.

4 Click **Behaviors**.

■ You can also press **Shift** + **F3** to open the panel.

■ The Behaviors panel opens.

5 Click 🔁.

6 Click **Web**.

7 Click **Go to Web Page**.

Can I specify how a Web page opens?

Yes. You can use the Open in menu in the
Go to URL dialog box to take users to other
files or Web pages. There are four different
targets you can specify. `_self` opens the
designated HTML page in the current frame
of the current browser window. `_blank`
opens the designated file in a completely
new browser window. `_parent` opens the
page in the parent of the current browser,
and `_top` opens the page in the top-level
frame of the current window.

lindsay@abc.com

E-MAIL US!

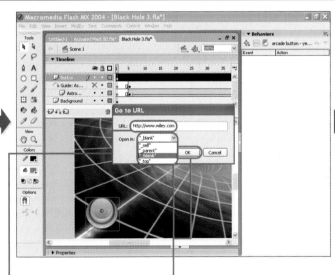

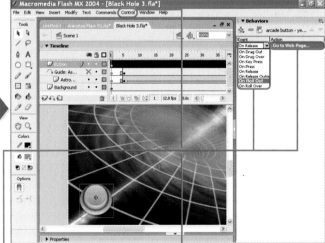

■ The Go To URL dialog box
opens.

8 Type the path to the Web
page you want to open.

9 Click the Open in ⌄ and
click a target.

■ You can select **_blank** to
open the Web page in a new
browser window.

10 Click **OK**.

■ Flash adds the behavior to
the list.

■ To change the event that
triggers the Web page, click
here and select another.

■ To test the behavior, click
Control, click **Test Movie**,
and then click the object to
activate the hyperlink.

ADD A COMPONENT

You can use components to add instant interactivity to your movie projects. *Components* are simply pre-built, complex movie clips for user interface elements such as radio buttons and list boxes. You can add just one of these components to a movie, combine them, or use all of them to create a very simple user interface for a Web page form.

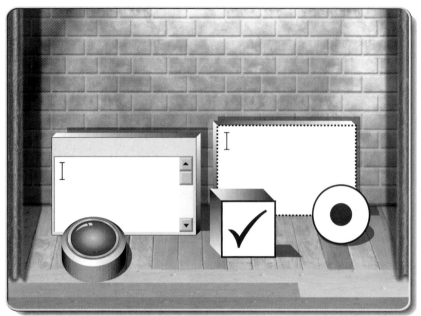

Once you add a component to the Stage, you can customize the data contained within the component. For example, if you add a combo box that offers the user a list of menu choices, you can control exactly what menu choices appear in the list.

ADD A COMPONENT

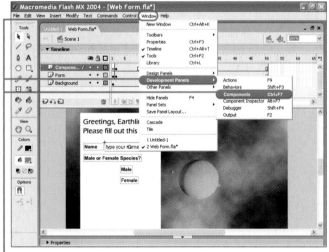

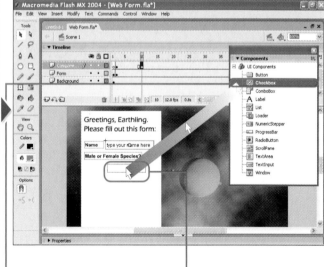

1 Click **Window**.

2 Click **Development Panels**.

3 Click **Components**.

■ The Components panel opens.

Note: You can undock and move the Flash panels around the screen. See hapter 1 to learn more about working with panels.

4 Click the component you want to add.

5 Trag the component onto the Stage.

What types of components can I use in my Flash movies?

Flash components include the following common user interface elements: radio buttons, check boxes, push buttons, combo boxes, scroll panes, text scroll bars, and list boxes. You typically find each of these elements in Web page forms and use them for basic navigation. When you insert a component instance on the Stage, Flash automatically adds the component's graphic elements to your movie's Library. Called *skins* in Flash terminology, you can edit the component's graphical elements to match the appearance of other elements in your movie.

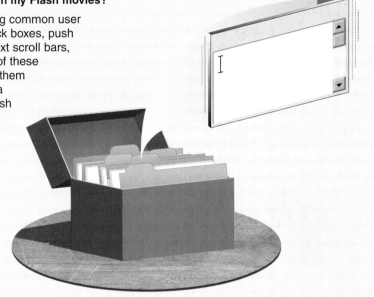

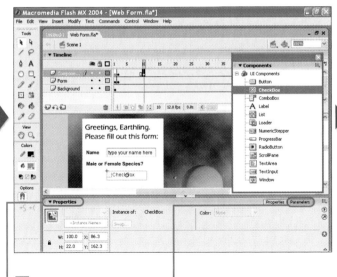

■-**6** Open the Properties inspector.

■ Press `Ctrl` + `F3` (`Shift` + `F3`) to display the Properties inspector.

■-**7** Click the **Parameters** tab.

■-**8** Type the component parameters you want to define.

■ Parameters vary for each component and may involve setting dimensions, labels, and values.

■ In this example, a check box label is needed.

■ You can add additional components to your movie to continue building an interactive form.

Shape-Changing

Animated

CHAPTER 11

Creating Interactive Buttons

You can add quick and easy interaction to your Flash movies using buttons. Buttons allow users to activate actions for controlling the movie. This chapter shows you how to add your own interactive buttons and make them stand out with animation effects.

Assign Action

PLAY MOVIE

FLASH BUTTONS

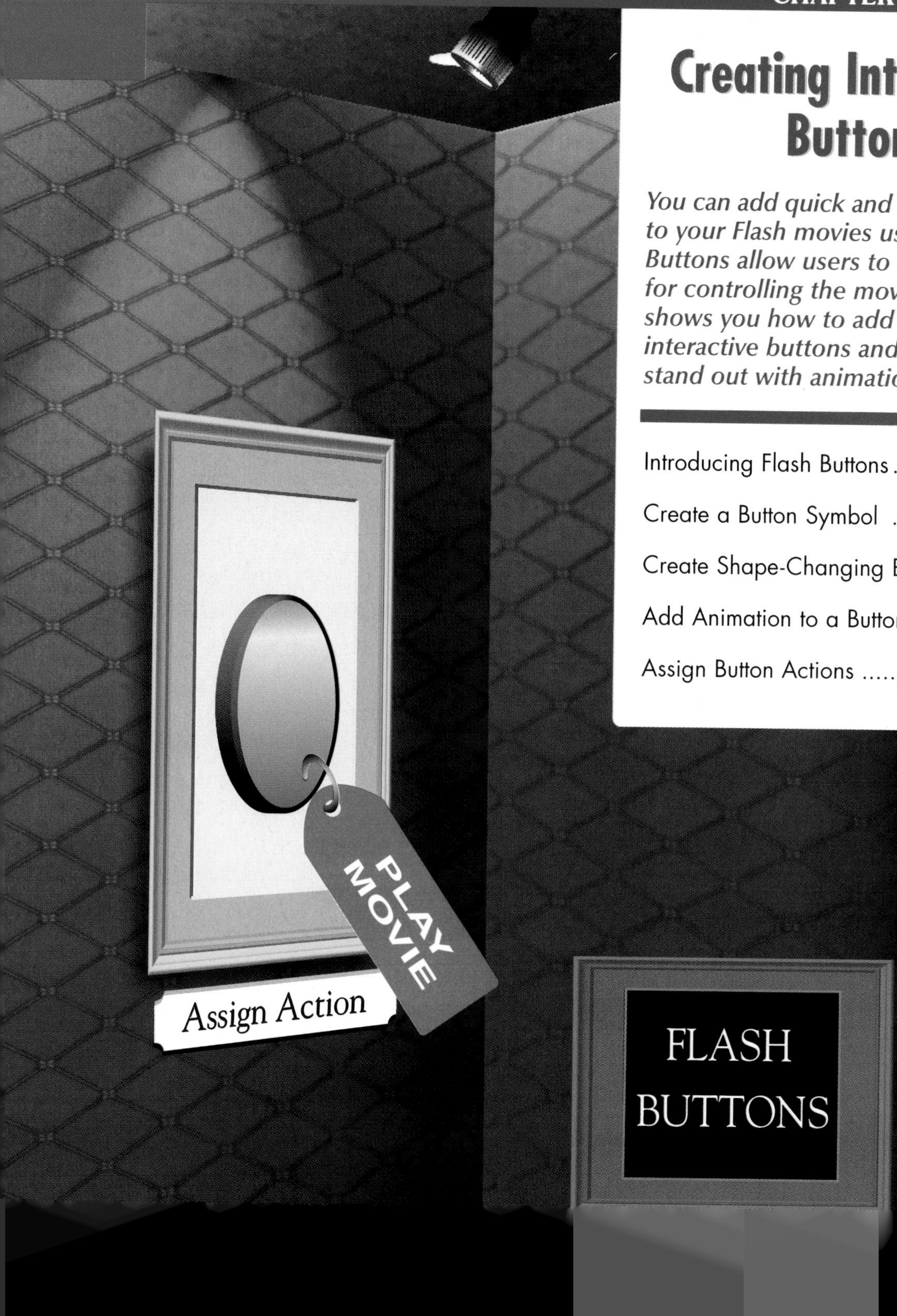

A popular way to enable users to interact with your Flash movies is through the use of *rollover buttons*. You can create a simple button that changes in appearance when the user rolls the mouse pointer over it, and changes appearance again when the user clicks it. Buttons are commonly employed on Web pages. You can create buttons in Flash that are static or animated.

Buttons Are Symbols

Buttons are a type of symbol to which Flash assigns *behaviors.* The behaviors are based on what happens when the mouse pointer interacts with the button. You can assign Flash actions to a button that trigger an action. You can turn any symbol you create in Flash into a button symbol or you can create a new button from scratch.

Button Frames

When you create a button in Flash, it comes with its own Timeline and four distinct frames: Up, Over, Down, and Hit. The four frames make up a mini-movie clip of the button's behavior. A button's timeline does not actually play like other Flash timelines, but rather jumps to the appropriate frame directed by the user's mouse action.

Up Frame

You use the Up frame to display what the inactive button looks like. This is the frame the user sees when the mouse pointer does not hover over the button. By default, the Up frame has an added keyframe.

Over Frame

The Over frame displays what the button looks like when the mouse pointer moves, or "rolls" over the button. For example, you can make the button turn bright red or emit a sound when the user pauses the mouse pointer over it, thereby alerting the user that the button is now active.

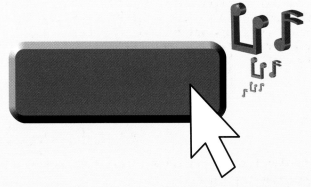

Down Frame

The Down frame displays what the button looks like when a user clicks the button. You can use the Down frame to make a button change color or appearance to indicate the user has clicked the button.

Hit Frame

The Hit frame defines the button area or boundary as a whole. This frame is often the same size and shape as the image in the Over and Down frames. The Hit frame differs from the other button frames in that the user never actually sees it.

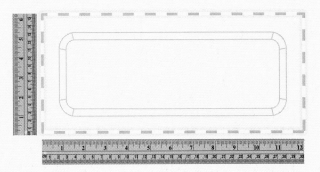

CREATE A BUTTON SYMBOL

You can create button symbols to add interactivity to your Flash movies. Buttons allow users to interact with movies by clicking to start or top an action. You can create new buttons or turn any symbol into a button.

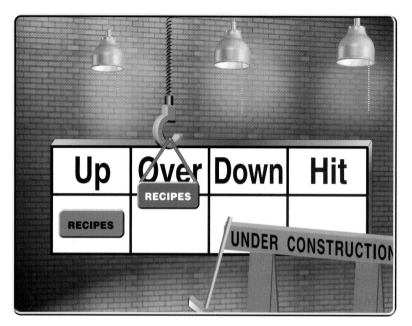

When you create a button, it includes a Timeline with four frames: Up, Over, Down, and Hit. You must assign an image or action to each of the four button states. You can make the image the same in each frame, or you can vary it to create the illusion of movement.

CREATE A BUTTON SYMBOL

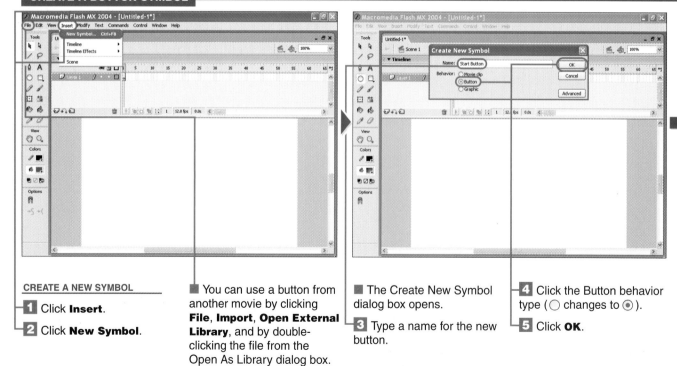

CREATE A NEW SYMBOL

1 Click **Insert**.

2 Click **New Symbol**.

■ You can use a button from another movie by clicking **File**, **Import**, **Open External Library**, and by double-clicking the file from the Open As Library dialog box.

■ The Create New Symbol dialog box opens.

3 Type a name for the new button.

4 Click the Button behavior type (○ changes to ⦿).

5 Click **OK**.

How do I display and use Flash's premade buttons?

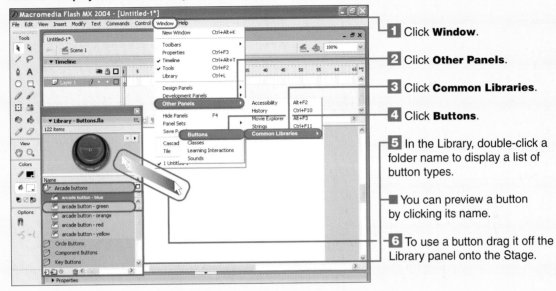

1 Click **Window**.

2 Click **Other Panels**.

3 Click **Common Libraries**.

4 Click **Buttons**.

5 In the Library, double-click a folder name to display a list of button types.

■ You can preview a button by clicking its name.

6 To use a button drag it off the Library panel onto the Stage.

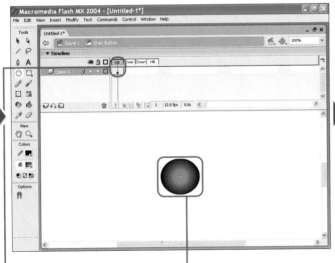

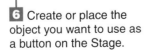

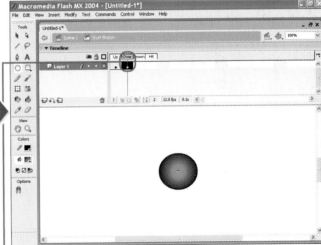

CREATE THE UP STATE

■ The button's Timeline opens in symbol-edit mode with four frames allowing you to create each frame's button state.

■ By default, Flash selects the Up frame and inserts a keyframe.

6 Create or place the object you want to use as a button on the Stage.

Note: See Chapter 2 to learn more about using the Flash drawing tools. See Chapter 4 to learn how to import graphics.

CREATE THE OVER STATE

7 Click the **Over** frame.

8 Press F6.

■ Flash insert a keyframe into the frame.

Note: See Chapter 8 to learn more about frames.

CONTINUED

CREATE A BUTTON SYMBOL

When deciding what you want your button to look like, consider your audience. Are they technologically savvy enough to recognize the image you use as a button onscreen, or do you need to keep the button simple and easy to understand? Although it is sometimes tempting to use detailed drawings as buttons, simple geometric shapes are always reliable for a general audience.

CREATE A BUTTON SYMBOL (CONTINUED)

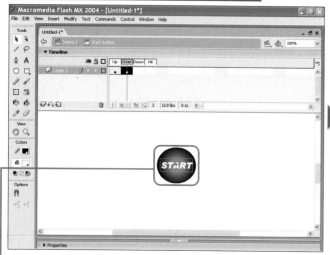

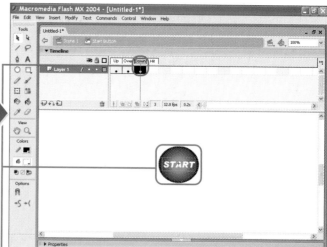

■ Flash duplicates the object from the Up keyframe.

■ You can make changes to the object.

■ This example adds a text box to describe the button.

Note: See Chapter 3 to learn more about editing objects and Chapter 5 to learn about adding text.

CREATE THE DOWN STATE

9 Click the **Down** frame.

10 Press **F6**.

■ Flash duplicates the object from the Over keyframe.

■ You can edit the object, if needed, such as adding a sound to the frame, or short animation.

Note: See Chapter 8 to learn how to create animation in Flash. See Chapter 12 to learn how to add sound clips to frames.

What edit mode am I in?

Flash switches you from movie-edit mode to symbol-edit mode when you create a button. You can always tell when you are in symbol-edit mode if you see the name of the symbol to the right of the scene name at the top of the Stage. To exit symbol-edit mode, click the scene name. You can also exit by pressing Ctrl + E (⌘ + E).

How do I preview a button?

In symbol-edit mode, click the button's Up frame, and then press Enter (Return). Watch the Stage as Flash plays through the four button frames. Any changes you make to frames appear during playback.

You can preview the button in movie-edit mode by pressing Ctrl + Alt + B (⌘ + Alt + B) and moving the mouse pointer over the button and clicking it to see the rollover capabilities.

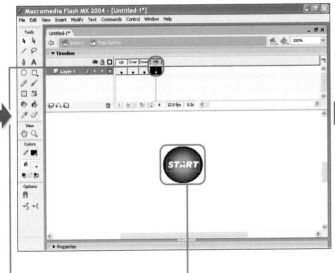

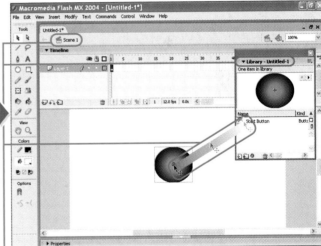

CREATE THE HIT STATE

11 Click the **Hit** frame.

12 Press F6.

■ Flash inserts a keyframe that duplicates the Down frame object.

■ Users cannot see the object contained in the Hit frame.

PLACE THE BUTTON ON THE STAGE

13 Click the Scene name to return to movie-edit mode.

14 Open the Library by pressing F11.

15 Click and drag the button from the Library to the Stage.

■ The newly created button appears on the Stage.

■ To test the button, you can click **Control**, **Enable Simple Buttons** and interact with the button.

237

CREATE SHAPE-CHANGING BUTTONS

You can create shape-changing buttons in your Flash movies for added graphical impact. Buttons are a great way to add interactivity to your Flash movies, and shape-changing buttons can make an ordinary button much more dynamic.

Creating a shape-changing button requires four different shapes. The Up, Over, and Down frames can each have a different shape, but the Hit frame needs a shape that encompasses all three of the other shapes. Although a user does not view the Hit frame, it defines a button's size.

CREATE SHAPE-CHANGING BUTTONS

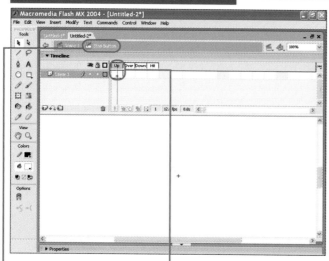

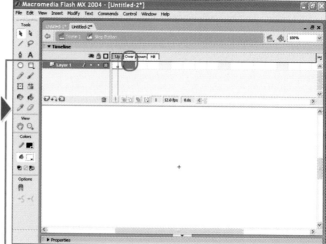

CREATE A NEW BUTTON

1 Start a new button symbol.

Note: See the section "Create a Button Symbol" to create a new symbol.

■ Flash switches to symbol-edit mode, and the button's name appears at the top of the Stage.

■ Flash selects the Up frame by default when you switch to symbol-edit mode.

2 Click the **Over** frame.

Can I use layers in my button?

Yes. The button's timeline works just like the main Timeline in movie-edit mode. You can add layers to organize various objects. If your button includes a text block, you may want to place it on another layer, or if your button uses a sound, place the clip on a separate layer. See Chapter 6 to learn about layers.

How do I toggle between symbol-edit and movie-edit mode?

You can quickly toggle back and forth between editing modes using a keyboard shortcut. Press Ctrl + E (⌘ + E).

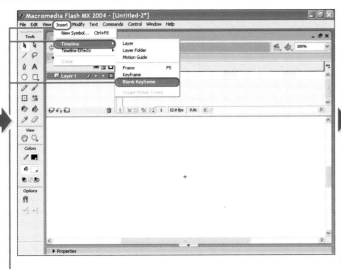

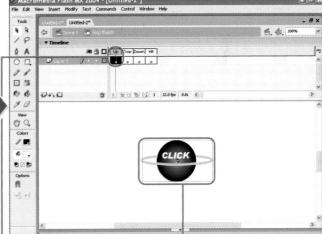

3 Click **Insert**.

4 Click **Timeline**.

5 Click **Blank Keyframe**.

■ You can also press F7 to insert a blank keyframe.

■ Flash inserts a blank keyframe.

6 Repeat steps **3** and **5** to add blank keyframes to the Down and Hit frames.

CREATE THE UP STATE

7 Click the **Up** frame to select it.

8 Create a new object or place an existing object on the Stage.

CONTINUED

CREATE SHAPE-CHANGING BUTTONS

If a button's image stays the same for all four frames in the button's timeline, users cannot distinguish between its active and inactive states. Changing the button's image for each state gives users some idea of the button's status. They can see a difference when the mouse pointer hovers over a live button or when they click the button.

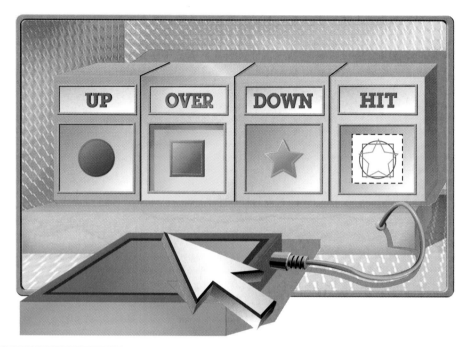

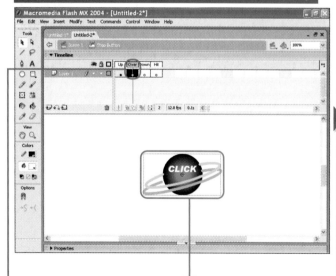

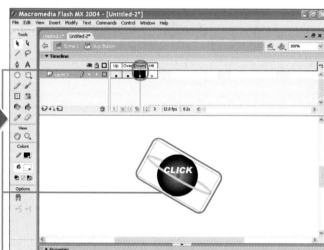

CREATE THE OVER STATE

9 Click the **Over** frame to select it.

10 Create a new object or place an existing object on the Stage to use as the active button state.

■ The object must differ from the object placed in the Up frame.

CREATE THE DOWN STATE

11 Click the **Down** frame to select it.

12 Create another new object or place an existing object on the Stage.

■ Make this object differ from the other two objects used in the previous frames.

240

Why do I need to draw a shape in the Hit frame?

Although the Hit frame is invisible to the user, it defines the active area of the button. You must make the object you draw big enough to encompass the largest object in the other button frames. If you do not, a user may click an area of the button that does not activate the button. If you have trouble guessing how large of an area to define, click the Onion Skin button (image) to see outlines of the shapes on all the other frames. Click image again to turn the feature off. For more information on the onion skinning feature, see Chapter 8.

How do I make changes to a button?

Double-click the button symbol to return to symbol-edit mode and make changes to the objects in each button timeline frame. For example, you may decide to use a different shape in your shape-changing button. After modifying your button, remember to check the Hit frame to make sure the defining shape size encompasses any new shapes in the other frames.

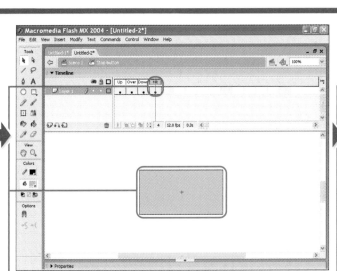

CREATE THE HIT STATE

13 Click the **Hit** frame.

14 Draw a geometric shape large enough to encompass the largest object size used in your button frames.

Note: If you do not define the Hit frame area properly, the user cannot interact with the button. Users cannot see the Hit frame's contents, but it is essential to the button's operation.

PREVIEW THE BUTTON

15 Click the **Up** frame to select it.

16 Press Enter (Return).

■ On the Stage, Flash plays through the four button frames and you can see the changing button states.

ADD ANIMATION TO A BUTTON

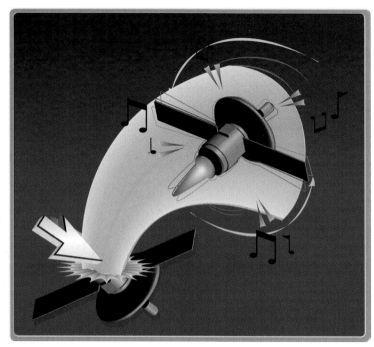

You can create animation effects for buttons, such as making a button seem to glow when the mouse pointer hovers over it. Spinning, jumping, and flashing buttons are all good examples of animation effects you can apply to help draw the user's attention to interactive buttons.

You can animate buttons by adding movie clips to your button frames. You must first create or import a movie clip and then assign it to a button state. Movie clips utilize their own timelines and play at their own pace. The button remains animated as long as the clip plays.

ADD ANIMATION TO A BUTTON

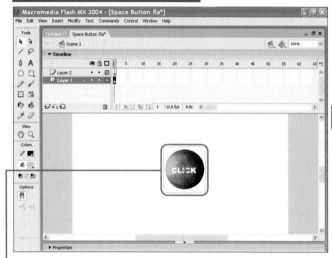

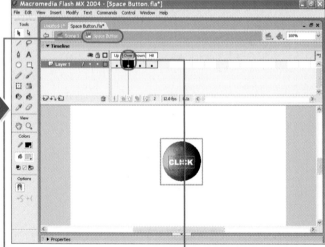

INSERT A MOVIE CLIP

1 Double-click the button to which you want to add an animation.

■ Flash switches you to symbol-edit mode.

■ The button's name appears above the Stage.

Note: See the section "Create a Button Symbol" to learn how to create a button.

2 Click the frame to which you want to add an animation, such as the **Up**, **Over**, or **Down** frame.

Note: Because the user cannot see the Hit frame it is not useful to animate this frame.

Should I add my movie clip to another layer in my button timeline?

You can utilize as many layers and layer folders as you need with a button to keep the various elements organized, including movie clips you add to the button. To learn more about timeline layers, see Chapter 6.

Is there a limit to the length of a button animation?

No. However, remember that the purpose of your button is to interact with the user. When you add a long animation sequence to a button state, you keep the user waiting to complete the action. It is a good idea to keep animation sequences short when applying them to buttons.

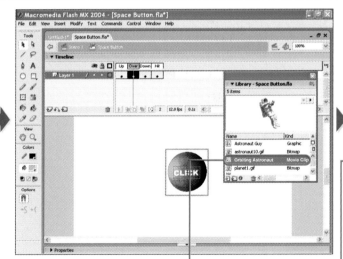

3 Press Ctrl + L (⌘ + L).

■ The Library panel opens.

4 Click the movie clip that you want to insert.

Note: See Chapters 8 and 9 to learn how to create animations and movie clips in Flash.

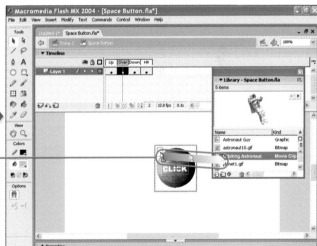

5 Drag the movie clip from the Library and place it on the Stage where the button appears.

CONTINUED ▶

ADD ANIMATION TO A BUTTON

You can add an animation to any button state. For example, you may want the user to see a spinning animation when the button is inactive, or you may want the object to spin only when the user rolls over the button with the mouse. The only frame you do not want to animate is the Hit frame because its contents are not visible to the user.

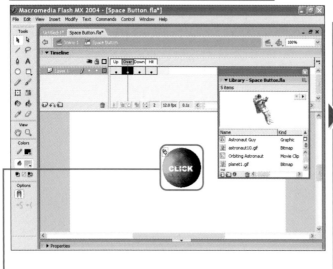

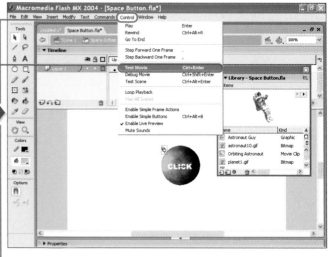

■ Flash inserts an instance of the clip on the Stage.

■ You can press **F11** to quickly toggle the Library panel open and closed.

TEST THE MOVIE CLIP

6 Click **Control**.

7 Click **Test Movie**.

■ To test the button states within the button timeline, press **Enter** (**Return**).

Can I add sounds to button frames?

Yes. You can add sound clips the same way you add movie clips. Try adding a
sound from Flash's Sounds Library. See Chapter 12 to learn more about sounds.

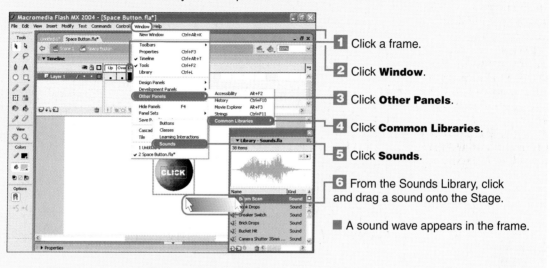

1 Click a frame.

2 Click **Window**.

3 Click **Other Panels**.

4 Click **Common Libraries**.

5 Click **Sounds**.

6 From the Sounds Library, click
and drag a sound onto the Stage.

■ A sound wave appears in the frame.

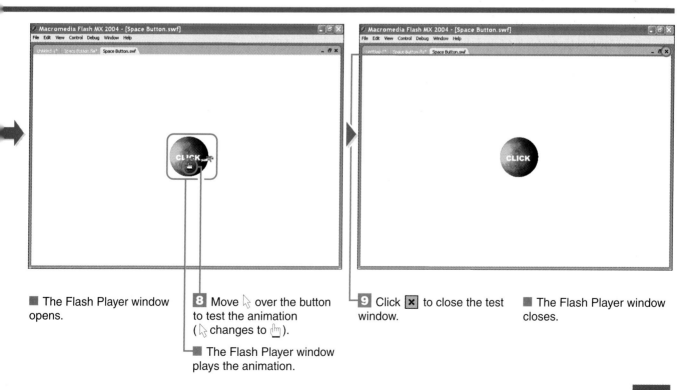

■ The Flash Player window
opens.

8 Move ⌖ over the button
to test the animation
(⌖ changes to ⌘).

■ The Flash Player window
plays the animation.

9 Click ✕ to close the test
window.

■ The Flash Player window
closes.

ASSIGN BUTTON ACTIONS

You can assign all kinds of actions to buttons you create. Buttons already utilize built-in actions, such as moving immediately to the Down frame when a user clicks the button. You can add other Flash actions, such as a `play` action that starts a movie clip playing when the user clicks the button.

In the case of buttons, you can assign frame actions that determine how the user interacts with the button. You add frame actions in movie-edit mode, not symbol-edit mode, and you add them to the frame containing the button.

ASSIGN BUTTON ACTIONS

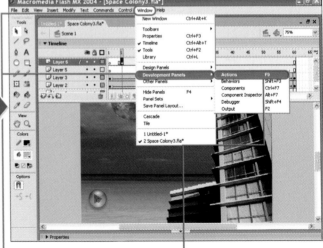

ADD AN ACTION TO A BUTTON

1 Click the button symbol to which you want to add an action.

Note: See the section "Create a Button Symbol" to learn how to create a button.

2 Click **Window**.

3 Click **Development Panels**.

4 Click **Actions**.

■ The Actions-Button panel opens.

What is an event handler?

An event handler, such as the `OnMouse Event`, manages the action. You can recognize the `OnMouse Event` in the Object Actions dialog box by the words `on`, such as `on release`. The words following the word `on` set the parameters for the event. You can add your own `On Mouse Event` handlers in the Actions panel. The script for the `on release` event, for example, appears as `on (release) {`.

I cannot select my button on the Flash Stage. Why?

If Flash activates the button when you move your cursor over the button, you have the Enable Simple Buttons feature turned on. Press `Ctrl` + `Alt` + `B` (`⌘` + `Alt` + `B`) to disable the feature and then click the button to select it.

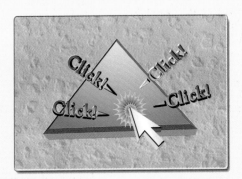

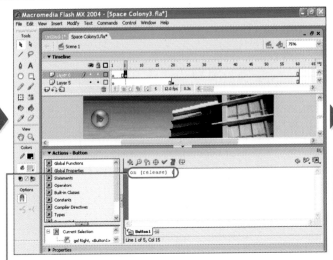

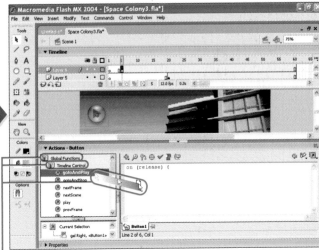

5 Type **on (release) {** in the Actions list box or script pane.

6 Press `Enter` (`Return`) to start a new script line.

7 Click an action category.

8 Click an action subcategory.

9 Click and drag the action from the list and drop it in the Actions list box.

■ You can also double-click the action name to immediately place it in the Actions list box.

Note: See Chapter 10 to learn how to work with Flash actions.

CONTINUED

ASSIGN BUTTON ACTIONS

Actions are simplified programming scripts that instruct Flash how to perform a certain task, such as activating a Web page link or stopping a sound clip. Using a basic programming language, actions include command strings to spell out exactly what action Flash must perform.

In addition to the action you assign, you must also assign a special event handler, called the On Mouse Event action, to the button. The On Mouse Event action acts as a manager to make sure whatever action you assign works properly with the button actions that are already built-in for the symbol type.

ASSIGN BUTTON ACTIONS (CONTINUED)

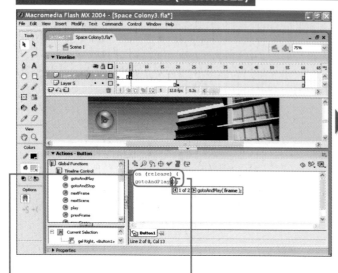

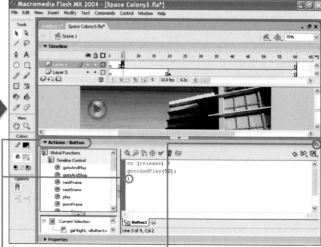

■ Flash adds the necessary action script to the Actions list.

🔟 Define any additional parameters required by the action you assigned.

■ In this example, a frame number is required.

1️⃣1️⃣ Press **Enter** (**Return**) to start a new line.

1️⃣2️⃣ Type }.

1️⃣3️⃣ Click the panel's title bar.

■ Flash minimizes the Actions panel.

■ You can also click the panel's Options menu button (📃) and click **Close Panel** to close the panel.

Can I add multiple actions to a button?

Yes. You can use the Actions-Button panel to add more actions to a button, either before or after an existing action. For example, you can add multiple actions to occur within one set of On/End actions, and Flash triggers all of the actions by a single mouse event. Be sure to add actions before the last line of the script, }, or your actions may not work properly.

How do I edit an action?

You can perform edits to your button actions in the Actions-Button panel. Click the line you want to edit in the Actions list. Depending on the action, different parameters are listed. To remove an action, select the line you want to delete and press 🗑. To add an action, click 🔩 and then select another action.

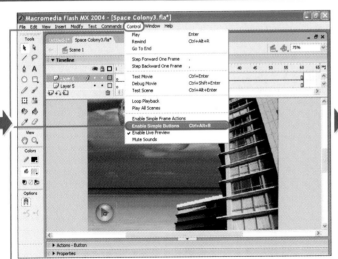

TEST A BUTTON ACTION

14 Click **Control**.

15 Click **Enable Simple Buttons**.

■ You can also test the button action in the Flash Player window.

■ You can click the **Control** menu and click **Test Movie** to open the Player.

16 Move the 🖑 over the button and click it.

■ Flash plays its associated action.

CHAPTER 12

Adding Sound

Does your animation need some sound? In this chapter, you learn how to add sound files to your animation frames and control how the sounds play.

IMPORT A SOUND CLIP

Although you cannot record sounds in Flash, you can import sounds from other sources for use with movies. For example, you can download an MP3 file from the Internet and add it to a movie, or import a saved recording to play with a Flash button. Flash supports popular sound file formats, such as WAV and AIF.

You add sounds to keyframes the same way you add graphics and buttons. However, before you can add a sound to a frame, you must first import it into your movie's Library.

Make sure that your sound clips are as short as possible by trimming excess parts of the clip or by using an audio clip that loops. When you use large sound files, such as background music, they take longer to download when users are accessing files from your Web site.

IMPORT A SOUND FILE

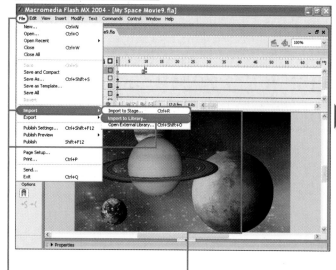

1 Click **File**.

2 Click **Import**.

3 Click **Import to Library**.

■ You can also click **Import to Stage** to import sound files directly to the Stage as well as the Library.

■ The Import to Library dialog box opens.

4 Click the sound file you want to import.

■ You can click ⊻ to look for the file in another folder or drive.

■ You can click ⊻ to look for a particular type of sound file.

Does Flash have any sounds I can use?

Yes. To display the Sounds library:

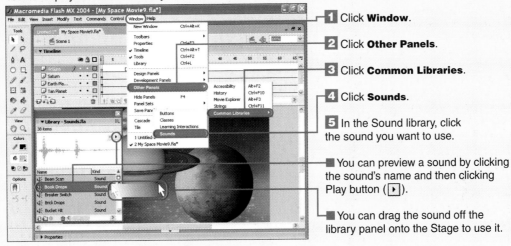

1 Click **Window**.

2 Click **Other Panels**.

3 Click **Common Libraries**.

4 Click **Sounds**.

5 In the Sound library, click
the sound you want to use.

■ You can preview a sound by clicking
the sound's name and then clicking
Play button (▶).

■ You can drag the sound off the
library panel onto the Stage to use it.

5 Click **Open**.

■ You can also double-click
the file to import
immediately.

■ Flash imports the sound
file and places it in the
Library.

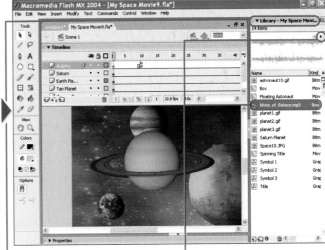

6 Press **F11**.

■ The Library panel opens.

*Note: See Chapter 7 to learn more
about using the Library.*

■ You can preview the
sound clip in the Library by
clicking the sound and then
clicking the Play button (▶).

ADD A SOUND LAYER

You can organize sounds in your movie using *layers*. By keeping your sound clips on a separate layer, you can more easily locate the sounds and see how they relate to items in other layers and easily edit them later. When you place sounds on separate layers, you can treat the layers as audio channels in your movie, and the various layers play together during playback.

ADD A SOUND LAYER

ADD A LAYER

1 Click the layer below where you want to insert a new layer.

■ Flash always adds a new layer to the Timeline directly above the active layer.

2 Click the Insert Layer button (image).

■ A new layer appears on top of the active layer.

Can I enlarge the size of my sound layer?

Yes. Enlarging a layer that contains a sound clip enables you to more easily view its waveform image in the Timeline:

1 Right-click the layer name.

2 Click **Properties**.

■ This opens the Layer Properties dialog box.

3 Click the Layer Height ⌄ and select a percentage.

4 Click **OK** to close the dialog box and apply the new size.

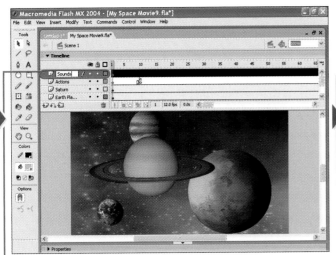

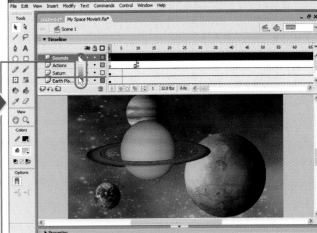

RENAME THE LAYER

3 Double-click the default layer name.

4 Type a name that identifies this layer as a sound layer.

5 Press **Enter** (**Return**).

■ Flash saves the new layer name.

■ To make the sound layer easy to find, you can drag the layer to the top or bottom of the Timeline layer stack.

Note: See Chapter 6 to learn how to work with layers and layer folders.

255

ASSIGN A SOUND TO A FRAME

You can enliven any animation sequence with a sound clip whether you add a single sound effect or an entire sound track. You save sound files as instances that you can insert into frames on the Timeline and use throughout your movie. Flash represents sounds as waveforms in frames.

Depending on the length of the sound clip, the sound may play through several frames of your movie. Unlike a graphic or button symbol, however, sound clips appear as outlines on the Stage and the waveform for the sound appears in the designated layer and frame in the Timeline.

ASSIGN A SOUND TO A FRAME

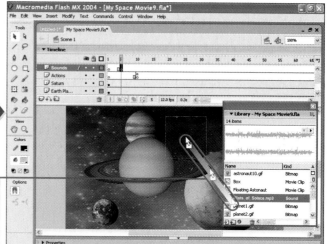

ADD A SOUND USING THE LIBRARY PANEL

1 Click the frame to which you want to add a sound.

Note: See the section "Import a Sound File" to learn how to add sound clips to the Library.

2 Press F6.

■ Flash inserts a keyframe.

3 Press F11.

■ Flash opens the Library panel.

4 Click and drag the sound clip from the Library and drop it onto the Stage (⇗ changes to ⇗).

■ The sound's waveform appears in the frame.

Note: By default, Flash assigns all sounds Event synchronization status unless you specify otherwise. See the section "Set Synchronization Properties" to learn more.

Can I enlarge the frames to better view the waveforms?

Yes. Click the Timeline menu button (⊞) and click another frame size to display.

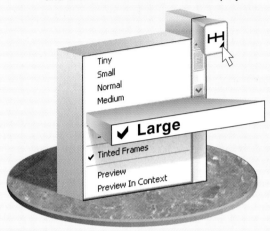

Why does my sound's waveform appear compressed into one frame?

If you assign a sound file to a keyframe that appears at the end of your movie, or if you have yet to add additional frames or keyframes to your movie, the sound's waveform appears only in the frame in which you assigned it, typically as a straight line.

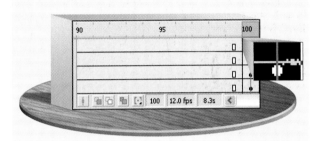

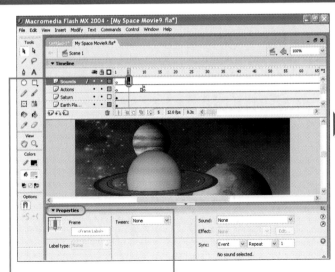

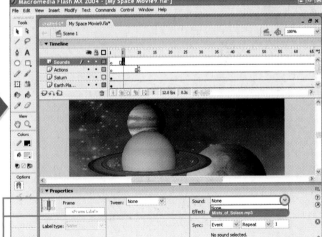

ADD A SOUND USING THE PROPERTIES INSPECTOR

1 Click the frame to which you want to add a sound.

Note: See the section "Import a Sound File" to learn how to add sound clips to the Library.

2 Insert a keyframe by pressing F6.

3 Open the Properties inspector by pressing Ctrl + F3 (⌘ + F3).

4 Click the Sound ⌄.

5 Click the sound you want to assign.

■ The sound's waveform appears in the frame.

Note: By default, Flash assigns all sounds Event synchronization status unless you specify otherwise. See the section "Set Synchronization Properties" to learn more.

SET SYNCHRONIZATION PROPERTIES

You can tell Flash how you want a sound to synchronize with your movie by setting sound properties. Sounds fall into two categories: *event driven* and *streamed*. You assign an event sound to a specific keyframe and it continues to play independently of your movie's Timeline. You use event sounds when you do not want to synchronize the sound with your movie.

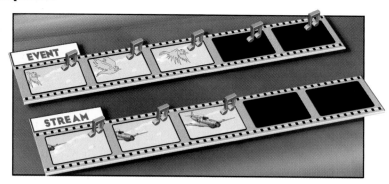

Streamed sounds download as they are needed, and start playing even if the rest of the clip has not yet loaded. Flash synchronizes streamed sounds with your movie's frames and attempts to keep any animation in sync with the streamed sound.

SET SYNCHRONIZATION PROPERTIES

■1 Click the frame containing the sound you want to edit.

Note: See the section "Add a Sound to a Frame" to learn how to assign sound clips.

■2 Press `Ctrl` + `F3` (`⌘` + `F3`).

■ Flash opens the Properties inspector.

■3 Click the Sound ▾.

■4 Click the sound you want to edit.

How do I remove a sound clip I no longer want in the movie?

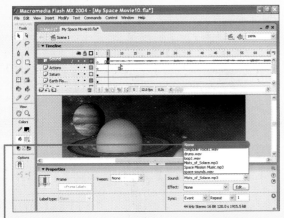

1 Follow steps **1** to **3** in this section.

2 Click **None**.

■ Flash no longer associates the sound with the keyframe, but it still stores the clip in your movie's Library.

If I repeat or loop a sound, does it affect my file size?

Yes. For example, if you repeat a streamed sound more than once, or loop it to play continually, your overall file size increases. For that reason, be careful in selecting sounds for your movie if your goal is to keep the overall file size down. Also, use caution when playing the sounds more than once.

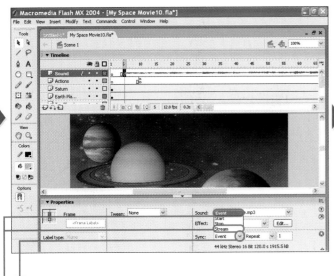

5 Click the Sync ▾.

6 Click **Event** or **Stream**.

■ You select **Event** to trigger a sound that plays independently of the movie timeline at a particular frame or action.

■ You select **Stream** to synchronize the sound clip to your movie frames.

Note: By default, Flash sets all sound to Event sounds unless you specify otherwise.

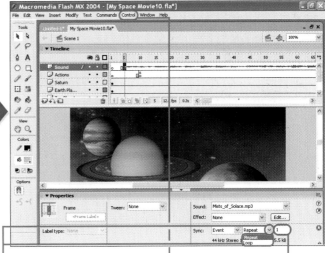

7 Click ▾.

8 Click **Repeat** or **Loop**.

■ If you select **Repeat**, specify how many times the clip should play.

■ If you select **Loop**, the clip plays continuously.

■ You can now click **Control**, and then **Test Movie** to open the Player window and test the sound.

You can use the Effect properties to adjust the way in which a sound clip plays in your movie. For example, you can make a sound appear to fade in or out, or you can simulate a stereo audio channel effect.

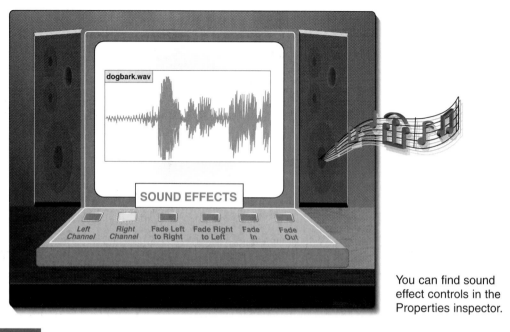

You can find sound effect controls in the Properties inspector.

ASSIGN A SOUND EFFECT

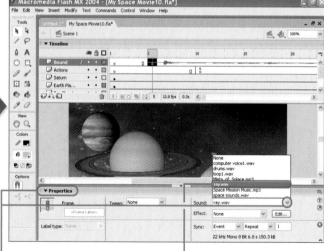

1 Click the frame containing the sound you want to edit.

Note: See the section "Add a Sound to a Frame" to learn how to assign sound clips.

2 Press `Ctrl` + `F3` (`⌘` + `F3`).

■ Flash opens the Properties inspector.

3 Click the Sound ⌄.

4 Click the sound you want to edit.

What are the sound effects I can apply?

You can select **Left Channel** or **Right Channel** to play sounds only in the left or right speaker. Selecting **Fade Left to Right** or **Fade Right to Left** makes the sound move from one speaker to another. When you select **Fade In** or **Fade Out,** Flash makes the sound gradually increase or decrease in volume.

How do I create a custom effect?

You can apply some rudimentary editing to your Flash sounds using the **Custom** sound effect control. For example, you can adjust the sound volume or length. See the section "Edit Sounds" later in this chapter to learn more about this control.

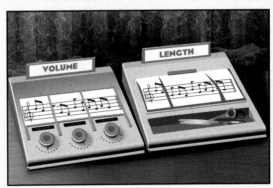

5 Click the Effect.

6 Click a sound effect.

■ Flash assigns the new sound effect to the clip.

7 Press **Enter** (**Return**).

■ Flash plays the sound effect and the playhead moves across the Timeline.

■ You can also click **Control**, and then **Test Movie** to open the Player window and test the sound.

261

ASSIGN A SOUND TO A BUTTON

You can add sounds to buttons to help people know how to interact with the buttons or just to give the buttons added flair. For example, you can add a clicking sound that the user hears when he or she clicks a button.

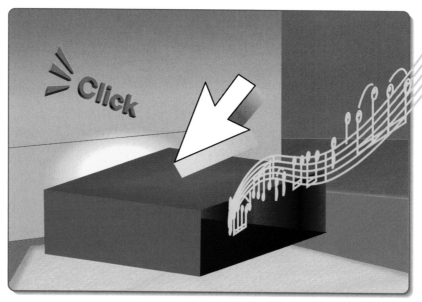

If your buttons are part of a graphic or page background, adding a sound to the button's rollover state helps users find the buttons on the page.

ASSIGN A SOUND TO A BUTTON

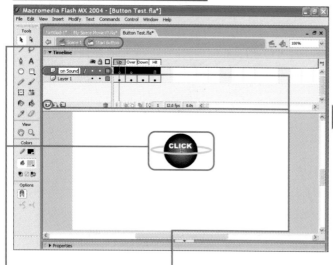

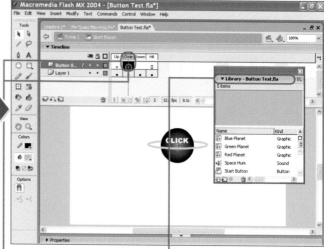

1 Open the button to which you want to add a sound in symbol-edit mode.

Note: See Chapter 11 to learn more about creating buttons.

2 Click 🔲.

3 Type a name for the layer.

Note: See the section "Add a Sound Layer" to learn how to add and name a layer.

4 Click the frame to which you want to add a sound.

5 If the frame does not already have a keyframe press F6.

■ Flash inserts a keyframe.

6 Press Ctrl + L (⌘ + L)

■ Flash opens the Library.

To which button frame should I assign a sound?

The most practical frames to use when assigning sounds are the Over and Down frames, but you can assign sounds to any button frame. For example, you may want the button to beep when the user rolls over the button with the mouse pointer. To do this, assign a sound to the Over frame. To learn more about the Over and Down frames, see Chapter 11.

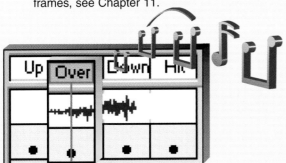

Flash does not let me add a sound to a frame. Why not?

You can add sounds to only keyframes, not to regular frames in the Timeline. Be sure you insert a keyframe before attempting to add the sound. See Chapter 8 to learn more about types of frames.

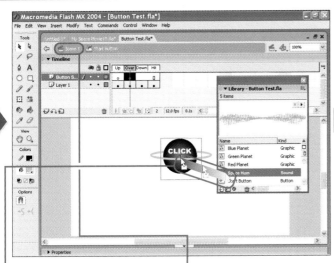

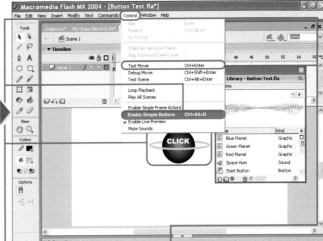

7 Click and drag the sound clip from the Library and drop it onto the Stage.

■ The sound's waveform appears in the frame.

8 Click the scene name.

■ Flash switches back to movie-edit mode.

Note: See Chapter 11 to learn how to enable buttons in movie-edit mode.

9 Click **Control**.

10 Click **Enable Simple Buttons**.

■ You can now move over the button or click the button to hear the assigned sound.

■ You can also test buttons using the Flash Player window.

■ Click **Control**, **Test Movie** to open the player.

LOAD A SOUND USING A BEHAVIOR

You can use the Load Sound from Library behavior to control the playback of a sound clip in your movie. Behaviors are prewritten ActionScript you can assign to an object in your movie to control another object, such as a sound clip. You can assign the behavior to a button that plays the sound clip when a user clicks the button.

Directions for behaving:
- Load Sound from Library
- Play Sound
- Stop Sound

To set up the Load Sound from Library behavior, you must first import a sound clip into your movie's Library and assign an identifier name to the clip.

LOAD A SOUND USING A BEHAVIOR

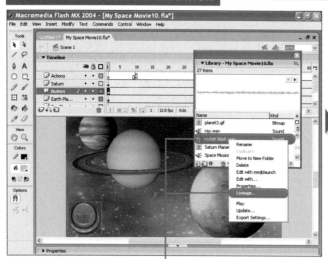

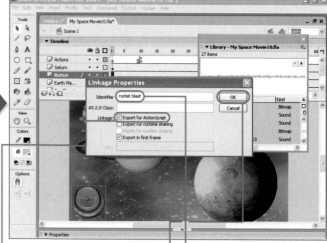

1 Press **F11**.

■ Flash opens the Library panel.

2 Right-click over the sound clip you want to use.

3 Click **Linkage**.

■ The Linkage Properties dialog box opens.

4 Click the **Export for ActionScript** option (☐ changes to ☑).

5 Type an identifier for the clip.

6 Click **OK**.

■ You can press **F11** to close the Library panel again.

Where do I find sound clips?

You can find lots of free sound clips on the Internet. Flash supports WAV, AIFF, MP3, and QuickTime file formats, to name a few. Flash includes a Sounds library you can use to add sound effects to your movie. To open the Library, click **Window**, **Other Panels**, **Common Libraries**, and then **Sounds**.

Is there a quicker way to open the Behaviors panel?

Yes. You can press **Shift** + **F3** on the keyboard to open the panel.

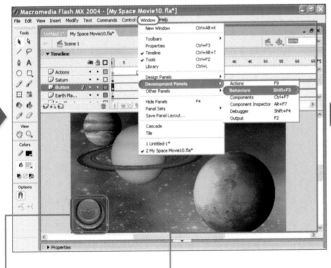

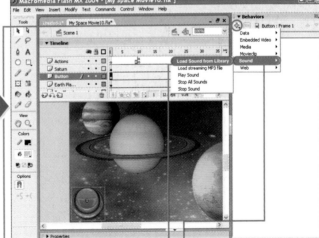

■7 Select the object to which you want to assign a sound behavior.

■ In this example, a button will trigger the sound.

■8 Click **Window**.

■9 Click **Development Panels**.

■10 Click **Behaviors**.

■ The Behaviors panel opens.

■11 Click the Add button (⊞).

■12 Click **Sound**.

■13 Click **Load Sound from Library**.

CONTINUED ▶

LOAD A SOUND USING A BEHAVIOR

You can control sound behaviors by specifying an event or action. By default, Flash assigns the `On Release` event to the behavior unless you specify another event. This means that the sound clip plays when the user clicks the button and releases the mouse pointer. You can also set up other events, such as `On Press` or `On Rollover`.

LOAD A SOUND USING A BEHAVIOR (CONTINUED)

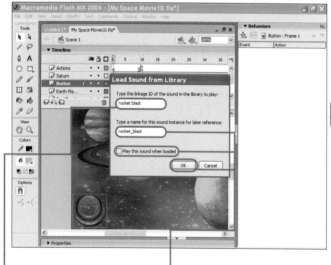

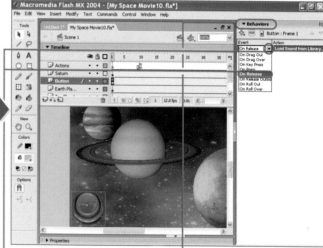

■ The Load Sound from Library dialog box opens.

14 Type the identifier name you typed in step **5**.

15 Type an instance name.

16 Deselect the **Play this sound when loaded** option (☐ changes to ☑).

17 Click **OK**.

■ Flash assigns the sound behavior.

■ To change the event handler, you can click here and select another.

■ You can click the panel's title bar to minimize the Behaviors panel.

266

How do I remove a sound behavior I no longer want?

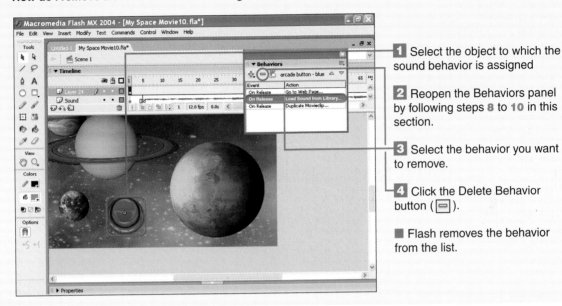

■1 Select the object to which the sound behavior is assigned

■2 Reopen the Behaviors panel by following steps **8** to **10** in this section.

■3 Select the behavior you want to remove.

■4 Click the Delete Behavior button ( ).

■ Flash removes the behavior from the list.

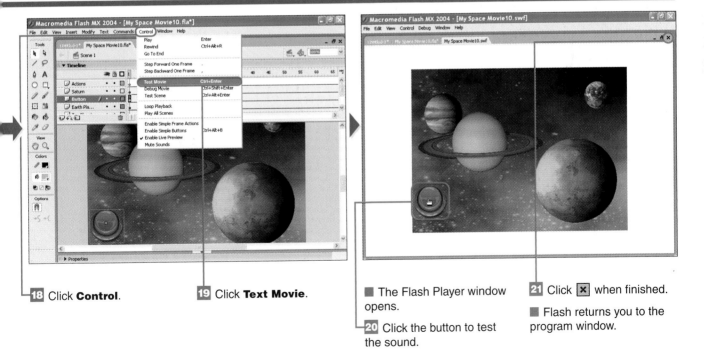

■18 Click **Control**.

■19 Click **Text Movie**.

■ The Flash Player window opens.

■20 Click the button to test the sound.

■21 Click × when finished.

■ Flash returns you to the program window.

ASSIGN START AND STOP SOUNDS

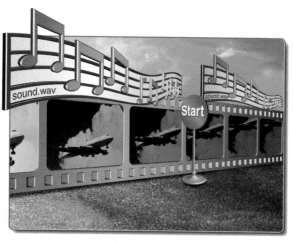

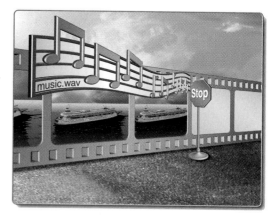

You can use the Flash Start and Stop sound controls to start and stop sounds in your movie.

Start Sound

Use the Start command to start a new instance of a sound. The Start command is handy when you want to synchronize a sound with your animation.

Stop Sound

Use the Stop command to stop a sound from playing. For example, if your animation ends on a particular frame, but your sound clip goes on much longer, you can place a Stop command in the frame to end the sound.

ASSIGN START AND STOP SOUNDS

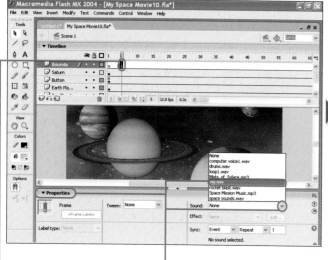

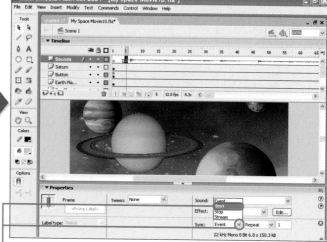

SET A START SOUND

1 Press **F6** where you want to start the sound again.

■ Flash inserts a keyframe.

2 Press **Ctrl** + **F3** (**⌘** + **F3**) to display the Properties inspector.

3 Click the Sound ⌄.

4 Click the sound you want to start.

5 Click the Sync ⌄.

6 Click **Start**.

■ Flash plays the clip from its beginning when the movie reaches the keyframe with the assigned Start control.

Do you have to place the Stop command in the same layer as the Start sound?

You can place a **Stop** command on any layer to stop the sound. The command immediately stops any playback of the sound regardless of where you assign the sound.

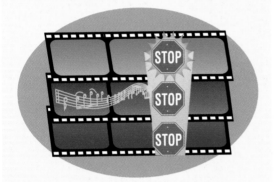

Can I use sound behaviors to start and stop sounds?

Yes. You can apply the **Play Sound**, **Stop Sound**, and **Stop All Sounds** behaviors to control sounds in your movies. To use behaviors with sounds, your sound clips require an identifier, a name to identify the sound object for ActionScript actions. To learn more about behaviors, see the section "Load a Sound Using a Behavior" earlier in this chapter.

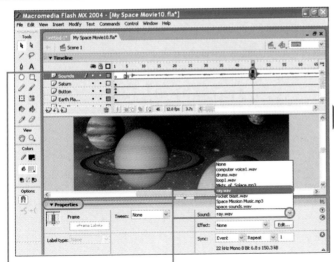

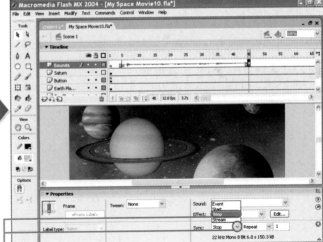

SET A STOP SOUND

1 Press **F6** where you want to stop the sound.

■ Flash inserts a keyframe.

2 Press **Ctrl** + **F3** (**⌘** + **F3**).

■ Flash opens the Properties inspector.

3 Click the Sound ⌄.

4 Click the sound you want to stop.

5 Click the Sync ⌄.

6 Click **Stop**.

■ Flash stops the clip from playing when the movie reaches the keyframe with assigned the Stop control.

EDIT SOUNDS

When you import a sound into Flash, its file includes information about the sound's length, volume, and stereo settings. You can fine-tune these settings using the Edit Envelope dialog box. Flash's sound-editing controls enable you to define start and end points for sounds, or to adjust the volume at different points in the sound.

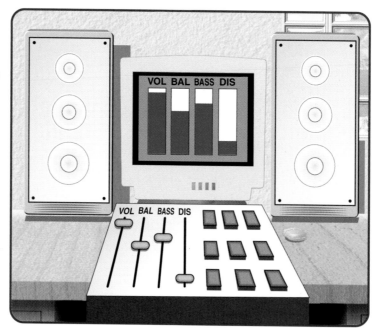

For example, you can make your sound files smaller in size if you define the exact point at which a sound starts to play, or define the point where the sound ends.

EDIT SOUNDS

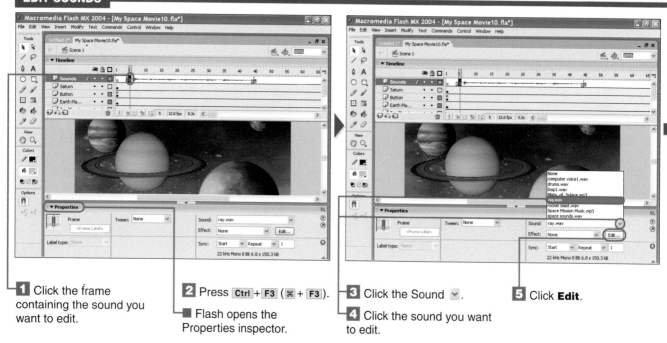

1 Click the frame containing the sound you want to edit.

2 Press Ctrl + F3 (⌘ + F3).

■ Flash opens the Properties inspector.

3 Click the Sound ⌄.

4 Click the sound you want to edit.

5 Click **Edit**.

How do I create start and end points for my sound?

In the Edit Envelope dialog box, click and drag the Time In control marker, located at the far left side of the Sound Timeline bar separating the two channels, to create a new start point for your sound. To create a new end point, click and drag the Time Out control marker, located at the far right side of the Sound Timeline bar.

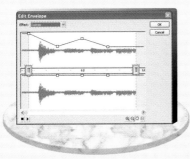

Can I change the panning for a sound channel?

Yes. *Panning* refers to the stereo effects of a sound, adjusting the left and right audio channels. You can adjust the volume by dragging envelope handles in either audio channel in the Edit Envelope dialog box to create panning effects for your movie.

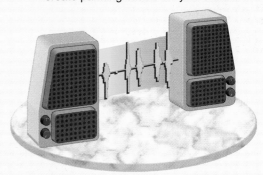

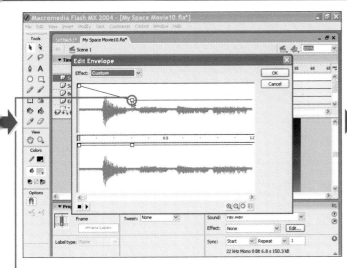

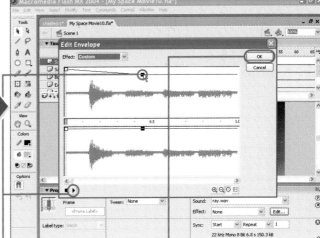

■ The Edit Envelope dialog box opens.

6 Click the waveform channel that you want to edit.

■ Flash places an envelope handle (☐) on the waveform.

■ You can add up to 8 envelope handles to either channel.

7 Click and drag ☐ up or down to adjust the sound's volume.

8 To hear the sound, click the Play button (▶).

■ Continue adjusting the sound as needed.

Note: For greater sound-editing controls, you may need a full-featured sound-editing program.

9 Click **OK**.

■ Flash applies your edits to the sound.

SET AUDIO OUTPUT FOR EXPORT

You can control how sounds are exported in your Flash files. You find options for optimizing your sound files for export in the Publish Settings dialog box.

Options include settings for compressing your sounds in ADPCM, MP3, or RAW format. By default, Flash exports sounds in MP3 format using a bit rate of 16 Kbps. MP3 is the emerging standard for distributing audio on the Internet.

SET AUDIO OUTPUT FOR EXPORT

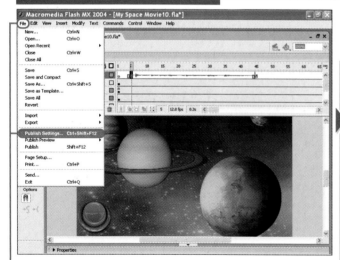

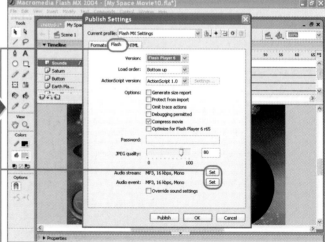

1 Click **File**.

2 Click **Publish Settings**.

■ The Publish Settings dialog box opens.

3 Click the **Flash** tab.

4 Click the **Set** button corresponding to the audio type you want to control.

■ You can control the export quality of both streaming and event sounds.

■ Clicking either **Set** button opens the Sound Settings dialog box.

What is a good bit rate for MP3?

MP3 efficiently compresses audio files, resulting in high bit rates — therefore better quality — and small file sizes. This is why MP3 is emerging as the standard for distributing sounds on the Internet, especially on Web pages. For large music files, try a setting of 64 Kbps. For speech or voice files, try 24 or 32 Kbps. To set near CD quality, use a setting of 112 or 128 Kbps. Use 16 Kbps settings for simple button sounds, or larger audio sounds where quality is not crucial.

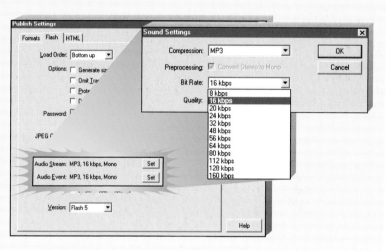

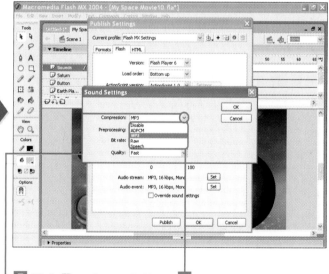

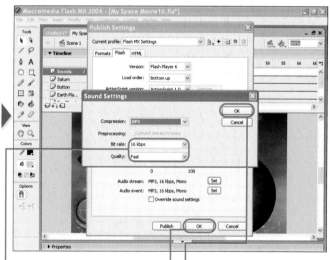

5 Click ☑ to view available compression formats.

6 Select a compression format to apply.

■ Depending on the format you select, the remaining options in the Sound Settings dialog box reflect settings associated with your selection.

■ You can make changes to the remaining settings.

7 Click **OK** to close the Sound Settings dialog box.

8 Click **OK**.

■ The Publish Settings dialog box closes and Flash saves your settings.

CHAPTER 13

Distributing Flash Movies

Are you ready to distribute your Flash creations to others? Learn how to export Flash files to the Web, to disks, or as self-playing files.

UNDERSTANDING DISTRIBUTION METHODS

You can distribute your Flash projects to an audience in several ways. You may publish a Flash movie to a Web page, save it as a QuickTime movie to send to another user via e-mail, or deliver the movie as a self-playing file. You can assign a distribution method using the Publish Settings dialog box, or you can export your movie as another file type using the Export Movie dialog box.

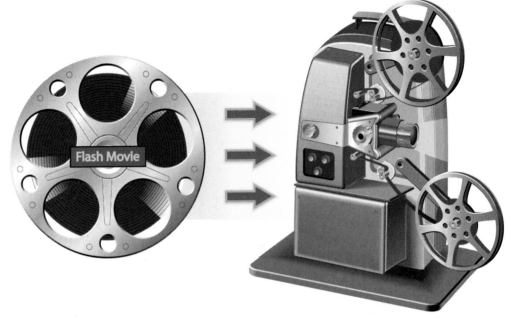

Start with an Authoring File

When you create content in Flash, you start by creating an *authoring file*. The authoring file is where you draw and animate your movie's content. This file contains all the elements that make up your movie, such as bitmap objects, sounds, symbols, buttons, text, and so on. The authoring file can be quite large in file size. Authoring files use the .FLA file extension.

Create an Export File

After you create the authoring file and get it working just the way you want, you can turn it into an *export file*. When you create an export file, you create a file that is separate from the authoring file. Flash offers two exporting features, Export Movie and Publish. The feature you select depends on what you want to do with your Flash content.

Export or Publish

When you export a movie using the Export Movie feature, you export your file as a specific file type for another program, such as QuickTime, to use. When you publish a movie, you turn your content into a file type viewable from the Web. The process of publishing compresses the file contents, making it easier for others to view the file. The resulting file is uneditable, so you cannot change its contents. Published Flash movie files use the .SWF file extension.

Publish in Flash Player Format

Your Flash creations really shine when you publish them in the original program format — Flash Player format. When you distribute a movie as a movie file, Flash saves it in the SWF file format, and the format requires the Flash Player application or plug-in for a user to view. The Flash Player is the most widely used player on the Web and comes preinstalled with most computers and all major Web browsers today.

Publish as a Projector

Another way to distribute your movie is to turn it into a *projector*. A projector is a standalone player that runs the movie without the need of another application. You use the Projector feature to distribute your Flash creations to users who do not have access to the Flash Player or plug-in. This method is great for distributing your movie on a CD-ROM

Using the Bandwidth Profiler

When preparing a movie for publishing, Flash offers a handy tool to help you check for quality and optimal playback. The Bandwidth Profiler is a valuable tool that can help you fix problem areas that hold up your movie while downloading into the browser window. You use the Profiler to help you fix problems before you post the Flash file on a Web page.

PUBLISH A MOVIE AS A FLASH MOVIE FILE

When you complete a Flash movie, you can publish the movie as a Flash movie file so you can share with others. You use two phases to publish your movie. First you prepare the files for publishing using the Publish Settings dialog box, and then you publish the movie using the Publish command.

By default, Flash publishes your movie as an SWF file, but you can publish it in other formats. For example, you may publish your movie as a GIF, JPEG, or PNG image, or as a self-playing Windows or Mac file, or as a QuickTime movie.

PUBLISH A MOVIE AS A FLASH MOVIE FILE

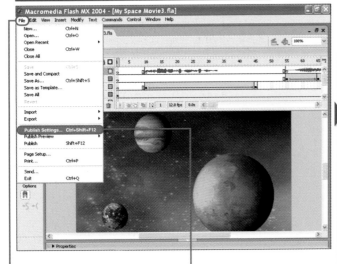

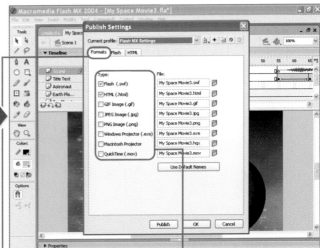

PREPARE FILES FOR PUBLISHING

1 Click **File**.

2 Click **Publish Settings**.

■ The Publish Settings dialog box appears.

Note: If you have already published your file, tabs from your last changes appear in the dialog box.

3 Click the **Formats** tab.

4 Click the Format option you want to use (☐ changes to ☑).

■ Depending on which format you select, additional tabs appear with options related to that format.

How does the Publish feature differ from the Export Movie feature?

You use the Publish feature specifically for publishing your work for use on the Web or to create a projector file. The Export Movie feature enables you to save your Flash project as another file type, so you can use it in another program. To learn more about these features, see the

Do I always have to publish a movie through the Publish Settings dialog box?

No. If you want to publish the movie using the previous settings you set up in the Publish Settings dialog box, you can click **File**, and then click **Publish**. Flash does not give you a chance to name the file if you want to publish directly and bypass the Publish Settings dialog box.

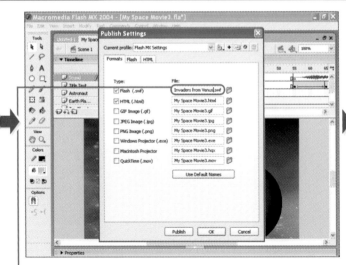

■ To assign a different filename other than the default supplied by Flash, you can click inside the Filename field and type a new name in the format's text box.

■ Flash publishes your files to the My Documents folder unless you specify another folder and filename path in the Filename box.

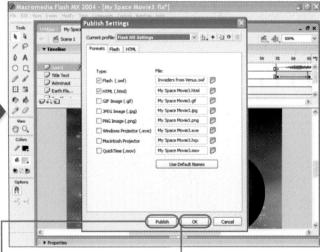

PUBLISH FILES

5 Click **Publish**.

■ Flash generates the necessary files for the movie.

6 Click **OK**.

■ Flash saves the settings and closes the Publish Settings dialog box.

PUBLISH A MOVIE AS A WEB PAGE

You can save a movie as a Web page and Flash generates all the necessary HTML code for you, including the tags you need to view your page in both Microsoft Internet Explorer and Netscape Navigator. You can then upload the document to your Web server.

Flash bases the HTML document you create on a template that contains basic HTML coding. By default, Flash assigns the Flash Only template, which is the simplest template to use to create an HTML document. You can select from other templates.

PUBLISH A MOVIE AS A WEB PAGE

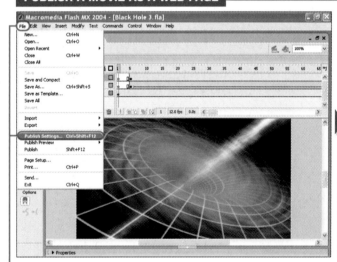

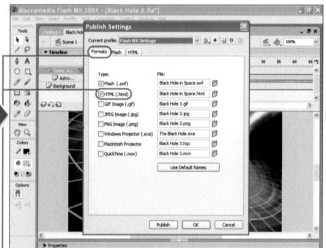

■1 Click **File**.

■2 Click **Publish Settings**.

■ The Publish Settings dialog box appears.

Note: If you have already published your file, tabs from your last changes appears in the dialog box.

■3 Click the **Formats** tab.

■4 Click the **HTML (.html)** format option (□ changes to ☑).

■ The Flash (.swf) format is selected by default.

Note: The Flash and HTML formats are selected by default the first time you use the Publish Settings dialog box.

What HTML tags does Flash insert into the HTML document?

The Publish feature inserts the tags necessary for playing a Flash movie file in the browser window, including the `OBJECT` tag for Microsoft's Internet Explorer browser and the `EMBED` tag for Netscape's Navigator browser. Flash also inserts the `IMG` tag for displaying the movie file in another format, such as animated GIF or JPEG. The `OBJECT`, `EMBED`, and `IMG` tags create the movie display window used to play the Flash movie.

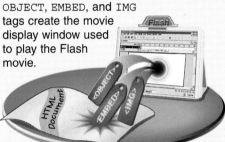

Can I make my own HTML templates for Flash?

Yes. You can set up your own HTML templates or customize existing templates. Be sure to save any HTML templates in the HTML subfolder within the Flash application folder on your computer system. Flash looks for all HTML templates in the HTML folder. The template must also include a title that starts with the recognized HTML title code $TT, such as $TTMy Template.

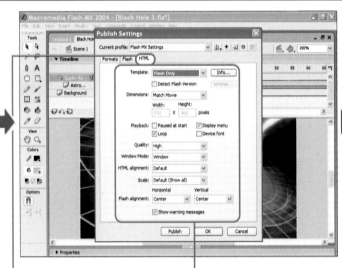

■5 Click the **HTML** tab.

■ Flash displays options associated with generating a Web page, such as playback options and movie dimensions.

■6 Select any options you want to apply.

■ The default Flash Only template allows other Flash users to view your movie.

■ Users without the Flash plug-in cannot view the movie.

■ You can click the Template and select another template from the list.

CONTINUED ▶

A MOVIE AS A WEB PAGE

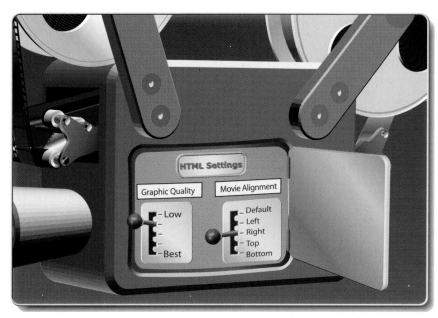

...lish
...as a
...s for
...how your movie
...the browser window.
...can set alignment,
dimensions, and even playback
options. Any changes you make
to the settings overrides any
previous settings for the file.

You can control exactly how a movie
starts, indicating whether the user
starts the movie manually or if the
movie loops continuously or not.
You can also specify new movie
dimensions that differ from the
movie's original screen size
dimensions.

PUBLISH A MOVIE AS A WEB PAGE (CONTINUED)

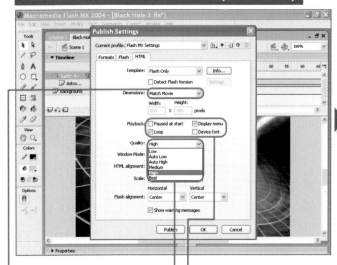

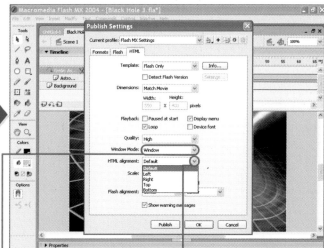

■ You can click the
Dimensions ⊻ to set
width and height attribute
values for the movie
display window — the
area where the Flash
plug-in plays the movie.

■ You can click a Playback
option to control how the
movie plays on the Web
page (☐ changes to ☑).

■ You can click the Quality
⊻ and select options for
controlling the image quality
during playback.

■ You can click the Window
Mode ⊻ and select options
for playing your movie on a
regular, opaque, or
transparent background
(Windows browsers only).

■ You can click the HTML
Alignment ⊻ and change
the alignment of your movie
as it relates to other Web
page elements.

How do I make my movie full-size in the browser window?

To make your Flash movie appear full-screen size in the browser window:

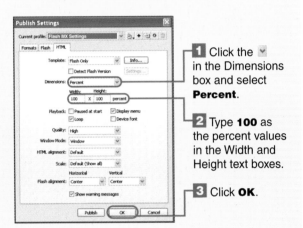

1 Click the ⌄ in the Dimensions box and select **Percent**.

2 Type **100** as the percent values in the Width and Height text boxes.

3 Click **OK**.

How can I tell which HTML template does what?

Select the template you want to know more about, then click **Info** in the Publish Settings dialog box to see a description of the selected template. You can click **OK** to exit the dialog box.

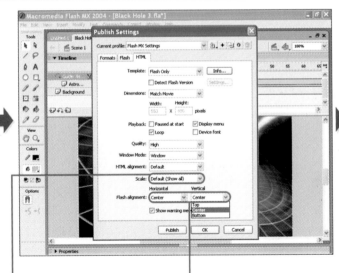

■ If you opt to set new dimensions for the movie, you can click the Scale ⌄ to rescale movie elements to fit the new size.

■ You can click the Flash Alignment ⌄ and designate how the movie aligns in the movie window area.

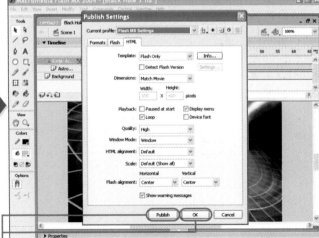

7 When you are ready to publish the movie using your settings, click **Publish**.

■ Flash generates the necessary files for the HTML document.

8 Click **OK**.

■ Flash saves the settings and closes the Publish Settings dialog box.

Note: By default, Flash publishes files to the same folder as the current Flash authoring file unless you specify another folder in the Formats tab.

PUBLISH A MOVIE AS A PROJECTOR FILE

You can publish a movie that plays in its own Flash Player window without the benefit of another application, which means that anyone receiving the file does not need to install the Flash Player application. Flash projectors are simply self-extracting, self-sufficient mini-applications designed to play movies in real time.

Because the projector files are self-sufficient, you can easily place the files on disks or send them as e-mail file attachments. The only catch is that you must publish the projector file to a format appropriate to the computer platform the end user needs.

PUBLISH A MOVIE AS A PROJECTOR FILE

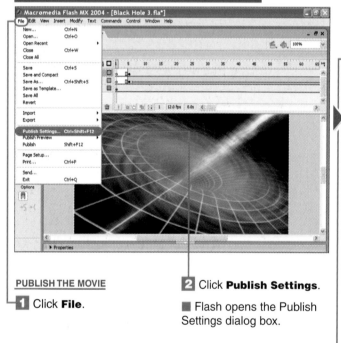

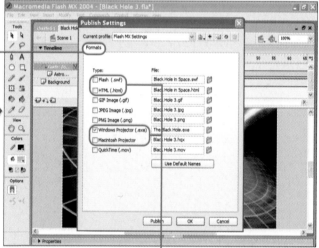

PUBLISH THE MOVIE

1 Click **File**.

2 Click **Publish Settings**.

■ Flash opens the Publish Settings dialog box.

Note: If you have previously published your file, tabs from your last changes appear in the dialog box.

3 Click the **Formats** tab.

4 Select either **Windows Projector** or **Macintosh Projector** as the format (☐ changes to ☑).

■ If you do not want to publish your movie for the Web, you can deselect the **Flash** and **HTML** format check boxes (☑ changes to ☐).

Do I need to worry about licensing my projector file?

Macromedia allows free distribution of its Flash Player and Projector product. If you are distributing your movie for commercial purposes, however, you need to check the Macromedia Web site for information about crediting Macromedia. Visit www.macromedia.com/ support/programs/mwm. You need to include the Made with Macromedia logo on your packaging and give proper credits on your credit screen.

What is the difference between a SWF file and a projector?

When you save a file as a Projector file, you are making an executable copy of your Flash movie. This file does not require a player or plug-in. It comes with everything necessary to run the movie. A regular SWF file packs only the movie data, not the player. Regular SWF files require the Flash Player in order to view the movie.

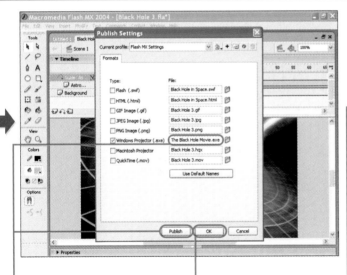

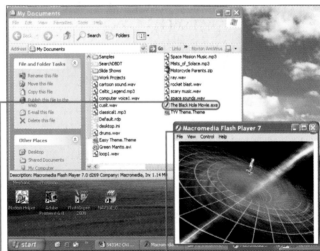

■ You can assign a different file name by typing directly in the File field.

5 Click **Publish**.

■ Flash generates the necessary files for the movie with an .EXE (Windows) or .HQX (Mac) file extension.

6 Click **OK**.

■ The Publish Settings dialog box closes and Flash publishes the movie.

PLAY THE MOVIE

1 Double-click the movie's name.

■ In this example, the file opens via Windows My Documents window.

■ The Flash Player window opens and plays the movie.

2 Click ☒ to close the window when the movie stops.

EXPORT TO ANOTHER FILE FORMAT

You can easily export a Flash movie into another file format for use with other applications. For example, you can save your movie as a Windows AVI file or as a QuickTime file, or perhaps you want to save each frame as a bitmap sequence. Flash allows for over a dozen different file formats for export in both Windows and Mac platforms.

The Export feature differs from the Publish feature in that it creates editable Flash content. You use the Publish feature when you want to generate Web-based content. Unlike the Publish feature, Export savings are not saved with the movie file.

EXPORT TO ANOTHER FILE FORMAT

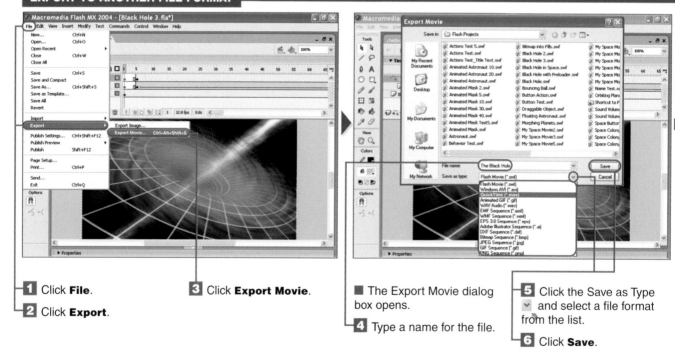

1 Click **File**.

2 Click **Export**.

3 Click **Export Movie**.

■ The Export Movie dialog box opens.

4 Type a name for the file.

5 Click the Save as Type and select a file format from the list.

6 Click **Save**.

What is the difference between exporting a movie and publishing a movie?

The two features share some of the formats and options, but when you publish a movie as opposed to exporting it, Flash saves information about the movie's Publish settings along with the movie file. When you export a movie, you are saving it to a single format. When you publish a movie, you can publish to Flash (SWF), Generator Template, HTML, GIF, JPEG, PNG, Windows Projector, Macintosh Projector, QuickTime, and RealPlayer formats. When you export a movie, you can save the file in over a dozen different file formats, such as Windows AVI or Animated GIF.

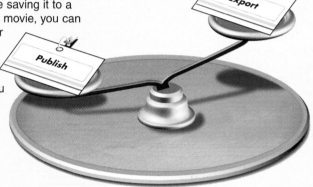

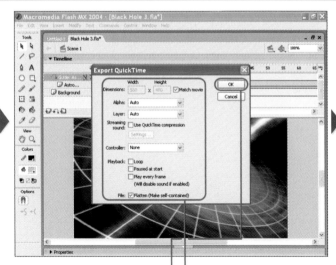

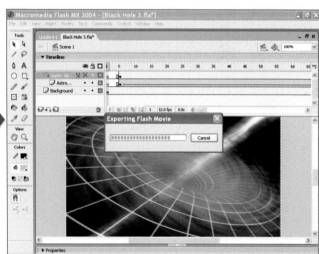

■ Depending on the file type you selected, an additional Export dialog box opens with options for size, sound, and video format.

■ You can make any selections necessary.

7 Click **OK**.

■ Flash exports the movie to the designated file type.

Note: Depending on the file type, another dialog box, may open first. Make any selections necessary, and click OK to continue exporting.

Note: Interactive elements you include in your Flash movies may not export to other file formats properly.

PLAY A FLASH MOVIE IN FLASH

You can use the Flash Player to play your published movie files. You can play movies from within Flash, or outside the confines of the program window by using the Flash Player window. The Flash Player, version 7, is installed when you install Flash onto your computer.

The Flash Player is a separate application for viewing Flash multimedia files. As such, when you download a Flash file, it opens into its own window along with several menu commands for controlling how a movie plays.

Note: The Flash Player window and test movie window are one and the same.

PLAY A FLASH MOVIE IN FLASH

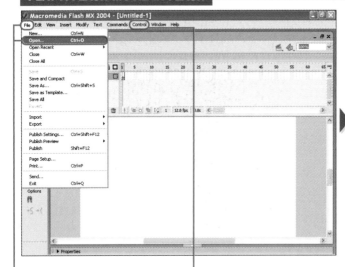

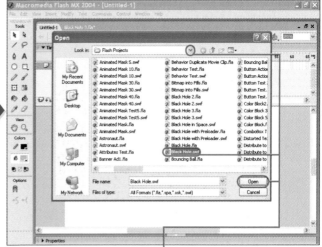

1 Click **File**.

2 Click **Open**.

■ You can also open the Flash Player by clicking **Control**, **Test Movie**.

■ The Open dialog box appears.

■ Published movie files use the SWF file extension and are identified by a different icon ( ) than the Flash authoring files ( ).

■ You can click here to navigate to the folder containing the Flash movie file you want to play.

3 Click the Flash movie file you want to play.

4 Click **Open**.

How do I stop the movie from looping?

The Flash Player window has a few tools you can use to control how the movie plays. Click **Control** to see the available commands. Flash has the Loop command turned on by default. To deactivate the command, click **Loop**. To stop the movie from playing, click **Stop** or just press `Esc`.

How do I open another movie to play in the Flash Player window?

As long as you have the Flash Player window open, you can view other Flash movies as well:

1 Follow steps **1** and **2** in this section.

2 In the Open dialog box, navigate to the next movie file you want to play.

3 Double-click the movie filename.

■ The movie starts playing in the Flash Player window.

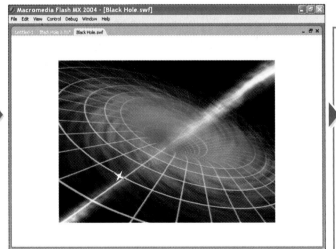

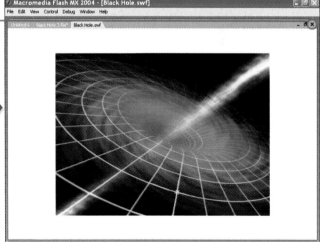

■ The Flash Player window opens and plays the movie.

■ When opening the Flash Player from within the Flash program, the Player fits inside the Flash program window and has a separate set of window controls and menu commands.

■ To stop the movie, you can press `Esc`.

■ To resume play again, you can press `Enter` (`Return`) again.

5 Click ✕.

■ The Flash Player application closes and you are returned to the Flash program window.

Note: To open a movie for editing, you must open the movie's FLA file.

PLAY A FLASH MOVIE IN A BROWSER

You can play a Flash movie using the browser's Flash plug-in. Most browsers, such as Microsoft Internet Explorer and Netscape Navigator, include the Flash Player plug-in program for playing SWF files.

Most Internet users can access Flash Web content without needing to download the Flash Player application separately, which makes the Flash Player the most widely used player on the Internet. Today's browsers and computer systems come with the Flash Player preinstalled.

PLAY A FLASH MOVIE IN A BROWSER

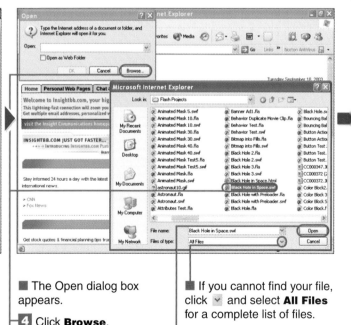

1 Open the browser you want to use.

■ This example uses Microsoft Internet Explorer.

2 Click **File**.

3 Click **Open**.

■ The Open dialog box appears.

4 Click **Browse**.

5 In the dialog box that opens, click the Flash movie file you want to play.

■ If you cannot find your file, click ∨ and select **All Files** for a complete list of files.

6 Click **Open**.

Can older browser versions view Flash movies?

It depends on how old the version of the browser program is. The latest version of the Flash Player plug-in is version 7, which is supported in Netscape Navigator, or Microsoft Internet Explorer. Earlier versions of these browsers do not include the Flash Player plug-in, however, you can download and install the player.

How do I control the movie's screen size?

The movie's screen size is set when you define the Stage area measurements. To learn how to set the Stage size, see Chapter 1. You can also control the size of the movie display window that appears inside the browser window when a Flash movie plays. You can find movie-display controls in the Publish Settings dialog box. Learn more about these controls in the section "Publish a Movie in HTML Format."

7 Click **OK**.

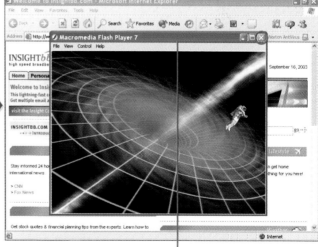

■ The Flash Player window opens and the movie begins playing.

8 Click ✕.

■ The Flash Player window closes.

TEST MOVIE BANDWIDTH

You can use the Flash Bandwidth Profiler to help you determine which movie frames may cause problems during playback on the Web. File size and the user's data-transfer rate affect how smoothly and quickly your movie downloads and plays.

With the Bandwidth Profiler you can test different modem speeds, and gauge which frames in your movie use the most bytes. This information helps you to see exactly where your movie might slow down during playback.

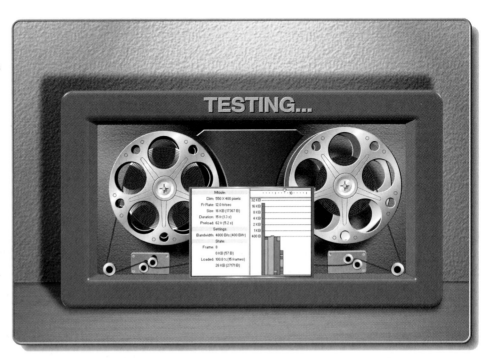

TEST MOVIE BANDWIDTH

<u>OPEN THE BANDWIDTH PROFILER</u>

1 Click **Control**.

2 Click **Test Movie**.

■ The Flash Player window opens and starts playing the movie.

■ You can press `Esc` to stop the movie from playing.

3 Click **View**.

4 Click **Download Settings**.

5 Select a download speed to test.

How do I customize the download speed I want to test?

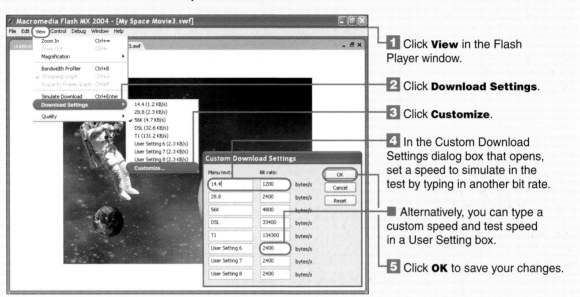

1 Click **View** in the Flash Player window.

2 Click **Download Settings**.

3 Click **Customize**.

4 In the Custom Download Settings dialog box that opens, set a speed to simulate in the test by typing in another bit rate.

■ Alternatively, you can type a custom speed and test speed in a User Setting box.

5 Click **OK** to save your changes.

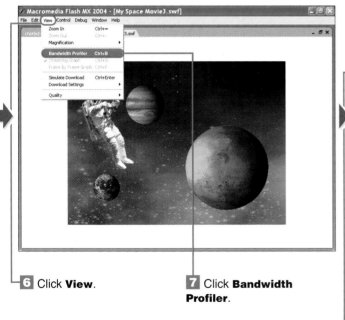

6 Click **View**.

7 Click **Bandwidth Profiler**.

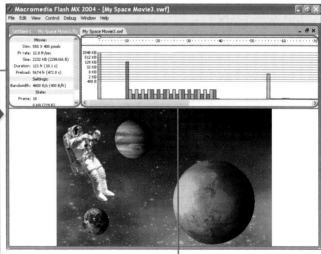

■ The Bandwidth Profiler appears at the top of the window.

■ The left side of the Profiler shows information about the movie, such as file size and dimensions.

■ The bars on the right represent individual frames and the total size, in bytes, of data in the frame.

CONTINUED ▶

TEST MOVIE BANDWIDTH

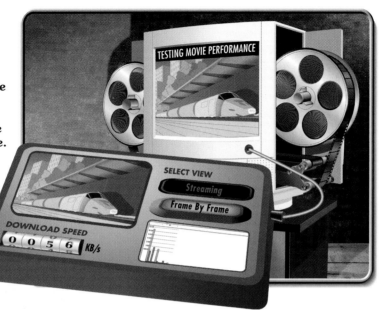

You can use two different views in the Flash Bandwidth Profiler to see how the frames play in your movie: Streaming Graph mode or Frame by Frame Graph mode. The default view is Streaming Graph mode. Depending on the view you select, the right section of the Profiler displays data differently.

A vertical bar on the graph represents a single frame in the movie. The bars correspond with the frame number shown in the timeline.

To make sure you are viewing all the movie's information on the left side of the Profiler, you can resize the Profiler graph. To check which frames may be causing a slow down, switch to Frame by Frame Graph mode.

TEST MOVIE BANDWIDTH (CONTINUED)

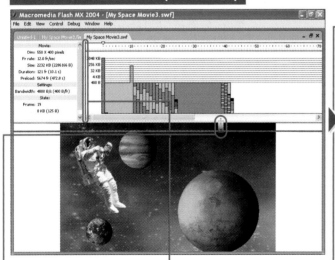

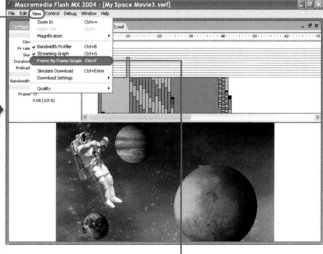

RESIZE THE GRAPH

8 Move the ⊳ over the bottom border until the pointer turns into ⬍.

9 Click and drag the border to resize the Profiler graph.

■ The Bandwidth Profiler resizes.

■ You can also drag the border between the panels to resize panels.

CHANGE THE GRAPH VIEW

10 Click **View**.

11 Click **Frame by Frame Graph**.

Does the Bandwidth Profiler test the exact modem speed?

No. The Profiler estimates typical Internet connection speeds to estimate downloading time. Modem speeds are typically never full strength. For example, a 28.8 Kbps modem can download 3.5 kilobytes of data per second under perfect conditions, but in real life, there are no perfect conditions when connecting to the Internet. In real life conditions, a 28.8 Kbps modem is lucky to download 2.3 kilobytes of data per second. Flash gears each modem test speed setting in the Profiler towards real-life connection speeds.

How do I view a specific frame in the Profiler?

You can use the scroll bar arrows ◄ ► to move left or right in the Profiler Timeline at the top of the Profiler graph. To view a specific frame, drag the playhead to the frame, or click the playhead where you want it to go.

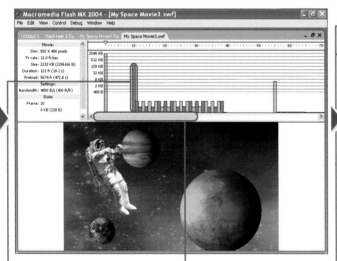

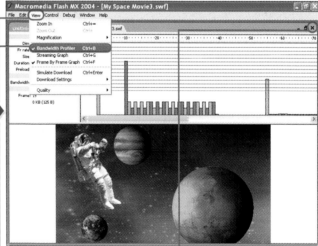

■ The Profiler graph displays Frame by Frame Graph mode.

■ Frames that have bars extending beyond the horizontal red line may cause loading delays for users downloading the movie.

■ You can use the scroll bar to scroll through the movie's Timeline and view other frames.

CLOSE THE PROFILER

⓬ Click **View**.

⓭ Click **Bandwidth Profiler**.

⓮ To close the Flash Player window, click ☒.

■ Flash closes the Bandwidth Profiler and the Player window.

PRINT MOVIE FRAMES

Some Flash projects may require you to print out a frame or series of frames. You may print out frame content to show a storyboard of the movie. You can use the Page Setup dialog box (Windows) or Print Margins dialog box (Mac) to specify a layout, and then use the Print dialog box to specify which pages to print.

You can specify a variety of printing options for frames. You can print a single frame and designate margins, alignment, page orientation and paper size for the printout. You can also print thumbnails—miniatures of your movie's frames.

PRINT MOVIE FRAMES

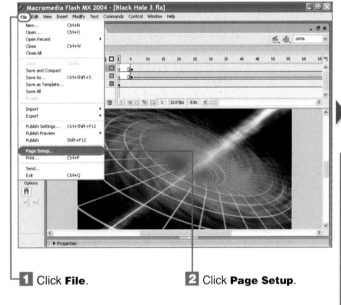

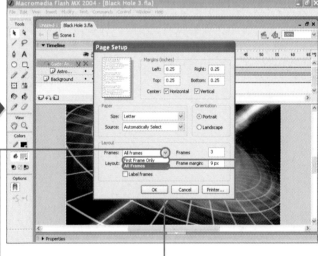

1 Click **File**.

2 Click **Page Setup**.

■ The Page Setup dialog box opens.

3 Click the Frames ⌄.

4 Click **All frames**.

■ You can use the **First Frame Only** option if you want to print just the first frame of the movie.

Can I add labels to each printed frame?

Yes. If you select one of the storyboard layout options in the Print dialog box, a Label frames check box appears. Click this check box (☐ changes to ☑) to print the scene and frame number for each frame you print out in the storyboard.

Does Flash print any symbols I have placed in the work area off of the Stage?

No. Flash prints only the symbols and objects found on the Stage area of any given frame. If you move a symbol off the Stage to place in a later frame or insert later, the symbol does not display in your printout.

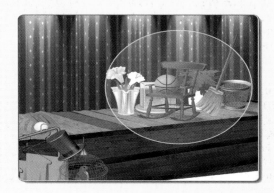

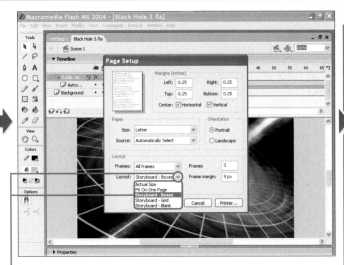

▬5 Click the Layout ⌄ to view layout options.

▬6 Click an option.

■ Select **Storyboard-Boxes** to print in storyboard boxes.

■ Select **Storyboard-Grid** to print in a grid pattern.

■ Select **Storyboard-Blank** to print only the graphic items of each frame.

▬7 Click **OK**.

■ The Page Setup dialog box closes.

▬8 Click **File**.

▬9 Click **Print**.

■ The Print dialog box opens.

■ From within the Print dialog box you can specify print options such as number of copies.

▬10 Click **OK**.

■ Flash prints the specified pages and layout.

INDEX

INDEX

INDEX

symbols
    add, 168–169
    animate along path, 184–187
    from another library, 121
    button, 119, 232
    create, 124–125
    edit, 130–131
    graphic, 119
    from Libraries, 193
    opacity, 172–175, 189
    size, 180–183
    spin, 176–179
    synchronization properties, 258–259

T

targets, 207
templates, HTML, 283
Test Movie, 115
text
    add with Text tool, 88–89
    align, 92
    break apart, 98
    distort, 57, 99
    font change, 91
    format, 90–91
    kern, 93
    Tools panel, 30
text boxes, 89, 94–97
Timeline, 6, 7, 106–107
Timeline buttons, 7
Title bar, 6
Tools panel, 6, 30
_top, 227

Trace Bitmap command, 80–81
transform gradient fill, 64–65
transparent instances, 129
tween effect
    create, 176–177, 180, 190–191
    layers, 184–185
    to masks, 200
    maximum, 183
    speed, 188–189
    test, 171
tweened animation, 135
tweened frames, 137

U

ungroup groups, 71

V

vector graphics, 78
vertical lines, 33, 49
video clips, import, 84–85
View tools, 31

W

Web pages
    color designs, 67
    link button to, 226–227
    publish movie as, 280–281

Z

Zoom tool button, 21

Read Less – Learn More™

Visual

Simplified®

Simply the Easiest Way to Learn

For visual learners who are brand-new to a topic and want to be shown, not told, how to solve a problem in a friendly, approachable way.

All Simplified® books feature friendly Disk characters who demonstrate and explain the purpose of each task.

Title	ISBN	Price
America Online Simplified, 2nd Ed.	0-7645-3433-5	$27.99
America Online Simplified, 3rd Ed.	0-7645-3673-7	$24.99
Computers Simplified, 5th Ed.	0-7645-3524-2	$27.99
Creating Web Pages with HTML Simplified, 2nd Ed.	0-7645-6067-0	$27.99
Excel 2002 Simplified	0-7645-3589-7	$27.99
FrontPage 2000 Simplified	0-7645-3450-5	$27.99
FrontPage 2002 Simplified	0-7645-3612-5	$27.99
Internet and World Wide Web Simplified, 3rd Ed.	0-7645-3409-2	$27.99
Microsoft Excel 2000 Simplified	0-7645-6053-0	$27.99
Microsoft Office 2000 Simplified	0-7645-6052-2	$29.99
Microsoft Word 2000 Simplified	0-7645-6054-9	$27.99
More Windows 98 Simplified	0-7645-6037-9	$27.99
Office XP Simplified	0-7645-0850-4	$29.99
PC Upgrade and Repair Simplified, 2nd Ed.	0-7645-3560-9	$27.99
Windows 98 Simplified	0-7645-6030-1	$27.99
Windows Me Millennium Edition Simplified	0-7645-3494-7	$27.99
Windows XP Simplified	0-7645-3618-4	$27.99
Word 2002 Simplified	0-7645-3588-9	$27.99

Over 10 million Visual books in print

with these full-color Visual™ guides

The Fast and Easy Way to Learn

Discover how to use what you learn with "Teach Yourself" tips

May 03

Teach Yourself VISUALLY™

For visual learners who want to guide themselves through the basics of any technology topic. *Teach Yourself VISUALLY* offers more expanded coverage than our bestselling *Simplified* series.

Title	ISBN	Price
Teach Yourself FrontPage 2000 VISUALLY	0-7645-3451-3	$29.99
Teach Yourself HTML VISUALLY	0-7645-3423-8	$29.99
Teach Yourself the Internet and World Wide Web VISUALLY, 2nd Ed.	0-7645-3410-6	$29.99
Teach Yourself Microsoft Access 2000 VISUALLY	0-7645-6059-X	$29.99
Teach Yourself Microsoft Excel 2000 VISUALLY	0-7645-6056-5	$29.99
Teach Yourself Microsoft Office 2000 VISUALLY	0-7645-6051-4	$29.99
Teach Yourself VISUALLY Access 2002	0-7645-3691-9	$29.99
Teach Yourself VISUALLY Adobe Acrobat 5 PDF	0-7645-3667-2	$29.99
Teach Yourself VISUALLY Adobe Premiere 6	0-7645-3664-8	$29.99
Teach Yourself VISUALLY Computers, 3rd Ed.	0-7645-3525-0	$29.99
Teach Yourself VISUALLY Digital Photography	0-7645-3565-X	$29.99
Teach Yourself VISUALLY Digital Video	0-7645-3688-5	$29.99
Teach Yourself VISUALLY Dreamweaver MX	0-7645-3694-7	$29.99
Teach Yourself VISUALLY E-commerce with FrontPage	0-7645-3579-X	$29.99
Teach Yourself VISUALLY Excel 2002	0-7645-3594-3	$29.99
Teach Yourself VISUALLY Fireworks 4	0-7645-3566-8	$29.99
Teach Yourself VISUALLY Flash MX	0-7645-3661-3	$29.99
Teach Yourself VISUALLY Flash 5	0-7645-3540-4	$29.99
Teach Yourself VISUALLY FrontPage 2002	0-7645-3590-0	$29.99
Teach Yourself VISUALLY Illustrator 10	0-7645-3654-0	$29.99
Teach Yourself VISUALLY iMac	0-7645-3453-X	$29.99
Teach Yourself VISUALLY Investing Online	0-7645-3459-9	$29.99
Teach Yourself VISUALLY Mac OS X v. 10.2 Jaguar	0-7645-1802-X	$29.99
Teach Yourself VISUALLY Macromedia Web Collection	0-7645-3648-6	$39.99
Teach Yourself VISUALLY More Windows XP	0-7645-3698-2	$29.99
Teach Yourself VISUALLY Networking, 2nd Ed.	0-7645-3534-X	$29.99
Teach Yourself VISUALLY Office XP	0-7645-0854-7	$29.99
Teach Yourself VISUALLY Photoshop 6	0-7645-3513-7	$29.99
Teach Yourself VISUALLY Photoshop 7	0-7645-3682-6	$29.99
Teach Yourself VISUALLY Photoshop Elements 2	0-7645-2515-8	$29.99
Teach Yourself VISUALLY PowerPoint 2002	0-7645-3660-5	$29.99
Teach Yourself VISUALLY Restoration and Retouching with Photoshop Elements 2	0-7645-2610-4	$29.99
Teach Yourself VISUALLY Windows 2000 Server	0-7645-3428-9	$29.99
Teach Yourself VISUALLY Windows Me Millennium Edition	0-7645-3495-5	$29.99
Teach Yourself VISUALLY Windows XP	0-7645-3619-2	$29.99
Teach Yourself VISUALLY Word 2002	0-7645-3587-0	$29.99
Teach Yourself Windows 95 VISUALLY	0-7645-6001-8	$29.99
Teach Yourself Windows 98 VISUALLY	0-7645-6025-5	$29.99
Teach Yourself Windows 2000 Professional VISUALLY	0-7645-6040-9	$29.99

The Visual™ series is available wherever books are sold, or call **1-800-762-2974.**

Outside the US, call **317-572-3993**